Recipes Rated Ten Plus

by M. Dolly Miller

THE BEST RECIPES FOR MEALS YOU LOVE TO EAT

A collection of outstanding recipes by famous chefs and individuals.

Additional copies of **RECIPES RATED TEN PLUS** may be obtained by sending a check for $11.95 plus $2.00 for postage and handling to:

RECIPES RATED TEN PLUS
P.O. Box 26610
Tempe, AZ 85282-0210

| First Printing | March, 1984 | 5,000 copies |
| Second Printing | May, 1985 | 5,000 copies |

Library of Congress Catalog Card Number 83-91315

ISBN: 0-9613120-0-9

Printed in U.S.A.
S.C. Toof & Co.
670 S. Cooper St.
Memphis, TN 38104

DEDICATION

This book is lovingly dedicated to my
husband, Donald; my children, Randy,
Wayne, Macrina and Fred; and my
deceased parents.

INTRODUCTION

This book is a collection of <u>outstanding</u> recipes, all of which can be cooked by anyone. The emphasis is on quality, not quantity. It is dedicated to the person who wants to have good, tasty, delicious meals.

These excellent recipes come from famous chefs, home economists and men and women I have known for many years who have that one "marvelous" recipe that you only occasionally are fortunate enough to discover. Also, some are my own which I have spent a great deal of time developing.

Every recipe has been personally tested by me, and rated from 1 to 10 by my husband and certain friends. When an exceptional recipe was tested, they said "that's a 10 plus"—which is how I derived the title—and recipes in the book.

The reason many meals are not as good as they should or can be is the recipe, not the cook. There are thousands, perhaps millions, of recipes in print today. My recipes are for those who want to be certain they have an outstanding recipe for any occasion before they begin.

If you are going to take the time and effort, why not use a recipe that you know will be outstanding?

The recipes with the symbol of the hat with "Dolly's Delights" are my creations.

This is what my book is all about.

Bon appétit,

M. Dolly Miller

ACKNOWLEDGEMENTS

Chefs

Chef Vincent Guerithault, Vincent's French Cuisine, Scottsdale, Arizona. French born; First North American Chef to receive International Wine and Food Society Citation of Excellence; recognized by *The New York Times* and *Bon Appetit;* Silver Cup Award, Arizona 1983 for Layered Mousse Dessert.

Chef Norbert Ruegg, Basin Street, Palm Bay, Florida. Swiss born; graduate, Belvour School, Zurich; Swiss Government Award as Second Best Chef Ever Certified in Switzerland; Palace Hotel, St. Moritz; Beachcomber Hotel, Queensland, Australia; Sawgrass Country Club, Jacksonville, Florida.

Chef William Maldonado, Maldonado's, Pasadena, California. Los Angeles Restaurant Writers' Association Four Star Award (highest award) four consecutive years; listed by *Bon Appetit* among top restaurants in 25 cities; recognized by *Gourmet, Bon Appetit,* and *L. A. Magazine.*

Chef Patrick Tombelaine, Golden Eagle, Phoenix, Arizona. Trained in France and Spain; apprenticed in San Francisco.

Chef Antonio Pologruto, Hyatt Regency, Memphis, Tennessee. Italian born; graduate, Culinary Institute of America; Chef in Zurich, Switzerland; Madrid, Spain; Philadelphia; Atlantic City.

Chefs Christian Planchon and Yves Labbe, La Vieille Mason, Boca Raton, Florida.

Chef Henri L. Labazee, Retired. French born; Barons de Rothschild; Abbey des Vaux-de-Cernay, France; Duchess of Marlborough, Blenheim Palace, England.

Chef Peter Wynkoop, Part Owner, Nannie Lee's Strawberry Mansion, Melbourne, Florida. Culinary Institute of America (Honors); Artistic Display Award, Brevard Chapter, Florida Restaurant Association, 1982.

Chef Debra Holt, Hyatt Regency, Memphis, Tennessee.

Chef Cornelius O'Donnell, Consumer Products Division, Corning Glass Works, Corning, New York.

Chef Mike Zyla, Paradise Valley Country Club, Paradise Valley, Arizona. Austrian born; Oak Hill Country Club, Rochester, New York.

Chef Robin Murphey, Nannie Lee's Strawberry Mansion, Melbourne, Florida. L'Academie de Cuisine, Bethesda, Maryland.

Chef Joseph Archazki, O'Shea's Restaurant and Lounge, Marco Island, Florida.

Chef Donald Schubert, Los Angeles Trade-Technical College, Los Angeles, California.

Chef Carmen Pons, San Juan, Puerto Rico.

Restaurants

La Vieille Maison, Boca Raton, Florida.

Casa Vecchia, Ft. Lauderdale, Florida.

Down Under, Ft. Lauderdale, Florida. Leonce Picot, Part Owner.

Griswold's Restaurant, Claremont, California.

Wesley's Restaurant, Virginia Beach, Virginia.

Paradise Valley Country Club, Paradise Valley, Arizona. David Dellefield, Banquet Manager.

Cuisine Food Supplies

Matthews 1812 House, Box 15, Whitcomb Hill Road, Cornwall Bridge, Connecticut 06754. Specializes in homemade gift cakes, including a Brandied Apricot Cake made in small batches without preservatives.

Gloria Pitzer, author of Gloria Pitzer's Secret Recipes, Box 152, St. Clair, Michigan 48079

Evelyn's Beer and Winemaking Supplies, 9220 N. 7th St., Phoenix, Arizona 85020.

Sahuaro Spices, 1015 N. 7th St., Phoenix, Arizona 85006.

Home Economists

Judy Casey   Florence Henningsen
Lana Hugo   Sandra Nicholas
Deanna Matthews   Gloria Pitzer
              Libby Lafferty

And to all of those that submitted those marvelous recipes for which I had no room.

TABLE OF CONTENTS

Pages 10-38

Pages 40-58

Pages 60-78

Pages 80-102

Pages 104-150

Pages 152-170

Pages 172-178

Pages 180-208

Pages 210-284

Pages 286-309

APPETIZERS

Broiled Shrimp in Bacon.......10
Creamy Shrimp Dip...........11
Crab and Cream Cheese
    Spread...................12
Smoked Oyster Spread........13
Deep Fried Zucchini with
    Creamy Garlic Dip.........14
Artichoke Squares............15
Nachos.....................16
Guacamole..................17
Spiced Ham Ball.............18
Liverwurst Pâté..............19
Sweet 'n Sour Meat Balls......20
Sauerkraut Balls.............21
Triple Cheese Ball...........22
Cheese Pitas................23
Party Stuffed Brie............24
Special Deviled Eggs.........25

SOUPS

Mom's Barley Soup...........26
Sebastian's Albondigas Soup....27
Seafood Curry Soup..........28
Norton's Favorite Bouillabaisse..29
Lobster Bisque...............30
Old Fashioned New England
    Clam Chowder.............31
Seafood Soup...............32
Austrian Cherry Soup.........33
Italian Minestrone............34
Italian Wedding Soup.........35
Crème de Laittues (Cream of
    Lettuce Soup).............36
Leek and Potato Soup and
    Vichyssoise...............37
Russian Cabbage Soup........38

CHEF NORBERT RUEGG
Basin Street Restaurant
Palm Bay, Florida

BROILED SHRIMP IN BACON

8 to 12 slices of bacon, halved
Hot spicy mustard
16 to 24 medium size raw
shrimp, shelled and deveined

1. Preheat broiler.

2. Place bacon on waxed paper and brush generously with mustard.

3. Wrap bacon around each shrimp (mustard facing shrimp) and secure each roll with a toothpick.

4. Broil on broiling pan until bacon is crisp, turning once. Serve hot.

Yield: 16-24
Preparation: 35 minutes
Broiling time: 7-10 minutes

Very, very tasty and different.

CREAMY SHRIMP DIP

FLORENCE HENNINGSEN
Tempe, Arizona

1 10³/₄-oz. can cream of shrimp
  soup
1 8-oz. package cream cheese
1 4¹/₂-oz. can shrimp, drained
6 green onions, chopped
¹/₄ cup celery, chopped fine
Broccoli and cauliflower
  flowerettes

Serves: 6
Preparation: 25 minutes
Cooking: 10 minutes

Umm—Great—hmm!

1. In a double boiler blend shrimp soup and cheese until melted and well blended. Heat thoroughly.

2. Add shrimp, onions and celery, again heat thoroughly and place in chafing dish. Serve with fresh broccoli and cauliflower flowerettes.

MERRIAM GOSWICK
Clearwater, Florida

CRAB AND CREAM CHEESE SPREAD

1 can crabmeat, drained and cleaned from any bones
1 8-oz. package cream cheese
1 ½ cups chili sauce, chilled
1 Tablespoon horseradish
1 teaspoon Worcestershire sauce
1 Tablespoon onion greens, chopped
1 Tablespoon lemon juice
Dash of Tabasco sauce
Parsley, chopped
Ritz crackers as garnish

Serves: 6-8
Preparation: 30 minutes

1. Clean crabmeat and set aside.

2. Slice cheese in half horizontally and place on a platter so that they touch side by side.

3. Mix chili sauce, horseradish, Worcestershire sauce, chopped onion greens, lemon juice and Tabasco sauce. Pour over cream cheese. Flake crabmeat over sauce and sprinkle top of crabmeat with chopped parsley.

4. Serve with your choice of crackers.

There are many versions of this—and this is our favorite. Thanks, Merriam.

SMOKED OYSTER SPREAD

BONNIE ZIPPERER
Kissimmee, Florida

3 3-oz. packages cream cheese
½ cup sour cream
½ teaspoon Worcestershire
  sauce
1 Tablespoon dried onion flakes
⅛ teaspoon garlic powder
½ Tablespoon onion greens
  or chives
1 can smoked oysters, drained
  and coarsely chopped

1. Mix all together and refrigerate for at least 2 hours to mellow flavor.

2. Serve with crackers of your choice.

Makes: 2 cups
Preparation: 20 minutes

Marvelous.

JUDY CASEY
Tempe, Arizona

DEEP FRIED ZUCCHINI WITH CREAMY GARLIC DIP

CREAMY GARLIC DIP:
1 cup buttermilk
1 cup mayonnaise
1 packet <u>Ranch</u> salad dressing
  mix
2 cloves minced garlic
¼ teaspoon oregano

DEEP FRIED ZUCCHINI:
1 or 2 medium fresh unpeeled
  zucchini, thinly sliced
  in circles
½ cup flour
2 eggs beaten
1-2 cups canned Italian
  seasoned bread crumbs

Serves: 4
Preparation: 30 minutes
Cooking: 10-15 minutes

Once you start eating these you can't stop.

1. Combine all Creamy Garlic Dip ingredients by <u>hand</u>, not blender, at least one day before using and refrigerate.

2. Next day, right before serving, coat zucchini slices with flour, then egg, then bread crumbs and deep fry at 375° until golden. Serve with Creamy Garlic Dip.

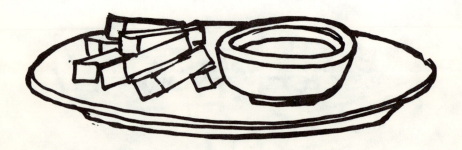

ARTICHOKE SQUARES

BRENDA LETSON
Warren, Ohio

2 6-oz. jars marinated artichoke hearts, chopped fine
1 small onion, chopped fine
1 clove garlic, minced
5 eggs
⅓ cup dry bread crumbs
¼ teaspoon salt
¼ teaspoon pepper
¼ teaspoon oregano
¼ teaspoon Tabasco
½ lb. sharp Cheddar cheese, grated
2 Tablespoons parsley, chopped
2 Tablespoons Parmesan cheese, grated (optional)

1. Drain marinade from 1 jar of artichokes into a frying pan.

2. Drain off remaining jar of artichokes.

3. Sauté chopped artichokes, onion and minced garlic in marinade until limp.

4. Beat eggs with fork, add bread crumbs, salt, pepper, oregano, Tabasco, Cheddar cheese and parsley.

5. Add sautéd artichoke mixture to egg mixture.

6. Pour into slightly buttered 7" x 11" baking pan. Sprinkle top with Parmesan cheese.

7. Bake in preheated 325° oven for 30 minutes. Remove from oven and cut into 1½" squares.

8. These can be served hot or cold.

Serves: 4-6
Preparation: 30 minutes
Baking: 30 minutes

Sensational!

NACHOS

MACRINA SUDIMACK
San Rafael, California

6 ripe avocados, peeled and mashed
1 pt. sour cream
1 package taco seasoning
2 lb. sharp Cheddar cheese, grated
2 lb. Jalapeno Jack cheese, grated
2 large tomatoes, chopped
2 bunches of green onions with tops, chopped
1 large can black olives, sliced
Tortilla chips

Serves: 10
Preparation: 30 minutes

Out of sight.

1. Mix well sour cream and taco seasoning mix and set aside.

2. On a large platter start with avocado on bottom and spread out in a circle.

3. Place mixed sour cream mixture on top of avocados and rest of ingredients in order given, except chips.

4. Place chips around Nacho mixture and serve. Serve with margaritas.*

   *See page 305.

GUACAMOLE

JUDY CASEY
Tempe, Arizona

3 large or 6 small avocados, scooped out of skin
1 Tablespoon green chilies, chopped
1 Tablespoon sour cream per avocado
1 Tablespoon cottage cheese per avocado
Dash of Tabasco
Dash of garlic salt
Dash of seasoned salt
Dash of pepper
1 Tablespoon lemon juice
1 Tablespoon lime juice
1 Tablespoon salsa
Diced bacon (optional)
Diced onion (optional)
Diced tomato (optional)

Makes: 3-4 cups
Preparation: 15 minutes

1. Mix all ingredients in blender or processor until smooth, except diced bacon, onion and tomatoes.

2. It isn't necessary to add bacon, onion or tomatoes. They are an added treat.

3. Cover with Saran Wrap (never tin foil) until ready to serve.

There are many recipes for this, but this one beats all.

17

BOB NICHOLAS
California, Maryland

SPICED HAM BALL

1 cup boiled ham, chopped fine
3 green onions (chop greens
  only)
1 8-oz. package cream cheese
½ cup pecans, chopped
Pinch of cayenne pepper
  (optional)
Fresh parsley flakes, chopped

Makes: 2 cups
Preparation: 20 minutes

Thanks, Bob, it's great.

1. Mix all except parsley flakes. Make into a ball. Roll in parsley and refrigerate at least 2 hours. Serve with crackers. Wheat Thins are best.

LIVERWURST PÂTÉ

RANDY ZIPPERER
Kissimmee, Florida

8 oz. Liverwurst
8 oz. Braunschweiger
1 stick butter, melted and cooled
1 can of ripe olives, drained and chopped
¼ cup brandy

1. Blend Liverwurst, Braunschweiger and butter together.

2. Mix in remaining ingredients and refrigerate in a crock.

3. Serve with crackers or party French bread.

Serves: 4-6
Preparation: 15 minutes

The best liver pâté I ever tasted.

SWEET 'N SOUR MEATBALLS

BETTE RUTTEN
Arcadia, California

MEATBALLS:
½ cup milk
1 slice bread
2 lb. ground beef
½ lb. ground pork
1 egg
2 teaspoons salt
Pepper to taste
3 Tablespoons salad oil

SAUCE:
1 can beef bouillon
2 Tablespoons soy sauce
1 No. 2 can pineapple chunks
½ teaspoon salt
½ cup chopped green pepper
1 teaspoon Accent
½ cup sugar
¼ cup wine vinegar
2 Tablespoons cornstarch

Serves: 10
Preparation: 35 minutes
Cooking: 30-35 minutes

1. For Meatballs: Pour milk over bread to soften. Add rest of ingredients and brown in salad oil.

2. Meanwhile, simmer all ingredients for sauce (except cornstarch) for 15 minutes.

3. Add cornstarch mixed with a little water to the sauce. Add meatballs and simmer for another 10-15 minutes. Serve in a chafing dish.

Many versions of these, but these are the best.

SAUERKRAUT BALLS

REV. MARY SAYLOR
Manhattan, Montana

½ lb. lean ham
½ lb. pork
½ lb. corned beef
1 medium onion
1 teaspoon parsley, minced
1 teaspoon dry mustard
2 cups flour
1 teaspoon salt
2 cups milk
2 lbs. sauerkraut, cooked and
    drained
Additional breading flour
2 eggs, slightly beaten
Dry bread crumbs

1. Put meat and onion through medium blade of food grinder; add parsley.

2. Blend well and sauté in 3 Tablespoons shortening until browned. Add 2 cups flour mixed with salt, dry mustard and milk; blend.

3. Cook, stirring constantly until thick.

4. Mix with sauerkraut and put mixture through food chopper. Mix thoroughly.

5. Return to skillet and cook, stirring constantly, until very thick. Cool.

6. Form into walnut-sized balls. Roll in flour, beaten eggs and bread crumbs.

7. Fry a few at a time in deep fat at 370° until browned. Drain on absorbent paper and serve piping hot.

Yield: 90 to 100 balls
Preparation: 1 hour

Super for New Year's Eve. Thanks, Mary.

TRIPLE CHEESE BALL

SHERRY BURDETTE
Temple City, California

1 8-oz. package cream cheese
1 3-oz. package Roquefort
cheese
1 5-oz. jar Red Kettle smoked
or Cheddar
1 Tablespoon Worcestershire
sauce
1 Tablespoon dried onion flakes
⅛ teaspoon garlic <u>powder</u>
Fresh parsley flakes as garnish
Chopped pecans as garnish

Makes: 2 cups
Preparation: 30 minutes

A spread that is liked by all.

1. Mix all except parsley flakes and chopped pecans. Shape into a roll or ball. Roll in fine chopped parsley and nuts.

2. Refrigerate overnight. Serve with crackers of your choice.

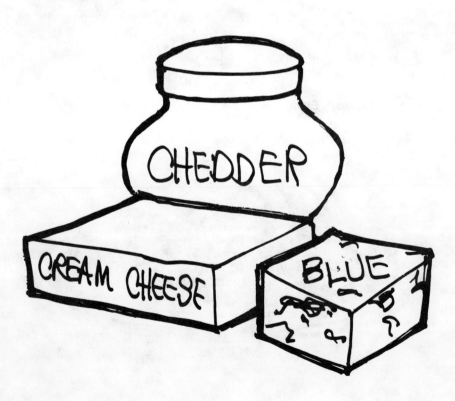

CHEESE PITAS

BONNIE ZIPPERER
Kissimmee, Florida

1 8-oz. package cream cheese
2 eggs, beaten
½ cup Romano cheese, grated
½ cup Parmesan cheese, grated
½ teaspoon salt
½ lb. butter, melted
1 package phyllo dough

1. Mix cream cheese, eggs, Romano cheese, Parmesan cheese and salt, blending well.

2. Lay one sheet of phyllo dough on table and brush with melted butter.

3. Cut dough into 4 strips lengthwise.

4. Place 1 teaspoon of cheese mixture on end of dough, fold side over side and roll to end of strip.

5. Place on greased cookie sheet and bake in preheated 350° oven for 10 to 15 minutes.

6. These can be made ahead of time and frozen on the cookie tray.

Yield: 24 to 30
Preparation: 1 hour
Baking: 10-15 minutes

They are worth every minute it takes.

PASTRY STUFFED BRIE

LANA HUGO
Tempe, Arizona

**2 4½-oz. rounds of Brie
cheese
4 pastry patty shells
(Pepperidge Farm, frozen)
½ cup slivered almonds
Assorted fruit as garnish**

1. I use a small 6" Pyrex pie plate or a "Sidekick" Corning Ware 4½" x 6¾" baking dish.

2. Roll out 2 patty shells and lay in buttered sidekick dish, overlap edges.

3. Place slivered almonds on top of pastry.

4. Place cheese on top of almonds. Press and spread cheese so that it fills the dish.

5. Roll out the other 2 patty shells to fit top, turn bottom edge over top layer and squeeze edge to seal.

6. Bake in preheated 350° oven for 20 to 30 minutes or until lightly browned. Remove from oven and turn over onto a platter to cool.

7. Can be served warm or cold with fruit wedges on the side.

Serves: 4-6
Preparation: 20 minutes
Baking: 20-30 minutes

A must for your next dinner party.

SPECIAL DEVILED EGGS

DON MILLER
Tempe, Arizona

6 hard boiled eggs, shelled
2 Tablespoons melted butter, cooled
3 Tablespoons mayonnaise
3 slices bacon fried crisp, cooled and crumbled
1 tsp. minced dried onion
2 Tablespoon chopped celery
¼ teaspoon Dijon mustard
¼ teaspoon salt
Dash of pepper
Paprika and parsley

Yield: 12 halves
Preparation: 40 minutes

1. Cut eggs in half lengthwise. Carefully remove yolks to a small bowl. Set whites aside.

2. Mash yolks, add remaining ingredients and mix well.

3. Generously fill whites, sprinkle with paprika and garnish with a sprig of parsley in center. Refrigerate until ready to serve.

Another old recipe—always requested.

MOM'S BARLEY SOUP

2 qts. chicken broth
1/2 cup barley
1 celery stalk, chopped
1 carrot, sliced thin
1/4 cup parsley sprigs, chopped
1 1/2 cups fresh mushrooms,
  sliced
Salt and pepper to taste
1 large onion, chopped
1/4 cup flour
1/8 teaspon garlic powder
1/2 cup milk
1 cup light cream
2 egg yolks

1. Simmer chicken broth and barley covered for about 1 hour 15 minutes. Stir to prevent sticking.

2. Add celery, carrots, parsley, mushrooms, onion and seasoning. Simmer for 20 minutes.

3. While vegetables are cooking, sauté onion in butter until limp. Add garlic powder and flour to thicken. Stir in milk gradually, as not to make lumpy.

4. Add some of broth to milk mixture until consistency is smooth, then pour into soup mixture.

5. Cook about 5 minutes until well blended.

6. Beat cream and egg yolks with a wire whisk and pour into soup mixture. Serve with garlic croutons on top.

Makes: 2 qts.
Preparation: 40 minutes
Cooking: 2 hours

Barley was a most popular grain in our meals on the farm.

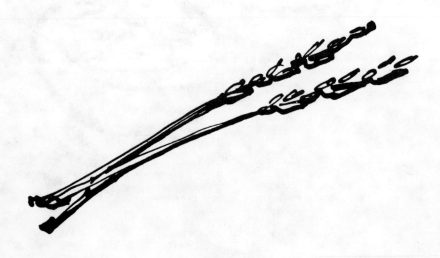

SEBASTIAN'S-ALBONDIGAS SOUP

MARY MACIAS
South Pasadena, California

1 Tablespoon oil
1 Tablespoon butter
1 large onion
1 clove garlic, minced
6 cups beef stock
1½ cups water
1 6-oz. can tomato paste
2 large potatoes, peeled and cubed
2 large carrots, peeled and sliced
1 large egg (or 2 small)
4 Tablespoons parsley, chopped
1 teaspoon salt
⅛ teaspoon pepper
½ teaspoon oregano
¼ teaspoon basil
1½ lbs. ground beef
⅓ cup long grain rice, uncooked
Chopped parsley as garnish
Hard rolls

Serves: 8-10
Preparation: 35 minutes
Cooking: 40-45 minutes

1. In a large kettle, sauté onion and garlic in butter and oil until tender and limp.

2. Stir in beef broth, water, tomato paste, potatoes and carrots. Bring to boil and simmer covered for 5 minutes.

3. In a bowl combine egg, 4 Tablespoons parsley, all spices, ground beef and rice. Form into 1" balls, drop into soup.

4. Return soup to boiling, turn down and simmer for about 35 minutes. Serve with a few chopped parsley sprigs on top and a roll on the side.

This is without a doubt the best Mexican soup you'll ever eat.

CHEF JOSEPH ARCHAZKI
O'Shea's Wharf Restaurant
Marco Island, Florida

SEAFOOD CURRY SOUP

2 qts. chicken stock
1 teaspoon curry powder
2½ Red Delicious apples, diced
2½ pears, diced
½ fresh pineapple, diced
½ cup raisins
½ cup coconut
½ teaspoon anise seeds
½ cup sugar
½ teaspoon nutmeg
1 teaspoon allspice
½ teaspoon cinnamon
3 Tablespoons butter
3 Tablespoons flour
1 pt. heavy cream
½ cup sherry
½ lb. shrimp, cleaned and washed
½ lb. scallops, cleaned and washed
½ lb. crab, cleaned and washed
2 Tablespoons butter
Toasted coconut and almond slices as garnish

Makes: 1½ qts. (approx.)
Preparation: 1 hour
Cooking: 3 hours (approx.)

1. In a large pot place first 12 ingredients. Bring to a boil, turn down heat to low and simmer for 2 hours. Strain, saving only stock.

2. Place cooked, strained stock back in container and boil until reduced to half (about 1 qt.)

3. In the meantime melt butter, add flour and mix until well blended. Add to reduced stock.

4. Add heavy cream and sherry and heat lightly.

5. Sauté cleaned shrimp, scallops and crab in 2 Tablespoons butter for a few minutes, or until done. Add to stock mixture. Serve in pineapple halves or in long-stemmed goblets with toasted coconuts and almond slices on top.

A very elegant rich, fruity soup with a curry touch. For those special, special guests.

HELEN NORTON
Kirkland, Washington

NORTON'S FAVORITE BOUILLABAISSE

4 Tablespoons butter
1 medium onion, chopped
½ cup Madeira
½ cup burgundy
2 16-oz. cans of tomatoes, crushed
1 10-oz. can of beef broth
½ teaspoon Bovril, meat base
1½ teaspoons oregano
¼ teaspoon basil
Pinch of thyme
1 bay leaf
1 clove of garlic, minced
1 teaspoon salt
⅛ teaspoon pepper
1 Tablespoon sugar
2 Tablespoons fresh parsley, chopped
2 lbs. of seafood, scallops, cleaned shrimp, sole, cleaned crab
Italian bread

Makes: 2½ qts.
Preparation: 20 minutes
Cooking: 30-35 minutes

1. Sauté onions in butter until limp, add Madeira and burgundy, cook briefly. Add the remaining ingredients except the fish and bread. Cover and simmer for 20 to 30 minutes.

2. Rinse seafood, pat dry on paper towel. Cut sole into bite size and add all to bouillabaisse, cooking 5 minutes more. Serve with Italian or French bread.

We love to dunk our bread in this bouillabaisse, and it is a meal in itself. Try frying the bread slices in butter and placing them in the soup bowl, pouring the soup on top of the bread—Yummy!

29

CHEF YVES LABBE
La Vieille Maison's
Boca Raton, Florida

LOBSTER BISQUE

1 2-lb. live lobster
2 qts. water
½ cup butter, divided
1 small onion, chopped fine
1 celery rib, chopped fine
1 small carrot, chopped fine
1 cup white wine
½ cup tomato puree
¼ cup long grain rice
6 peppercorns
1 bay leaf
¼ teaspoon thyme
¼ teaspoon salt
⅓ cup brandy
1 cup heavy cream

1. Place live lobster on cutting surface with backside down. Using a sharp knife, cut lobster in half at joint between body and tail. Cut off large claws and small legs on each side of body.

2. Bring water to a boil and cook lobster tail and claws 10 minutes. Remove lobster and reduce liquid by ½ by boiling 15 minutes. Reserve and set aside. Remove meat from claws and tail, dice and set aside.

3. In a large saucepan melt 4 Tablespoons butter. Chop body (including tomalley) into small pieces and sauté with onion, celery and carrot over medium heat for 10 minutes or until lobster turns pink. Add reserved cooking liquid, wine, tomato puree, rice and seasonings. Simmer 45 minutes. Remove shells and press soup and vegetables through a food mill. Pour into a blender and blend until smooth.

4. Return soup to a saucepan, add brandy. Bring to a boil over medium heat, stirring constantly. Add more seasoning if needed. Add remaining 4 Tablespoons butter, cream and reserved lobster meat. Heat through (do not boil) and serve.

Makes: 6 cups
Preparation: 1 hour
Cooking: 1 hour, 30 minutes

This recipe was among those selected for 'A Taste of America', the presentation of food from great U.S. restaurants, held during the Reagan Inauguration in Washington.

CHEF NORBERT RUEGG
Basin Street Restaurant
Palm Bay, Florida

OLD FASHIONED
NEW ENGLAND CLAM CHOWDER

1 can clams, chopped or
Fresh clams, chopped
¼ lb. salt pork, chopped fine
¼ cup butter
1½ cups bottled clam juice,
  if needed
2 potatoes, diced
1 onion, chopped
1 quart milk
1 Tablespoon corn starch
1 Tablespoon parsley, chopped,
  as garnish

Serves: 4-6
Preparation: 30 minutes
Cooking: 20-30 minutes

So good on a chilly evening.

1. Sauté salt pork and onion in butter (do not brown), add potatoes and clam broth and simmer until potatoes are soft.

2. Combine corn starch with ¼ cup milk and add to the pot of pork and onion along with the rest of the milk.

3. Bring chowder to a boil and simmer for 5 minutes. Add clams and cook another 3 minutes. Serve with chopped parsley.

SOUPS

SEAFOOD SOUP

CHEF CHRISTIAN PLANCHON
The Down Under Restaurant
Ft. Lauderdale, Florida

1 large carrot, cut into ¼" dice
3 medium celery ribs, cut into
  ¼" dice
1 large onion, chopped fine
1 medium leek, chopped fine
1½-2 lbs. red snapper, or
1½-2 lbs. striped bass, boned
  with frames reserved (cut
  fillets into ½" squares)
1 cup dry white wine
4 garlic cloves, crushed
6 sprigs of parsley
2 cups heavy cream
3 Tablespoons unsalted butter
8 oz. bay scallops
Salt
White pepper
2 tomatoes, peeled, seeded
  and roughly chopped
Cayenne pepper
¼ cup fresh basil, shredded

1. Combine the carrot, celery, onion and leek. Reserve 4 cups of the diced vegetables. Place any remaining diced vegetables in a stock pot or large Dutch oven. Add fish frames, wine, garlic, parsley and 4 cups of water. Bring to a boil, reduce heat and simmer, uncovered, for 20 minutes to make fish stock.

2. Meanwhile in a large saucepan, cook the cream over moderately low heat until reduced by half (about 15 minutes).

3. In a large skillet, melt the butter over moderately high heat. Add the fish and scallops and sauté, stirring until just white and opaque, about 4 minutes. Remove from heat and season lightly with salt and white pepper.

4. Strain the fish stock through a fine sieve, discard solids. Return the stock to the pot, add the reserved vegetables and bring to a boil. Reduce the heat and simmer uncovered for 4 minutes. Add the reduced cream, tomatoes and sautéed seafood. Season with salt, white pepper and cayenne to taste.

5. To serve, place a generous pinch of basil in each bowl and cover with piping hot soup.

Serves: 6-8
Preparation: 35 minutes
Cooking: 45-55 minutes

An elegant winner.

32

AUSTRIAN CHERRY SOUP

CHEF MIKE ZYLA
Paradise Valley Country Club
Paradise Valley, Arizona

4 cups water
1 orange, sliced
4 cloves
1 cinnamon stick
½ cup sugar
2 cups sauterne wine
2 cans cherry pie filling
1 pt. heavy cream, whipped
Whipped cream as garnish

1. Boil water, orange slices, cloves, cinnamon stick and sugar for 25 minutes. Strain and refrigerate until thoroughly chilled.

2. Add the wine, cherry pie filling and whipped cream. Blend well and put back in refrigerator until ready to serve.

3. Serve <u>cold</u> in long stemmed glasses with a dollop of whipped cream on top. May serve as an appetizer or dessert.

Serves: 8
Preparation: 15 minutes
Cooking: 25 minutes

So delicate and special.

33

ITALIAN MINESTRONE

1 ½ lbs. cut-up beef
2 Tablespoons oil
1 clove garlic, minced
1 large onion, chopped
2 carrots, sliced
2 stalks celery, chopped
¼ cup fresh parsley, chopped
3½ qts. water
1 8-oz. can tomato sauce
½ teaspoon thyme
½ teaspoon oregano
1 bay leaf
1 Tablespoon salt
½ teaspoon black pepper
1 10-oz. package frozen green
   beans
1 10-oz. package frozen peas
2 cups cabbage, chopped
1 16-oz. can kidney beans
½ lb. macaroni
Parmesan cheese as garnish
   (optional)

Serves: 10
Preparation: 30 minutes
Cooking: 2 hours

1. Sauté beef in oil until brown. Add garlic and sauté only 2 to 3 minutes. Add onion, carrots, celery, parsley, water, tomato sauce, thyme, oregano, bay leaf, salt and pepper. Bring to a boil, turn down heat, cover and simmer for 1½ hours, stirring occasionally.

2. Add remaining ingredients and simmer for 20 minutes or until macaroni is al dente. Serve with Parmesan cheese on the side and a loaf of Italian bread.

You'll never taste a better minestrone than this.

ITALIAN WEDDING SOUP

4 large chicken breasts
3 qts. of water
1 large onion, chopped
1 carrot, chopped
2 Tablespoons parsley,
  chopped
1 Tablespoon salt
½ teaspoon ground pepper
2 bunches of endive, cooked,
  squeezed and drained
1 lb. ground beef
2 Tablespoons Parmesan
  cheese, freshly grated
1 Tablespoon parsley, chopped
¼ teaspoon garlic powder
2 Tablespoons fine bread
  crumbs
2 eggs
Grated Parmesan or Romano
  cheese as garnish

Makes: 3½ to 4 qts.
Preparation: 1 hour
Cooking: 1 hour 15 minutes

1. In a large kettle cook chicken breasts, water, chopped onion, celery, carrot, parsley and salt and pepper. Bring to a boil. Simmer for 35 minutes. Remove chicken breasts; set aside to cool.

2. Make sure endive is cooked in separate container. Squeeze completely dry. Chop very fine (by hand). Add to chicken broth.

3. Clean chicken from skin and bone (throw away). Chop meat into 1″ pieces. Add to soup.

4. In a bowl combine ground beef, cheese, parsley, garlic powder, bread crumbs and eggs. Mix thoroughly, shape into 1″ balls and drop into broth. Cook soup for another 30 minutes. Add more seasoning if necessary. Serve with grated cheese on the side and Italian bread.

Always requested for special occasions—For Randy.

35

CHEF HENRI LABAZEE
Palm Beach, Florida

CREME de LAITUES (CREAM OF LETTUCE SOUP)

1 head of lettuce, washed and blanched in salt water
1½ cups milk, scalded
4 Tablespoons butter
½ cup flour
2 cups chicken broth
1½ medium sliced onions
1 carrot sliced
Sprig of parsley
1 teaspoon salt
Pinch of pepper
Fried garlic croutons as garnish
A little chervil as garnish

1. After boiling lettuce for 7 minutes, drain and coarsely chop. Add to hot bechamel.

2. Bechamel: Cook broth, onions, carrots and parsley for 15 to 20 minutes. Strain.

3. In a separate pan melt butter, gradually add flour, hot broth and milk. Add seasoning and chopped lettuce. Simmer until lettuce is quite tender. Serve immediately with garlic croutons (and chervil, if desired).

4. To make garlic croutons, simply cut a slice of white bread into 1" cubes, fry in butter with minced garlic clove until golden on each side of cube.

5. We like this soup with cream or Half and Half in substitute of milk and flour. Add in with broth (do not scald). Just a matter of choice, either way it's marvelous.

Serves: 4
Preparation: 30 minutes
Cooking: 20-25 minutes

Chef Labazee made this soup for the Gallerie Wildenstein in New York.

LEEK AND POTATO SOUP AND VICHYSOISSE

DR. KATIE SPANGERBERG
Laguna, California

3 large leeks including greens, washed and chopped fine
½ cup butter
1½ qts. chicken broth
2 lbs. potatoes, peeled and diced
1 cup Half and Half
Salt and white pepper to taste
Fresh chives, chopped (garnish)

1. Melt ¼ cup butter in kettle and add leeks. Reduce heat, cover and cook leeks for 5 minutes or until they sweat. Do not fry or brown.

2. Add broth, potatoes, salt, pepper and simmer for 45 minutes until potatoes are very soft.

3. Put soup mixture in blender and purée the soup. If mixture is too thick, add a little more chicken broth.

4. Just before serving, add the remaining ¼ cup butter and cream. Heat and serve with chopped chives.

5. For vichysoisse, do not add cream until chilled in the refrigerator several hours. Blend in cream, mixing thoroughly and serve with chopped chives.

Serves: 8
Preparation: 1 hour
Cooking: 45 minutes-1 hour

Another exceptional dish.

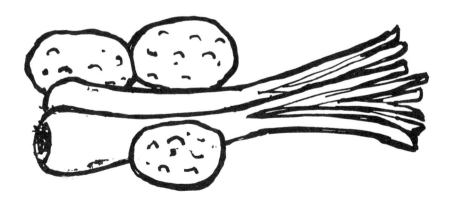

37

NICK HULYK
KATHERINE HULYK
Kiev, Russia

RUSSIAN CABBAGE SOUP

FIRST HALF:
2-2½ lbs. beef stew or roast
  beef, cut into cubes
¼ cup butter
2½ qts. water
2 bay leaves
1 teaspoon salt
½ teaspoon black pepper
1 teaspoon garlic powder
1 teaspoon thyme
1 large onion, chopped
2 celery stalks, chopped
2 carrots, chopped
¼ cup fresh parsley, chopped

1. Melt the butter in a large kettle, add beef and brown lightly. Add the remaining ingredients. Bring to a boil, cover, and simmer over a low heat for 2 hours. This stock is necessary for the elegant flavor. Then add the remaining ingredients. (There are some ingredients that are repeated, in the second part of cooking, but they are to be repeated.

SECOND HALF:
1-2 lb. head of cabbage, sliced
  thin)
¼ cup fresh parsley, chopped
2 carrots, chopped
2 medium onions, chopped
4 celery stalks, chopped
2 Tablespoons Bovril
  meat base
1 32-oz. jar sauerkraut, washed
  and drained
2 16-oz. cans stewed tomatoes
⅛ teaspoon cayenne pepper
4 Tablespoons firmly packed
  brown sugar
1½ teaspoons salt
  (more if needed)

1. Cover and cook over medium heat for 1 more hour, stirring every 15 minutes.

2. Serve with rye bread, or your favorite hard crusted bread.

Yields: 4 qts.
Preparation: ½ hour
Cooking: 3 hours

Many a cold winter night we enjoyed this delicious hearty soup—you will also.

SALADS

Hearts of Palm Salad 40
Caesar Salad 41
Grandpa's Antipasto Salad 42
Brutus Salad 43
Cauliflower Zucchini Salad 44
Marinated Broccoli and
    Cauliflower 45
Spinach Salad with Hot Bacon
    Dressing 46
Spinach Salad 47
Salad des Asperges aux
    Echalotes 48

Joan's "Hell I Don't Know"
    Salad 49
Summer Fruit Salad 50
Summer Fresh Fruit Salad 51
Flaming Spinach Salad 52
Mandarin Cashew Salad 53
Cucumbers in Sour Cream 54
Uncle Johnie's Cole Slaw 55
Mediterranean Salad 56
Overnight Layered Salad 57
Cranberry Salad 58

HEARTS OF PALM SALAD

BETTE RUTTEN
Arcadia, California

DRESSING:
⅓ cup salad oil
2 Tablespoons lemon juice
1 teaspoon sugar
½ teaspoon salt
1 teaspoon aromatic bitters
(bought in liquor store)
¼ teaspoon paprika
1 Tablespoon celery, chopped
very fine
2 Tablespoons green olives,
chopped very fine

SALAD:
1 14-oz. can hearts of palm,
drained and cut into 1″
pieces
4 cups Bibb lettuce, torn into
bite size

Serves: 4-6
Preparation: 15 minutes

Wonderfully tasty.

1. Mix all ingredients for dressing, place in a jar, shake well and refrigerate for at least 2 hours.

2. Toss hearts of palm, lettuce and dressing and serve.

CAESAR SALAD

CHEF NORBERT RUEGG
Basin Street Restaurant
Palm Bay, Florida

2 heads romaine lettuce,
washed, dried and torn
in pieces
1 clove garlic
½ teaspoon salt
¼ teaspoon dry mustard
¼ teaspoon fresh ground
pepper
½ cup Parmesan cheese,
grated
½ cup olive oil
Juice of 2 or 3 lemons
4 or 5 anchovy fillets, chopped
in small pieces
2 eggs at room temperature
or cooked for 1 minute
1 cup French bread croutons,
browned in oil

Serves: 4-6
Preparation: 20 minutes

1. Rub garlic clove all around in salad bowl. Add salt, mustard, ground pepper, cheese, oil, lemon juice and anchovy fillets; mix well.

2. Add eggs and whisk until well blended. Toss in romaine lettuce gently but thoroughly. Just before serving add the 1 cup of croutons; toss briefly.

You will never make any other Caesar Salad after this one—a ten plus, plus.

41

GRANDPA'S ANTIPASTO

½ head escarole lettuce, torn
   to bite size
1 head Bibb lettuce, torn to
   bite size
1 can ripe olives, sliced and
   drained
1 can garbanzo beans, drained
1 green pepper, cleaned and
   cut into 1" pieces
1 medium tomato, cut into
   small pieces
½ lb. salami,* cut into julienne
   strips
½ lb. Mozzarella cheese, cut
   in julienne strips
10 cherry peppers (optional)

DRESSING:
½ cup olive oil
¼ cup wine vinegar
⅓ cup Romano or Parmesan
   cheese, grated
⅛ teaspoon garlic powder
½ teaspoon salt
1½ teaspoons dry mustard
Pepper, freshly ground

Serves: 6-8
Preparation: 30 minutes

1. Combine all dressing ingredients in a jar. Shake well and refrigerate until ready to use.

2. Pour over salad and serve.

   *See page 137.

Good enough as a main meal with some Italian bread and wine.

42

BRUTUS SALAD

CHEF CHRISTIAN PLANCHON
The Down Under Restuarant
Ft. Lauderdale, Florida

4 heads Bibb lettuce
2 tomatoes, peeled and sliced
in ⅛ ths.
¼ cup green onions, chopped
½ cup bacon, fried and
crumbled
1 cup croutons
1 garlic clove
½ cup Romano or Parmesan
cheese, fresh grated
1 cup olive oil
Juice of 2½ lemons
½ teaspoon ground pepper
¼ teaspoon oregano
1 egg at room temperature
¼ teaspoon fresh mint,
chopped

Serves: 4-6
Preparation: 20 minutes

Scrumptious.

1. In a large wooden salad bowl, pour 2 Tablespoons of good imported olive oil. Sprinkle with salt, rub firmly with garlic.

2. Remove garlic, add tomatoes, then Bibb lettuce, green onions, cheese and bacon.

3. Make dressing. Pour oil, lemon juice, pepper, mint and oregano in a mixing bowl. Add coddled egg and whip vigorously. Pour over greens and toss. Top with croutons and serve.

43

CAULIFLOWER ZUCCHINI SALAD

BARBARA ROTH
Las Vegas, Nevada

1 head cauliflower, broken into flowerets
1 red onion, sliced thinly and separated into rings
4 zucchini, sliced about 1/8" thick
1 green pepper, diced
2 celery stalks, diced
1 6-oz. can olives, sliced and pitted
1 teaspoon fresh parsley, chopped
3/4 cup sugar

DRESSING:
3/4 cup oil
1/2 cup red wine vinegar
1/2 cup cider vinegar
2 teaspoons salt
1 teaspoon celery seed
1 teaspoon dry mustard

Serves: 6
Preparation: 30 minutes
Cooking: 5 minutes

This will please all salad lovers.

1. Combine all vegetables in a bowl and sprinkle sugar over vegetables.

2. Place all dressing ingredients in a saucepan and bring to a boil. Pour hot dressing over vegetables, cover and marinate at least 4 to 24 hours in the refrigerator.

3. Serve on a lettuce leaf.

CHEF NORBERT RUEGG
Basin Street Restaurant
Palm Bay, Florida

MARINATED BROCCOLI AND CAULIFLOWER

1 bunch of broccoli cut into flowerets
1 head of cauliflower cut into flowerets
1 cup olive oil
½ cup white vinegar
½ Tablespoon oregano
½ Tablespoon thyme
1 clove garlic, minced
1 teaspoon M.S.G. or Swiss Knorr all purpose seasoning
Salt and pepper to taste

Serves: 6-8
Preparation: 15 minutes

A distinctive delightful salad.

1. Mix all together and marinate at least 4 hours before serving.

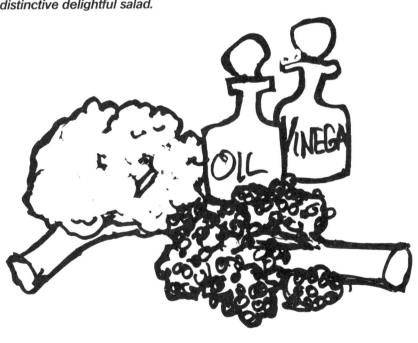

45

JUDY CASEY
Tempe, Arizona

SPINACH SALAD WITH HOT BACON DRESSING

DRESSING:
6 slices bacon
½ cup sugar
¼ teaspoon salt
Fresh ground pepper
⅛ teaspoon garlic powder
¼ cup red wine vinegar
½ teaspoon Worcestershire
   sauce
1 to 2 Tablespoons cornstarch

SALAD:
1 bunch spinach greens or red
   leafed lettuce
2 to 3 hard boiled eggs, sliced
1 bunch green onions with tops,
   chopped

Serves: 4-6
Preparation: 15 minutes
Cooking: 10 minutes

1. Dice bacon and sauté. Save grease. Sprinkle bacon over salad greens.

2. Combine grease and remaining ingredients until slightly thickened.

3. Serve over greens, garnish with egg and onion.

One of our favorites and good with everything.

46

SPINACH SALAD

FRED DAILY
Winter Garden, Florida

1 bunch spinach, chopped, cleaned, drained and de-stemmed or
1 bunch leaf lettuce
¼ lb. fresh bean sprouts
4 hard boiled eggs, sliced
4 slices bacon, crisped and crumbled

DRESSING:
1 cup salad oil
¾ cup sugar
1 cup catsup
Salt
½ cup vinegar
2 Tablespoons Worcestershire sauce
1 medium onion
1 teaspoon celery seed

Serves: 6
Preparation: 30 minutes

This has a sweet-sour taste and always a hit.

1. Mix dressing by placing in blender and pour over ingredients. Part of eggs and bacon may be used for garnishing.

2. This dressing will keep 2 weeks in the refrigerator.

CHEF VINCENT GUERITHAULT
Vincent's French Cuisine
Scottsdale, Arizona

SALADE DES ASPERGES AUX ÉCHALOTES

(Warm Asparagus Salad with Shallots)

DRESSING:
1 Tablespoon Dijon mustard
4 Tablespoons sherry vinegar
(more if desired)
12 Tablespoons olive or
vegetable oil
Salt and pepper to taste
4 large shallots, chopped,
rinsed and dried

SALAD:
40 fresh small asparagus (10
per person)
Red leaf lettuce, or
Fresh spinach, or
Endive
1 large tomato, blanched,
peeled, seeded and chopped

Serves: 4
Preparation: 35 minutes
Cooking: 2-3 minutes

1. Mix mustard and sherry vinegar, whisking 2 Tablespoons of oil at a time slowly so that the dressing doesn't break. It if breaks, start slowly again. Add salt and pepper. Add shallots. Store in Tupperware until ready to use.

2. Boil water in large pan. Salt heavily and submerge asparagus that has been tied in a bundle. Cook 2 minutes or until tender. Refresh in ice.

3. Arrange lettuce on plate. When ready to serve, submerge asparagus again in hot water quickly, just to heat. Toss through dressing. Arrange on lettuce and top with shallots, tomatoes and rest of dressing.

So elegant and special. Superb taste.

48

LANA HUGO
Tempe, Arizona

JOAN'S "HELL I DON'T KNOW" SALAD

1 8-oz. bottle olive oil
1 jar marinated artichokes, chopped
1 Tablespoon artichoke liquid
1 small can anchovies and oil, mashed
1 clove garlic, minced
1 small 7-8-oz. jar green olives, drained
1 small can ripe olives, drained
1 can garbanzo beans, drained
Freshly ground pepper to taste
1 package onion garlic croutons
1 head of romaine lettuce torn to bite size

Serves: 6-8
Preparation: 25 minutes

A delicious blend of flavors.

1. Stir together oil, artichokes, artichoke liquid, anchovies and garlic. Marinate for 4 to 6 hours.

2. Add green and ripe olives and garbanzo beans when ready to serve. Mix well and toss with romaine lettuce. Serve with croutons on top.

SUMMER FRUIT SALAD

FLORENCE HENNINGSEN
Tempe, Arizona

1 3¾-oz. regular vanilla
    pudding mix
1 20-oz. can pineapple chunks
1 can mandarin oranges
1 cup pineapple juice
Cantaloupe, cubed
Fresh honeydew, cubed
Seedless grapes
Fresh cherries
Bananas, sliced
Coconut, toasted or plain
Nuts, chopped

1. Drain pineapple in a cup to measure 1 cup juice. Set pineapple aside.

2. Drain mandarin oranges. (If you need more liquid to make 1 cup of juice, use some of the mandarin juice.) Set oranges aside.

3. Mix juice with vanilla pudding in sauce-pan over low-medium heat and stir constantly until thickened. For micro-wave, put on medium power for 3 to 4 minutes, stirring after 2 minutes.

4. Place pudding mixture in refrigerator for at least 4 hours.

5. Put pineapple (well drained) and mandarin orange in plastic container and refrigerate until ready to use.

6. When ready to serve, drain any juice left in pineapple and orange sections. Add pudding mixture and as much fresh fruit as you desire. Place on a lettuce leaf, top with coconut and nuts. This goes well with anything.

Serves: 4-6
Preparation: 30 minutes
Cooking: 4-10 minutes

This is truly a winner.

MARY WALKER
McDonald, Pennsylvania

SUMMER FRESH FRUIT SALAD

½ pineapple, cleaned and
   chopped in ½" cubes
1 cup sugar
1 6-oz. can pineapple juice
1 grapefruit, skinned, seeded
   and cubed
1 large Sunkist orange, skinned
   and cubed
2 kiwi, skinned and cubed
1 small cantaloupe, skinned,
   seeded and cubed
1 small honeydew melon,
   skinned, seeded and cubed
2 cups seedless green grapes
1 large pear, cored and cubed
   with skin on
1 large Delicious apple,
   cored and cubed with skin on
3 medium plums, seeded and
   cubed
2 cups sweet black cherries,
   seeded
1 large (1-qt., 14-oz.) can of
   apricot nectar
Bananas, strawberries, blueberries for garnish

Makes: 1 gallon
Preparation: 1 hour, 30 minutes

1. Mix all (except garnish) and refrigerate at least 24 hours so that all juices
and fruit can marinate. Serve with a
few slices of banana, strawberries and
blueberries on top. (You could put 1
cup of blueberries in the salad.)

A blend of marvelous fruits and excellent for any time of the year.

51

WAYNE C. ZIPPERER
Syracuse, New York

FLAMING SPINACH SALAD

8 oz. spinach leaves, washed and dried
3 slices bacon
1 teaspoon sugar
2 teaspoons vinegar
3 teaspoons A-1 sauce
3 teaspoons Worcestershire sauce
Juice of ½ lemon
1 oz. brandy or cognac
Freshly ground pepper
1 hard-boiled egg, finely chopped
2 Tablespoons turkey, chopped (can use more)
1 Tablespoon almonds, toasted

1. After cleaning spinach leaves, put in a large bowl and set in the refrigerator until ready to use.

2. Chop bacon and sauté until almost done. Add the sugar, vinegar, A-1 sauce, Worcestershire sauce, lemon juice and stir constantly.

3. Add brandy or cognac (at this point you can flame, not really necessary). If you don't flame, let it sauté for about 2 to 3 minutes, then pour over the spinach leaves. Add chopped egg, turkey and almonds.

4. Toss gently and divide into 2 bowls. Serve with French or Italian bread and a glass of wine.

Serves: 2
Preparation: 30 minutes
Cooking: 5-10 minutes

A spectacular salad.

MANDARIN CASHEW SALAD

ANNA LEE SMITH
Warren, Ohio

4 chicken halves, cooked, boned and skinned
½ teaspoon ginger
1 bunch leaf lettuce, chopped in ½" strips
1 bunch green onions, chopped (greens also)
1 cup cashews, toasted in oven and cooled
½ cup sesame seeds, toasted in oven and cooled
¼ package Mai Fun rice sticks
1 can mandarin oranges, drained, patted dry and cut in half

SALAD DRESSING:
5 Tablespoons sugar
1 teaspoon soy sauce
¼ cup red wine vinegar
½ cup salad oil
¼ teaspoon pepper
Salt to taste
Salad Shells*

Serves: 4-6
Preparation: 45 minutes

1. Cut chicken breasts into 1" cubes. Sprinkle ginger over top and mix well. Cover and put in the refrigerator to chill.

2. Put chopped lettuce and onions in another bowl and set in refrigerator.

3. Fry rice sticks a small amount at a time and drain on paper towel. Set aside.

4. Mix salad dressing ingredients in a saucepan over medium heat for a few minutes until all is melted and blended. Cool completely.

5. Mix chicken, lettuce, onions, cashews, sesame seeds, rice sticks, mandarin oranges and dressing in a large bowl; toss lightly. Put into individual bowls or salad shells and serve with rolls.

*See page 289.

A scrumptious delight for lunch or as a main entree.

CUCUMBERS IN SOUR CREAM

**2 medium cucumbers, peeled
and sliced
5 green onions, chopped
(including greens)
1 cup sour cream
1 Tablespoon sugar
1 teaspoon salt
2 Tablespoons vinegar
Paprika (garnish)**

1. Mix sour cream, sugar, salt and vinegar until well blended. Pour over cucumbers and onions. Cover and refrigerate at least 2 hours before serving. Serve in individual salad plates. Sprinkle top with paprika.

Serves: 4-6
Preparation: 15 minutes

This was and is a family favorite since childhood.

UNCLE JOHNIE'S COLE SLAW

JOHN LEBER
Pt. Pleasant Beach, New Jersey

½ head cabbage, chopped
½ green pepper, chopped
1 small onion, chopped
2 stalks of celery, chopped
1 carrot, grated
1 Tablespoon oil
1 Tablespoon white vinegar
½ teaspoon salt
¼ teaspoon pepper
3 Tablespoons sugar
2 Tablespoons milk
½ cup mayonnaise

1. Mix cabbage, pepper, onion, celery and carrot together. Pour oil and vinegar over all, mix and let sit for 10 minutes. Drain.

2. Whisk together salt, pepper, sugar, milk and mayonnaise. Pour over slaw. Mix well and serve.

Serves: 4
Preparation: 30 minutes

This cole slaw tops them all.

55

MEDITERRANEAN SALAD

MURIEL SCHAFFER
Phoenix, Arizona

**2 Tablespoons parsley,
 chopped
8 cups torn lettuce
6 green onions, chopped
½ cup celery, chopped
¾ cup sharp Cheddar cheese,
 shredded**

**DRESSING:
½ cup oil
¼ cup fresh lemon juice
½ teaspoon salt
½ teaspoon dill weed
¼ teaspoon fresh ground
 pepper**

Serves: 4-6
Preparation: 15 minutes

Easy and so refreshing.

1. Mix all salad dressing ingredients in a jar and place in refrigerator until ready to use.

2. When ready to use, toss salad and pour dressing over top. Garnish with more cheese on top.

MARION CARDONES
Warren, Ohio

OVERNIGHT LAYERED SALAD

1 head of lettuce, chopped
1 bunch of green onions
   including greens, chopped
1 large green pepper, chopped
1 cup celery, chopped
1 10-oz. package frozen peas,
   uncooked
1 can water chestnuts, drained
   and chopped
1 can ripe olives, chopped
1 can green olives, chopped
2 cups mayonnaise
2 Tablespoons sugar
4 hard boiled eggs, shelled
   and chopped
½ lb. bacon, fried crisp and
   crumbled
¼ lb. Monterey cheese, grated
¼ lb. Cheddar cheese, grated

Serves: 12-15
Preparation: 1 hour

1. Use a large container such as 13" x 20" x 4" flat casserole.

2. Lay in vegetables in order given starting with lettuce on the bottom. (You can cut this recipe in half, also.)

3. Spread mayonnaise over top of vegetables, sprinkle on sugar, then crumble on bacon and cheeses. Refrigerate overnight. Do not toss when ready to serve.

This is a dynamite combination of vegetables that is outstanding.

57

RANDY ZIPPERER
Kissimmee, Florida

CRANBERRY SALAD

1 small package cherry Jello
1 cup hot water
1 cup sugar
1 Tablespoon lemon juice
1 cup drained crushed
   pineapple (save juice)
1 cup raw ground cranberries
   (save juice)
1 orange, chopped
1 cup celery, chopped
½ cup pecans, chopped

Serves: 6
Preparation: 30 minutes

A must at our house on Holidays.

1. Dissolve Jello in hot water. Add sugar and all juices, then all other remaining ingredients.

2. Chill in oiled pan.

SEAFOODS

Shrimp in Creamed Mustard
Sauce. 60
Sautéed Scampi in Garlic
Sauce. 61
Shrimp or Scallops Sauté. 62
Shrimp Pernod. 64
Coquille St. Jacques. 65
Pasta Prawns and Scallops. 66
Scallops and "Shrimp
Marseilles". 67
Flounder A La Maison. 68

Stuffed Flounder in
Wine Sauce. 69
Barbecue Sole. 70
Lobster Thermidor Fondue. 71
Crab Crêpe Maxims. 72
Crêpes A La Crab. 73
Lemon Sole Dumplings. 74
Tish's Salmon Loaf. 74
Mimi's Tuna Casserole. 76
Suzie's Tuna Casserole. 77
Stuffed Clams Casino. 78

CONNIE ZIPPERER
Syracuse, New York

SHRIMP IN CREAMED MUSTARD SAUCE

2 lbs. fresh shrimp, peeled
  and deveined
1 cup fish stock*
½ cup dry white wine
1½ Tablespoons Dijon
  prepared mustard (or more
  to your taste)
2½ Tablespoons flour
4 Tablespoons butter
1 cup whipping cream,
  unwhipped
½ teaspoon salt
1 teaspoon fresh parsley,
  chopped
2 cups cooked rice

1. Heat and cook fish stock and wine to ¾ cup. Set aside.

2. Sauté shrimp in butter until lightly pink, 3-4 minutes.

3. Remove with slotted spoon and set aside.

4. Add flour, stirring constantly and alternate liquid with whipping cream.

5. Stir until slightly thickened, then add salt, pepper, mustard and chopped parsley. Mix well.

6. Add shrimp and serve over the bed of cooked rice, garnished with parsley on the side.

*See page 290.

Serves: 4
Preparation: 30 minutes
Cooking: 30 minutes

The oh's and ah's will be never ending.

SAUTÉED SCAMPI IN GARLIC SAUCE

CHEF NORBERT RUEGG
Basin Street Restaurant
Palm Bay, Florida

8 jumbo shrimp, cleaned and
  deveined, or
16 medium shrimp, cleaned
  and deveined
1 cup flour
2 Tablespoons fresh lemon
  juice
1 Tablespoon Worcestershire
  sauce
3 Tablespoons butter
1 green onion, chopped
4 or 5 fresh mushrooms, sliced
3 cloves of garlic, minced

Serves: 2
Preparation: 15 minutes
Cooking: 5-7 minutes

A favorite. Thanks, Norbert.

1. Dredge the shrimp in flour quickly and sauté them in the butter 2 minutes on each side. Remove and set aside and keep warm.

2. Add chopped onion, mushrooms, lemon juice and Worcestershire sauce. Boil 1 minute, add garlic and boil another minute. Add shrimp to get hot only. Remove and serve with rice on the side.

61

SEAFOOD

SHRIMP OR SCALLOPS SAUTÉ

"CORNELIUS"
Corning Ware
Corning, New York

2 Tablespoons olive oil
2 leeks,* chopped, or
1 small onion, chopped
1 clove garlic, minced
1 teaspoon dried tarragon,** or
2 teaspoons fresh tarragon,
   chopped
¼ cup fresh parsley, chopped
1 Tablespoon butter
Salt
Pepper
⅓ cup dry white wine, or
⅓ cup sherry
2 lbs. large raw shrimp,
   shelled, or
2 lbs. scallops

TOPPING:
¼ cup butter
¼ cup bread crumbs (made
   from fresh bread in blender
   or food processor)
2 Tablespoons Parmesan
   cheese, fresh grated
Lemon wedges for garnish
Paprika (optional)

1. Heat oil in 10" Rangetoppers skillet on medium heat. Add leeks, garlic, tarragon, parsley, and sauté lightly until onion is transparent.

2. Add 1 Tablespoon butter, salt and pepper to taste and white wine. Increase heat to medium high. Cook until bubbly.

3. Add shrimp and toss quickly, cooking until shrimp are just pink (about 5 minutes). The scallops should take about 3 minutes or until they turn opaque.) Do not overcook. Remove from heat.

4. In a small pan melt ¼ cup butter. Add bread crumbs and Parmesan cheese. Over medium high heat toss mixture until it begins to brown. Sprinkle over shrimp and run under broiler until browned. Serve with lemon wedges and dot the top with paprika, if you like, before serving.

(continued)

62

Shrimp or Scallops Sauté (continued)

*Wash split leeks well to remove all grit. Dry on paper towel.

**Soak dried tarragon in a Tablespoon of the white wine (or vermouth) for 10 minutes before adding to the pan.

Cornelius says "We seem to be eating more seafood these days. One reason is that now fresh seafood is available even in the landlocked area in which I live. Since this isn't a budget dish, I use it for special company or family occasions. Serves 4 as a main dish, 6-8 as an elegant first course."

Serves: 4 or 8
Preparation: 25 minutes
Cooking: 10-15 minutes

A ten plus-plus. Superb!

CHEF PATRICK TOMBELAINE
Golden Eagle Restaurant
Phoenix, Arizona

SHRIMP PERNOD

16 to 20 shrimp (prawns)
1 cup mushrooms, sliced
8 shallots, chopped fine
1 clove garlic, finely diced
1 oz. Pernod
1 cup brown sauce (1 Knorr
  Swiss-Hunter Sauce)
¼ cup heavy cream
Cooked rice pilaf or fettuccine

1. Make brown sauce and set aside. Melt enough clarified butter to cover the bottom of a heavy heated skillet and sauté together shrimp, garlic, shallots and mushrooms stirring constantly.

2. When shrimp have turned red in color, add Pernod and cook slightly.

3. Put the brown sauce and cream in with the shrimp and stir until well blended.

4. Serve with rice pilaf or fettuccine.

Serves: 4
Preparation: 20 minutes
Cooking: 10-20 minutes

A very unique and special entrée—another 10 plus.

COQUILLE ST. JACQUES

MARION CARDONES
Warren, Ohio

SEAFOOD MIXTURE:
1/4 lb. each scallops, shrimp,
  crab, fillet of sole
4 Tablespoons butter
1/2 lb. fresh mushrooms, sliced
6 green onions with tops,
  chopped
Juice of 1/2 lemon
1 1/2 cups dry white wine
1 teaspoon salt
1/8 teaspoon white pepper
1 bay leaf
3 Tablespoons butter, melted
2 Tablespoons flour
1 1/2 cups Half and Half
3 egg yolks
1 cup Swiss cheese, shredded

POTATO MIXTURE:
1 1/2 cups instant potatoes
1 1/4 cups hot water
6 Tablespoons butter
1/2 cup Half and Half
1/2 teaspoon salt
2 egg yolks
Fresh parsley as garnish

1. Sauté mushrooms, onions, lemon juice in 4 Tablespoons butter for about 3 to 4 minutes.

2. Add seafood that has been washed, drained and cut into bite size, wine, salt, bay leaf and pepper and bring to a boil.

3. Reduce heat and simmer for 2 minutes.

4. Remove all ingredients with slotted spoon except bay leaf and set aside.

5. Boil liquid until reduced to about 1 cup.

6. Discard bay leaf. Blend in 3 Tablespoons melted butter and flour. Cook until smooth and lightly thickened.

7. Beat 3 egg yolks and add to 1 1/2 cups Half and Half. Blend into hot wine mixture stirring constantly. Do not boil.

8. Add seafood mixture and pour into well buttered 9" x 13" pan or 8 to 10 individual ramekin dishes.

9. Mix instant potato mixture in order given and pipe edge of seafood mixture with potato mixture.

10. Sprinkle top of casserole with shredded Swiss cheese. Place under broiler (about 8" down) until golden and garnish with fresh parsley sprig before serving.

Serves: 8-10
Preparation: 45 minutes
Baking: 10-15 minutes

Believe me, this is absolutely divine.

65

CHEF ANTONIO POLOGRUTO
Hyatt Regency Hotel
Memphis, Tennessee

PASTA, PRAWNS AND SCALLOPS

6 large shrimp
6 large scallops
4 oz. fresh mushrooms, sliced
½ teaspoon shallots
6 oz. garlic butter
3 oz. brandy
3 oz. Amaretto*
4 oz. heavy cream
8 oz. spinach fettuccine
  cooked al dente
Parsley (garnish)

1. Sauté shrimp, scallops, mushrooms and shallots in garlic butter about 3 minutes. Remove and set aside.

2. Add brandy and Amaretto and cook about 3 minutes again. Add cream and cook until reduced about half.

3. Add shrimp and scallops. Heat in cream mixture for a few minutes.

4. Remove shrimp and scallops from sauce and set on side of platter.

5. Toss fettuccine in sauce and pour in center of platter. Arrange scallops and shrimp on top of fettuccine, sprinkle with chopped parsley and serve.

*See page 308.

Serves: 2
Preparation: 20 minutes
Cooking: 10-15 minutes

Exquisitely elegant.

SCALLOPS AND SHRIMP "MARSEILLES"

CHEF ANTONIO POLOGRUTO
Hyatt Regency Hotel
Memphis, Tennessee

8 large shrimp, peeled and
   deveined
Flour
8 large scallops
6 oz. fresh mushrooms, sliced
3 oz. olive oil
1 clove garlic, minced
½ teaspoon shallots
½ to ¾ teaspoon basil, or
2 fresh basil leaves
4 oz. white wine
Salt
Pepper
2 medium tomatoes, blanched,
   peeled, seeded and
   chopped
Cooked rice

Serves: 2
Preparation: 20 minutes
Cooking: 10-15 minutes

Easy—elegant—an Italian classic.

1. Dust shrimp in flour. Sauté shrimp, scallops and mushrooms in oil for 3 minutes. (Remove and keep warm.)

2. Add garlic, shallots, salt, pepper and basil. Sauté for another 3 minutes.

3. Add wine and chopped tomatoes and reduce liquid (about 2 to 3 minutes of cooking). Add shrimp, scallops and mushrooms.

4. Arrange on a bed of rice and serve.

CHEF NORBERT RUEGG
Basin Street Restaurant
Melbourne, Florida

FLOUNDER
A LA MAISON

4 flounder fillets (1 per person)
1 teaspoon lemon juice
1 teaspoon Worcestershire
   sauce
Pinch of salt
Pinch of pepper
1 cup sifted flour
½ cup butter

SAUCE DRESDEN:
1 cup sour cream
½ teaspoon fresh chives,
   chopped fine, or
½ teaspoon onion greens,
   chopped fine
½ teaspoon horseradish, fresh,
   grated fine
Pinch of salt
Pinch of pepper

GARNITURE:
Lemon slices
Pimento strips
Parsley sprigs
Jumbo black olives

Serves: 4
Preparation: 20 minutes
Cooking: 10-20 minutes

1. Make Sauce Dresden. Combine all ingredients and put in refrigerator to keep cool.

2. Mix lemon juice, Worcestershire sauce, salt and pepper. Dip flounder fillets into mixture, then coat with flour.

3. Sauté flounder in foaming, melted butter until golden brown.

4. Sesrve immediately on warm plate topped with Sauce Dresden and garnish.

Try pompano fish also with this recipe. A rare, delicious treat with either fish.

STUFFED FLOUNDER IN WINE SAUCE

WAYNE C. ZIPPERER
Syracuse, New York

STUFFING:
½ cup chopped onions
8 medium mushrooms, sliced
6 Tablespoons butter
(no substitute)
1 7½-oz. can crabmeat,
drained
12 single 2" x 2" square saltine
crackers, crushed
2 Tablespoons parsley,
chopped (fresh)
½ teaspoon salt
¼ teaspoon white pepper

4 flounder fillets, washed and
patted dry

SAUCE:
4 Tablespoons butter
3 Tablespoons flour
½ teaspoon salt
1½ cups Half and Half
½ cup dry white wine
½ teaspoon lemon zest
1 cup shredded Swiss cheese
Paprika
½ Tablespoon chopped
parsley as garnish

Serves: 4
Preparation: 30 minutes
Baking: 35 minutes

Easy, elegant and so delicious.

1. Sauté onions and mushrooms in butter until limp. Add rest of ingredients and cook about 4 minutes more.

2. Divide stuffing into two parts, shape and press together to size of the two fillets.

3. Lay 2 fillets on well buttered baking dish. Top each fillet with the 2 divided stuffings. Top the 2 stuffings with remaining 2 fillets. Then cut the stuffed fillets in half—making 4 servings.

4. Make a roux with butter and flour. Gradually add Half and Half, stirring constantly. Then slowly add wine and lemon zest. Cook until slightly thickened.

5. Pour over stuffed flounder and bake at 400° 25 minutes.

6. Remove from oven. Sprinkle Swiss cheese over the top, sprinkle paprika lightly and return to oven for 10 minutes. Garnish with chopped parsley.

Could use sole or bass in substitute of flounder.

69

BARBECUE SOLE

4 large fillets of sole, washed
   and dried
1 medium onion, chopped
4 Tablespoons butter
1 clove garlic, minced
½ cup ketchup
⅓ cup water
4 Tablespoons brown sugar
   (or more if desired)
1 Tablespoon Dijon prepared
   mustard
1 Tablespoon vinegar
1 Tablespoon Worcestershire
   sauce
Zest of ½ a lemon
Lemon slices and parsley
   sprigs as garnish

1. Butter a 9" x 13" baking pan and lay fillets on bottom, trying not to overlap.

2. Sauté onion in butter, add garlic and sauté until onion is limp.

3. Add rest of ingredients except the lemon slices and parsley sprigs. Simmer until sightly thickened, about 10 minutes.

4. Pour over sole fillets (can use red snapper, flounder or bass also) and bake uncovered in preheated 350° oven for 30-35 minutes. You can also broil them 5 to 7 minutes on each side. Spread sauce on each side if you broil them. Either way, they are tasty. Remove and garnish with lemon slices and parsley sprigs.

Serves: 4
Preparation: 30 minutes
Baking: 30-35 minutes

I use this sauce for all my barbecues, chicken, pork and beef. We love it.

LOBSTER THERMIDOR FONDUE

CONNIE ZIPPERER
Syracuse, New York

¼ cup butter
¼ cup onions, chopped
1 cup mushrooms, washed
  and sliced
2 Tablespoons flour
1 cup Half and Half
½ cup milk
8 oz. Velveeta cheese, cut
  in cubes
½ cup ripe olives, sliced
⅛ teaspoon cayenne pepper
⅛ teaspoon dry mustard
2 Tablespoons light dry wine
  (optional)
2 cups fresh or frozen lobster,
  cut in chunks (crab can be
  substituted, or even a
  combination of both)
⅛ teaspoon nutmeg
Salt to taste

Serves: 6
Preparation: 35 minutes
Cooking: 15-20 minutes

A ten plus, plus.

1. Sauté onions and mushrooms in butter until limp, about 5 minutes.

2. Add flour to make a thickening. Blend well.

3. Add Half and Half and milk slowly with cheese, stirring constantly over low-medium heat.

4. Add rest of ingredients and cook 5 minutes more. Pour into a chafing dish and serve. (Can be served as an appetizer also.)

5. Serve on the side French bread cut into 1" cubes, a green salad and wine.

71

CRAB CRÊPE MAXIM'S

CHEF BILL MALDONADO
Maldonado's
Pasadena, California

½ cup flour
½ teaspoon salt
½ cup Half and Half
1 egg, lightly beaten
1 Tablespoon cooking oil
4 teaspoons butter
1½ cups Alaskan crabmeat
  chunks
1 cup sour cream
1 fresh lime
1 Tablespoon catsup
½ teaspoon Dijon mustard
4 drops Tabasco sauce
¼ teaspon salt
Paprika
1 boiled egg, chopped
1 Tablespoon chives, chopped
8 thin center slices of lemon
8 bits of truffles, or
8 olive halves

1. To prepare crêpes: sift flour with salt, stir in Half and Half. Blend well. Add egg and oil, whisk only until blended. Batter should be thin enough to make crêpes not over ⅛" thick. Add flour or Half and Half as needed to correct. Heat a crêpe or an 8-9" omelette pan. Melt butter until bubbly but not brown. Make 4 crêpes. Do not cook crêpes on the top side. They should be lightly brown underside, glossy but firm on top. Place on wax paper.

2. To prepare crab filling: divide meat onto crêpes. Squeeze ¼ lime on each and add 1 heaping Tablespoon sour cream. Roll lightly.

3. To prepare sauce: lightly blend remaining sour cream, catsup, mustard, Tabasco and salt. Spoon over filled crêpes. Gently sprinkle a little paprika over sauce, followed by chopped egg and chives.

4. Garnish each crêpe with 2 slices of lemon which have been slit to the center, twisted and dotted with truffle bits or olive halves. Can be prepared one or two hours before serving. Refrigerate up to ½ hour before serving. Best when not too cold.

Serves: 4
Preparation: 35 minutes

Marvelous—a true 10 plus.

CRÊPES À LA CRAB

DR. KATIE SPANGERBERG
Laguna, California

1 6-oz. package fresh or frozen snow crab or king crabmeat
¼ cup butter or margarine
⅓ cup green onions, chopped
1 cup celery, chopped
1 cup mushrooms, sliced
3 Tablespoons flour
1½ cups Half and Half
⅔ cup Swiss cheese, grated
3 Tablespoons sherry
¼ teaspoon salt
⅛ teaspoon white pepper
⅛ teaspoon nutmeg
¼ cup Parmesan cheese, grated
8 cooked crêpes*

1. Thaw crabmeat. Retain liquid and separate into chunks.

2. In saucepan sauté onions, celery and mushrooms in butter for 2 to 3 minutes.

3. Remove with slotted spoon and set aside.

4. Stir flour into liquid until smooth. Add Half and Half and crab liquid and cook until thickened.

5. Stir in Swiss cheese, salt, pepper and nutmeg.

6. In a small bowl toss together crab, onions, celery, mushrooms and ⅓ of the sauce.

7. Add sherry to remaining sauce and set aside.

8. Spoon equal amounts of filling across the center of each crêpe and roll up or fold over.

9. Place in well buttered shallow baking pan and spoon remaining sherry sauce over the top.

10. Sprinkle with Parmesan cheese and bake in preheated 350° oven for 15 minutes.

*See page 293.

Serves: 4
Preparation: 30 minutes
Cooking: 30 minutes

An impressive, elegant, tasty dish.

LEMON SOLE DUMPLINGS

1½ lbs. fillet of sole, or
1½ lbs. fillet of flounder
½ cup butter
1 cup water
¼ teaspoon salt
1 cup flour
3 eggs
⅛ teaspoon nutmeg
¼ teaspoon lemon rind, grated
¼ teaspoon white pepper
Buttered casserole

SAUCE:
4 Tablespoons butter
3 Tablespoons flour
1 cup very dry vermouth
1 can chicken broth
1½ cups whipping cream, or
1½ cups Half and Half
2 heaping teaspoons
   apple jelly
3 teaspoons Knorr Swiss
   chicken granules
Juice of ½ lemon
Zest of 1 lemon
Salt to taste
Pepper to taste
1 cup Swiss cheese, grated
Parsley sprigs (garnish)
Lemon wedges (garnish)

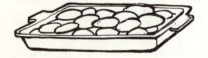

Serves: 6-8
Preparation: 1 hour, 30 minutes
Baking: 30 minutes

1. Pat fillets dry with paper towel over and over until no more moisture comes out and they are completely dry. Chop in food processor.

2. In a small saucepan bring to a boil the butter and water. Remove from heat, add flour and mix thoroughly. Add one egg at a time, beating well after each. Add nutmeg, salt, pepper and chopped fish. Cover and refrigerate for 1½ hours.

3. When the 1½ hours are up, boil water in a 10" x 2" skillet, shape dumplings by using two large spoons, making them oval shaped and dropping about 4 in the water at a time. Cook about 7 minutes on each side. Remove carefully to a well-buttered 9" x 13" baking pan. Set aside until sauce is made.

4. In a skillet melt butter, add flour and make a roux. Add remaining ingredients (except Swiss cheese) and cook about 10 minutes over medium heat until well blended and thickened. (You can make this ahead and freeze up to this point, or refrigerate until ready to bake. Bake straight from freezer at 400° for 20 minutes, reduce heat to 350° the last 10 minutes.)

5. Bake in preheated 350° oven for 20 minutes, remove from oven, sprinkle cheese over top and bake for another 10 minutes. Remove, top with parsley sprigs and lemon wedges on the side.

Very appealing to those of refined cuisine taste.

TISH'S SALMON LOAF

JOHN WALKER
McDonald, Pennsylvania

1 16-oz. can of salmon, drained
and flaked
1 egg, slightly beaten
1 cup grated Cheddar cheese
½ cup Half and Half
3 Tablespoons butter or
margarine, melted
1 Tablespoon lemon juice
½ teaspoon dillweed
¾ cup crushed cornflakes
or bread crumbs

DILL SAUCE:
2 cups mayonnaise
1 cup sour cream
4 Tablespoons fresh Parmesan
cheese, grated
1 teaspoon dillweed
¼ cup onion, finely chopped
1 Tablespoon vinegar
1 teaspoon pepper, freshly
ground
1 Tablespoon fresh lemon juice
2 teaspoons Worcestershire
sauce
2 garlic cloves, minced

GARNISH:
Dill sauce, hard boiled eggs
(sliced), tomato wedges and
asparagus, cooked and
chilled

Serves: 8
Preparation: 1 hour
Baking: 30 minutes

1. Make dill sauce and blend well in blender. Refrigerate until ready to use.

2. Mix all ingredients for salmon loaf and shape into loaf. Put into well buttered 10" x 6" or 9" x 5" pan. Bake in preheated oven at 350° for 30 minutes. Cool loaf 5 minutes. Wrap in Saran Wrap when cooled and refrigerate until serving time. Slice into 8 pieces.

3. Place on plates with leaf lettuce, garnish with dill sauce, sliced hard boiled eggs, tomato and cooked asparagus.

4. Salmon and dill sauce can be made up to a couple days before and refrigerated.

Sensational for brunch or for a hot summer evening entrée.

LANA HUGO
Tempe, Arizona

MIMI'S TUNA CASEROLE

1 cup rice, cooked
1 6½-oz. can tuna
  (can use crab)
5 hard boiled eggs, chopped
1 cup mayonnaise
½ teaspoon salt
⅛ teaspoon cayenne pepper
Dash of black pepper
⅛ teaspoon tarragon, crushed
1 Tablespoon fresh parsley,
  minced
2 teaspoons onions, chopped
  fine
1 5⅓-oz. can evaporated milk
½ cup Cheddar cheese, grated

Serves: 4
Preparation: 20 minutes
Baking: 45 minutes

Easy, quick and delicious!

1. Combine all ingredients except cheese and place in a well buttered 1½-quart casserole. Sprinkle top with grated cheese.

2. Bake in preheated 350° oven for 45 minutes.

SUZIE'S TUNA CASEROLE

MACRINA SUDIMACK
San Rafael, California

1 8-oz. package medium noodles (about 3 cups), cooked al dente and drained
1 6-oz. can of tuna, drained
½ cup mayonnaise
1 medium onion, chopped
4 oz. sharp cheddar, shredded, or
4 oz. Velveeta cheese, shredded
4 Tablespoons green pepper, chopped
2 stalks celery, chopped
2 Tablespoons canned pimento, chopped
1 small can evaporated milk
1 10½-oz. can of cream of mushroom soup
Salt and pepper to taste
Cheddar cheese, grated, as garnish

Serves: 6
Preparation: 25 minutes
Baking: 20 minutes

1. Mix and heat the canned milk, soup, salt, pepper and the 4 oz. of cheese.

2. Pour over the remaining ingredients (except the garnish grated cheese).

3. Put in a well-buttered casserole. Sprinkle garnish grated cheese over the top and bake uncovered in a 425° oven for 20 minutes. Serve with a salad.

For that quick, easy meal that you need in a hurry. You will enjoy it.

CHEF JOE ARCHAZKI
O'Shea's Restaurant
Marco Island, Florida

STUFFED CLAMS CASINO

6 fresh clams
1 6½-oz. can chopped clams, drained
1 small green pepper, diced
1 small onion, diced
1 teaspoon garlic clove, minced
1 stick of butter, melted
1½ cups fine bread crumbs
2 oz. wine
2 oz. lemon juice
1 2-oz. jar diced pimento
½ teaspoon M.S.G.
½ teaspoon cayenne red pepper
½ teaspoon Tabasco
1 teaspoon salt
5 strips of bacon

1. Scrub clams and steam off (1 extra can of chopped clams can be substituted for fresh clams, plus the can mentioned). Dice meat from fresh clams and wash shells again.

2. Sauté green pepper, onion and garlic in the stick of butter. Cool.

3. Mix all the ingredients except bacon in pepper and onion mixture.

4. Stuff clam shells (either fresh ones or ones that you may have had.)

5. Cut bacon into small strips. Top clams with bacon.

6. Bake in preheated 350° oven for 15 to 20 minutes and serve with a salad, Bear Claws* and a light, white wine.

*See page 155.

Yield: 12 shells (2 per person)
Preparation: 25 minutes
Baking: 15-20 minutes

Excellent tasting—easy to prepare—a true compliment will be given by all.

POULTRY

Sautéed Breast of Chicken
and Shrimp. 80
Poulet Au Citron. 81
Chicken Breast with
Raspberry Sauce. 82
Mary Beth's Chicken. 83
Indonesian Chicken Broil. 84
Poulet Geneviese. 85
Ginger Chicken. 86
Chicken Divan. 87
Chicken Kiev. 88
Chicken Scampi. 89
Saffron Cream Chicken. 90

Big Bucket in the Sky Fried
Chicken. 91
Stuffed Chicken Florentine. 92
Thin Man's Barbecue Chicken. . . 94
Sweet and Sour Chicken Wings. . 95
African Chicken Stew. 96
Italian Chicken Stew. 97
"Asopaito" Carmen's Style. 98
Duck of the Bay. 100
Cornish Hens Stuffed with Orange
Pecan Stuffing and Sauce
Bechamel. 101
Chicken Enchiladas or Crêpes. . 102

CHEF TONY POLOGRUTO
Hyatt Regency Hotel
Memphis, Tennessee

SAUTÉED BREAST OF CHICKEN AND SHRIMP OSCAR

4 large chicken breasts, deboned and skinned
Flour
1 beaten egg
Fine bread crumbs
Salt
Pepper
6 oz. butter
1 clove garlic, minced
1 teaspoon chopped shallots
8 asparagus spears, blanched about 3 minutes
8 large shrimp, cleaned and deveined
1 cup Béarnaise Sauce*
¼ cup toasted almonds, sliced

Serves: 4
Preparation: 30 minutes
Cooking: 20-30 minutes

1. Dip chicken breast in flour then egg, then bread crumbs and season.

2. Sauté in 6 oz. of butter, garlic and shallots until golden on each side, about 10 minutes.

3. Add shrimp and asparagus spears, cook shrimp and asparagus only a few minutes or until shrimp are pink.

4. Arrange chicken on individual plates with shrimps and 2 asparagus spears on each. Top with Béarnaise Sauce* and sprinkle with toasted almonds.

*See page 293.

Elegant, and a sure way to please guests.

JUDY CASEY
Tempe, Arizona

POULET AU CITRON
(Chicken with Fresh Lemon)

8 chicken breasts, boned
and skinned
8 Tablespoons butter
(no substitutes)
¼ cup brandy or cognac
Grated rind of 2 lemons
4 garlic cloves, minced
Salt and pepper
1 teaspoon tomato paste
(generous)
1 teaspoon Bovril broth and
seasoning base (generous)
5 Tablespoons flour
1¼ cups chicken broth
Juice of 1 medium lemon
1 cup sour cream at room
temperature
1 cup whipping cream,
unwhipped
1 teaspoon guava jelly
(or crabapple)
3 Tablespoons grated
Parmesan cheese

1. Sauté chicken in 5 Tablespoons butter until just lightly brown, add brandy and let cook a minute.

2. Remove chicken.

3. Add 3 Tablespoons butter, lemon rind, garlic, salt and pepper and cook briefly,

4. Remove from heat and stir in tomato paste, meat base and flour.

5. Mix and return to heat and cook about 5 minutes.

6. Add chicken broth and lemon juice. Stir until sauce comes to a boil over low heat.

7. Remove from heat and cool slightly.

8. Fold in sour cream, heavy cream and jelly slowly.

9. Place chicken in well buttered casserole, pour sauce over chicken and sprinkle with cheese. Bake uncovered 15-20 minutes at 350.°

Serves: 8
Preparation: 35 minutes
Cooking and Baking: 30-40 minutes

This is so elegant and superb. Serve with hard French rolls and a white wine.

CHEF NORBERT RUEGG
Basin Street Restaurant
Palm Bay, Florida

CHICKEN BREAST WITH RASPBERRY SAUCE

6 chicken breasts, skinned
and deboned
6 Tablespoons flour (or more
if needed)
Salt to taste
White pepper to taste
6 Tablespoons butter
1 cup raspberry juice (purée
and strain frozen berries)
1 cup currant jelly
2 Tablespoons cornstarch
1 oz. kirsch
1 cup heavy cream
1 pint fresh raspberries
(if available)
Parsley sprigs as garnish

Serves: 4-6
Preparation: 25 minutes
Cooking: 30 minutes

1. Coat cleaned chicken breasts very lightly in flour, sauté in butter and season with salt and white pepper. Cook about 8 to 10 minutes on each side.

2. In a saucepan bring to a boil raspberry juice and currant jelly. Mix cornstarch with kirsch and add to the mixture, stirring constantly. Reduce heat, add cream and stir until thoroughly heated.

3. Arrange chicken on silver tray, pour raspberry sauce on top and lay fresh raspberries on top of sauce. Serve with rice on the side and a salad.

Not only is this a beautiful presentation, but a superb combination of taste.

MARY BETH'S CHICKEN

MARY BETH HARLAN
Phoenix, Arizona

6 chicken breasts, boned and skinned
1 stick of butter, melted
1 package Good Season's Italian dressing mix (dry)
Juice of ½ lime

Serves: 6
Preparation: 10 minutes
Baking: 1 hour

1. Wash and pat chicken dry and put in 9" x 13" pan.

2. Mix rest of ingredients and pour over chicken.

3. Bake uncovered at 350° 1 hour.

This is so easy and so outstanding—you will agree.

83

INDONESIAN CHICKEN BROIL

NANCY F. MACHTOLF
Glendale, California

4 to 6 large chicken breasts, skinned
5 Tablespoons crunchy peanut butter
1 small onion, chopped fine
1 celery stalk, chopped fine
5 Tablespoons soy sauce
1½ Tablespoons brown sugar
Dash of hot pepper sauce
1 cup Lambrusco (Italian light red wine)

1. Slash 3 times with a knife on each breast of chicken. Place in flat container.

2. Mix remaining ingredients well.

3. Pour over chicken and marinate for 2 to 4 hours, covered in refrigerator.

4. Cover broiler pan with tin foil and spray with Pam. Place chicken breasts on tin foil and all of marinade on tops of chicken.

5. Broil on second shelf from the top of oven for 12 minutes, turn and place marinade on top of chicken and broil another 12 minutes.

6. Remove from oven, place on platter with remaining marinade over chicken and serve. Serve with Peking Oriental Rice.*

*See page 161.

Serves: 4-6
Preparation: 20 minutes
Cooking: 25 minutes

A crunchy, moist, flavored chicken entrée. Thanks, Nancy, it's superb!

JUDY CASEY
Tempe, Arizona

POULET GENEVIESE
(Chicken with Gin)

8 chicken breasts, boned, skinned
8 Tablespoons butter
½ cup gin
2 Tablespoons juniper berries, ground in blender or by hand
3 garlic cloves, minced
1 teaspoon Bovril meat glaze (generous amount)
½ teaspoon tomato paste (generous amount)
4 Tablespoons flour
1 cup chicken stock
Salt and pepper
1 cup cream at room temperature
3 Tablespoons fresh Parmesan cheese, grated

1. Sauté chicken in 4 Tablespoons butter until just brown.

2. Add gin.

3. Remove chicken and add 4 Tablespoons butter to pan.

4. Add crushed juniper berries and garlic. Remove from heat and stir in tomato paste, meat glaze and flour.

5. Mix and return to heat and cook about 5 minutes.

6. Add chicken broth and bring to a boil.

7. Cook slightly and then add cream a little at a time and salt and pepper.

8. Pour sauce over chicken, sprinkle with cheese. Bake at 350° for 15-20 minutes.

9. This dish can be made a couple days before and refrigerated until ready to use. (Serve with parslied potatoes and French bread.)

Serves: 6-8
Preparation: 40 minutes
Baking: 15-20 minutes

For all of you gin lovers—there are no words for this except 'Elegant.'

85

GINGER CHICKEN

LANA HUGO
Tempe, Arizona

4 Tablespoons butter
4 whole chicken breasts boned
and cut into bite size pieces
1/2 cup flour
1 Tablespon ginger, freshly
grated or
2 teaspoons ground dry ginger
1 teaspon salt and pepper
Rice, cooked

SAUCE:
1/2 cup orange juice
1/4 cup lemon juice
1 Tablespon honey
3 Tablespoons soy sauce
1/2 cup chicken stock
1/2 cup white wine

Serves: 6-8
Preparation: 30 minutes
Cooking and Baking: 1 hour

An oriental savory taste.

1. Mix flour, ginger, salt and pepper together in a bowl.

2. Roll chicken in flour mixture.

3. Brown in butter.

4. Place in buttered casserole.

5. Mix all sauce ingredients and pour over chicken.

6. Bake in preheated 350° oven 45 minutes.

7. Serve over a bed of rice.

CHICKEN DIVAN

BARBARA SHAER
Upland, California

2 10-oz. packages frozen broccoli or fresh broccoli
2 cups cooked chicken, cut into bite size pieces
2 cans condensed cream of chicken soup
1 cup mayonnaise or salad dressing
1 teaspoon lemon juice
½ teaspoon curry powder
6 Tablespoons sherry
1 cup shredded sharp Cheddar processed cheese
½ cup soft bread crumbs
2 Tablespoons butter, melted
Pimento strips (garnish)

Serves: 6-8
Preparation: 35 minutes
Cooking: 35 minutes

Marvelous as main entrée or brunch.

1. Cook broccoli as directed on package.

2. Arrange stalks in buttered 9" x 13" baking dish. Place chicken on top.

3. Combine soup, mayonnaise, lemon juice, sherry and curry powder; pour over chicken.

4. Sprinkle with cheese.

5. Combine crumbs and butter; sprinkle over all. Bake uncovered at 350° 25 to 30 minutes or until thoroughly heated.

6. Trim with pimento strips, if desired.

CHICKEN KIEV

JUDY CASEY
Tempe, Arizona

CHICKEN:
4 chicken breasts, skinned,
  boned and halved
1 stick butter, frozen and cut
  into 8 sticks
½ cup parsley, minced
½ cup green onions, minced, or
½ cup chives, minced
Garlic salt
Fresh ground pepper
½ cup flour
2 eggs, beaten
1 cup fine Italian bread crumbs
¼ cup butter
Parsley sprigs

MUSHROOM SAUCE:
¼ cup butter
1 medium onion, chopped
2 cloves garlic, minced
½ lb. mushrooms, sliced
1 Tablespoon lemon juice
2 Tablespoons white wine
½ teaspoon seasoned salt
Salt and pepper to taste
1 cup sour cream
½ lb. fine noodles, cooked
  and drained

Serves: 8
Preparation: 1 hour
Cooking and Baking: 15-20 minutes

Excellent gourmet entrée and a 10 plus.

1. Gently pound chicken breast, bone side up. Sprinkle with garlic salt and pepper then with parsley and green onions.

2. Top with butter stick. Roll up, tucking in ends. Secure with toothpicks.

3. Dip in flour, then egg, then crumbs. Cover and chill in the refrigerator.

4. Brown chicken in butter for 5 minutes and transfer to baking dish. (Can be done ahead of time and refrigerated until ready to bake.)

5. Bake in preheated 400° oven for 15 to 20 minutes. Prepare sauce while chicken is baking.

6. Sauté onion and garlic in butter in pan chicken was browned in. Add mushrooms and seasonings. Cook 5 minutes, remove from heat and stir in sour cream.

7. Mix half of the sauce with the noodles and place on serving platter. Top with chicken and garnish with parsley sprigs. Serve remaining sauce in separate bowl.

CHICKEN SCAMPI

GREG CARDONES
Warren, Ohio

6 Tablespoons butter
3 stalks celery, chopped
1 medium onion, chopped
½ lb. fresh mushrooms, sliced
2 cloves garlic, minced
2 Tablespoons fresh parsley, chopped
1 teaspoon oregano
½ teaspoon each salt and pepper (more if desired)
4 chicken breasts, deboned, skinned and cut into 1" pieces
3 Tablespoons flour
1 10-oz. can chicken broth
1 6½-oz. can minced clams and juice
Juice of 1 lemon
½ cup white wine
2 Tablespoons Parmesan cheese (garnish)
Lemon wedges (garnish)
Parsley (garnish)
½ lb. linguine, cooked

Serves: 4
Preparation: 1 hour
Cooking: 30 minutes

1. Sauté celery, onions, mushrooms until limp. Add minced garlic, oregano pepper and parsley. Sauté 3 minutes.

2. Remove vegetables with slotted spoon and set aside.

3. Sauté chicken 10 minutes, turning often. Remove chicken, set aside.

4. Add flour to pan to make a roux and gradually add chicken broth to make a smooth liquid.

5. Add clams, chicken, vegetables, lemon juice and wine; cover and simmer for 15 minutes, stirring often.

6. Serve over linguine, top with grated cheese, lemon wedges and parsley sprigs.

Greg's creation—delightfully tasty and judged by many to be superb.

89

SAFFRON CREAM CHICKEN

4 large chicken breasts, deboned and skinned
1 large onion, sliced
3 Tablespoons butter (no substitute)
½ teaspoon cumin
½ teaspoon black ground pepper
2 teaspoons chicken granules or bouillon
2 cups chicken broth
2 cloves garlic, minced
½ teaspoon saffron
½ cup sour cream
1 cup heavy cream
3 Tablespoons flour
¼ cup milk
Salt, if needed

Serves: 4
Preparation: 25 minutes
Cooking: 35-45 minutes

1. Slice the chicken into 1″ strips and sauté chicken and onion in butter until chicken is no longer pink (about 15 minutes). Add cumin and pepper, remove from skillet and set aside.

2. Add next six ingredients and mix well. Heat thoroughly, bringing to a slight simmer and stirring constantly.

3. Mix flour and milk in a small bowl. Add to mixture and mix until well blended. Add chicken and onions and heat until mixture is heated thoroughly and thickened slightly. (You can substitute curry to your taste for curry chicken. Leave out saffron.) Serve with noodles on the side and a salad.

The saffron and cumin gives this such a unique, marvelous taste!

GLORIA PITZER'S
SECRET RECIPES
P.O. Box 152
St. Clair, Michigan 48079

BIG BUCKET IN THE SKY FRIED CHICKEN

1 cut up chicken or
6 chicken legs or
6 chicken breasts
(Do not remove the skin)
½ stick of butter or margarine,
melted (or more if needed)

COATING INGREDIENTS:
1½ cups self-rising flour
½ Tablespoon paprika
1 envelope Lipton Tomato
Cup-A-Soup powder
1 package Good Seasons
Italian seasoning mix
½ teaspoon seasoning salt

1. Mix coating ingredients well. Shake in a double plastic bag.

2. Spray 9″ x 13″ pan with Pam.

3. Run chicken pieces under cold water and drain in a colander.

4. Dredge pieces in coating mixture 1 piece at a time and arrange skin side up on prepared pan.

5. Apply melted butter in "dabs" with 1″ wide pastry brush (drizzle does not work) until all butter or margarine is used.

6. Bake in preheated oven uncovered at 350° 1 hour or until golden brown and tender.

Serves: 4-6
Preparation: 30 minutes
Baking: 1 hour

Gloria says "We have tried for over eight years to duplicate the best fried chicken—just like the 'Colonel' would prepare it. This method gives results identical to the original but without frying!" Yummy—we love it!

CHEF DON SCHUBERT
Torrance, California

STUFFED CHICKEN FLORENTINE

8 chicken legs with thighs attached
Spinach stuffing (recipe below)
2 cups bread crumbs
Flour
Salt and pepper to taste
2 egg whites
1 cup milk
Clarified butter
Clarified oil
Cherry sauce (recipe below)

SPINACH STUFFING:
1/3 lb. bacon, diced
1 10-oz. package frozen spinach, thawed and chopped
1/4 teaspoon salt
2 egg yolks, lightly beaten
1/2 cup onion, finely chopped
2 cups seasoned croutons
1/4 teaspoon nutmeg

CHERRY SAUCE:
1 Tablespoon of butter
1/2 cup sugar
1/2 cup orange juice
1/2 cup lemon juice
1 16-oz. can pitted black cherries
1 cup dry sherry wine
1/4 cup cornstarch

1. Prepare chicken by placing it skin side down and removing the thigh bone from each piece. This is done by cutting the meat from around the bone and detaching the thigh bone at the joint.

2. Prepare Spinach Stuffing. Cook bacon until 2/3 done. Drain off half of fat, add onion and sauté until transparent. Add spinach and croutons, cook another 3 to 4 minutes.

3. Add nutmeg, salt and blend in egg yolks. Be sure to refrigerate stuffing before using in chicken.

4. Add about 1/3 cup of spinach stuffing to the space left when the thigh bone was removed.

5. Overlay meat and skin to close the pocket. Wrap stuffed chicken and freeze until ready to use.

6. When ready to cook, dust with flour, salt and pepper and pass through egg wash that was made by mixing egg whites and milk.

7. Dredge in bread crumbs.

8. Sauté chicken in clarified butter and oil until golden brown on all sides.

(continued)

92

Stuffed Chicken Florentine *(continued)*

9. Bake in a uncovered, buttered casserole in a preheated 400° oven for 55 to 60 minutes.

10. Remove to heated platter. Spoon some of the Cherry Sauce over chicken and serve. Serve remaining sauce on the side.

11. While the chicken is baking, make the Cherry Sauce. Combine in a saucepan butter, sugar, juices and also juice from cherries.

12. Heat until liquid comes to a simmer and sugar is dissolved. Combine sherry and cornstarch. Stir into hot mixture, stirring constantly until thickened.

13. Add cherries and continue heating until cherries and sauce are hot.

Serves: 8
Preparation: 1 hour, 30 minutes
Baking: 55-60 minutes

Magnificent entrée.

THIN MAN'S BARBECUE CHICKEN

TOPPING:
1/3 teaspoon celery seed
3/4 teaspoon turmeric
1 teaspoon M.S.G.
2 teaspoons soy sauce
4 Tablespoons brown sugar
(firmly packed)
1 teaspoon paprika
1/2 teaspoon dry mustard
8 chicken breasts or your
favorite parts of chicken

BARBECUE SAUCE:
1 cup catsup
1/2 cup brown sugar
(firmly packed)
3 1/2 Tablespoons soy sauce
1 1/2 teaspoons liquid smoke
1 teaspoon garlic powder
1/8 teaspoon onion powder

Serves: 4 to 6
Preparation: 15 minutes
Baking: 1 hour

1. Mix the topping ingredients and rub on both sides of chicken. Place in Pam sprayed 9" x 14" baking dish.

2. Mix the Barbecue Sauce and, using a pastry brush, brush tops and bottom of chicken parts. Be liberal with sauce, using about 3/4 of it.

3. Bake uncovered in a preheated 350° oven for 30 minutes. Remove from oven.

4. Baste top of chicken with remaining 1/4 Barbecue Sauce and bake another 30 minutes.

5. Serve with French fries and cole slaw.

6. Use on spareribs also. Bake ribs for 2 1/2 hours at 350.° The last hour baste with sauce as directed for chicken.

Florida's most sought after chicken—for Don. (Try this sauce on spare ribs also; put on the last hour of baking).

SWEET AND SOUR CHICKEN WINGS

4 lbs. chicken wings
1 cup teriyaki sauce
(by Kikkoman)
1 cup sweet and sour sauce
(by Lawry)

1. Line cookie sheet twice with tin foil, covering sheet over edges, also. Remove tips of chicken wings and lay wings on cookie sheet.

2. Pour teriyaki sauce over chicken wings and marinate 12 or more hours in refrigerator, turning once.

3. Bake in preheated 375° oven for 30 minutes. Remove from oven. Brush wings with sweet and sour sauce, bake another 30 minutes.

4. Could bake without sweet and sour sauce if desired. Bake the full hour.

Serves: 4-6
Preparation: 15 minutes
Baking: 1 hour

These really are finger lickin' good.

95

AFRICAN CHICKEN STEW

LOIS GILLILAND
Kenya, Africa

**6 chicken breasts, skinned
and deboned, or
6 chicken legs and thighs,
skinned and deboned
¼ cup peanut oil, or
¼ cup palm oil
1 large can tomatoes
1 medium can tomatoes
1 small can tomato paste
2 Tablespoons peanut butter,
heaping
3 large onions
2 cups chicken broth
Rice, cooked**

Serves: 8-10
Preparation: 25 minutes
Cooking: 45-55 minutes

1. Cut chicken into 1″ strips and brown in oil in a large saucepan. Remove chicken and set aside.

2. In a blender, purée both cans of tomatoes, tomato paste, peanut butter and onions.

3. Pour purée into saucepan along with the chicken broth and cook for 30 minutes over medium heat.

4. Add chicken and cook another 10 to 15 minutes. Serve with rice on the side and a green salad.

The peanut butter gives the sauce such an outstanding taste! Thanks, Lois.

ITALIAN CHICKEN STEW

LOIS DEFELICE
Palm Bay, Florida

2 Tablespoons oregano
3 chicken legs
3 chicken breasts
1 cup celery, diced
2 to 3 cloves of garlic, minced
½ lb. mushrooms, sliced
3 Tablespoons oil
¼ cup apple cider vinegar
1 12-oz. jar mancini sweet red peppers (you can buy these in an Italian deli)
1 7-oz. jar Spanish green olives with seeds
1 teaspoon capers
Salt and pepper to taste
½ cup burgundy (optional)

1. Clean out little bones from chicken breasts. Set aside.

2. Sauté celery, garlic and mushrooms in oil until limp.

3. Add chicken legs and breasts, vinegar and oregano. Simmer covered 45 minutes.

4. Pour any water formed on lid back into chicken. Stir and turn chicken every 15 minutes.

5. Add peppers that have been cut into ½" strips, drain olives and break with a mallet leaving seed in. Add capers, salt, pepper and burgundy. Cook another 15 to 20 minutes.

6. Serve with Parmesan noodles.

Serves: 4-6
Preparation: 30 minutes
Cooking: 1 hour

Very Italian and delicious. Thank you, Lois, for sharing an old family recipe.

CARMEN L. PONS
San Juan, Puerto Rico
Submitted by Governor and
Mrs. Rafael Hernández-Colón

"ASOPAITO" CARMEN'S STYLE

MARINADE:
1 teaspoon oregano
½ teaspoon thyme
4 cloves of garlic, chopped
1 bay leaf
¼ teaspoon fresh ground
  pepper
¼ cup wine vinegar
½ cup stuffed olives, rinsed
  and drained
¼ cup capers, washed and
  drained
2 chicken bouillon cubes
½ cup virgin olive oil
2 sprigs of cilantro, chopped, or
2 sprigs of parsley, chopped
12 pieces of chicken, cut up
  to your preference

1. Mix all these ingredients, place in plastic container and refrigerate overnight. (May also be prepared and frozen until ready to use.) The next day complete with the following:

(continued)

"Asopaito" Carmen's Style (continued)

NEXT DAY:
2 cups short grain rice
1 Tablespoon virgin olive oil
2 sliced chorizos or Italian
  sausage, or
4 strips of bacon, chopped
  (or both bacon and sausage)
2 green peppers, chopped
2 large onions, chopped
2 29-oz. cans tomatoes
1 cup dry red wine, or
1 cup water
3 12-oz. cans beer, or
36 oz. water
1 jar sweet red peppers, sliced
  in strips
1 10-oz. package frozen peas
1 10-oz. package frozen
  green asparagus

Serves: 12
Preparation: 45 minutes
Cooking: 1 hour

2. Wash and rinse rice well. Cover with water and let sit for 45 minutes. Set aside.

3. Heat oil in a large pot, brown sausage and bacon strips. Add peppers and onions and sauté until limp. Add chicken marinade mixture and brown well.

4. Add tomatoes, wine and beer. Cook 10 minutes. Add rice (<u>well drained</u>) and cook for 25 minutes or until rice is tender. Add more seasonings and salt at this time if desired. (If mixture is too thick, add more bouillon or water.)

5. Ten minutes before serving, add sweet, canned red peppers, frozen peas and asparagus. Serve with a salad.

The taste of this entrée is outstanding. You will reach for seconds and thirds.

DUCK OF THE BAY

CHEF PETE WYNKOOP
Strawberry Mansion
Melbourne, Florida

2 4-4½-lb. ducklings
Garlic powder

SAUCE:
1 cup fresh or frozen orange
juice
1 17-oz. can fruit cocktail
2 Tablespoons brown sugar
1 teaspoon cinnamon
½ teaspoon curry powder
(or more)
2 Tablespoons chutney
1 Tablespoon arrowroot, or
1 Tablespoon cornstarch
¼ cup water

1. Thaw, remove and discard neck, wing tips and gizzard bag. Cut off excess fat from both ends of duck.

2. Season duck with granulated garlic powder. (Garlic powder should be shaken evenly over duck to prevent duck from burning.)

3. Place ducks, breast side up, on racks inside roasting pan (make sure ducks don't <u>touch</u> each other). Bake in pre-heated 400° oven for 1½ hours until brown. Remove roaster, pour off fat into <u>metal</u> container. Return to oven, reduce heat to 325° and bake for another 45 minutes to 1 hour.

4. In the meantime make the sauce in a small saucepan. Mix orange juice, juice drained from fruit cocktail (reserve fruit for later), brown sugar, cinnamon and curry powder. Bring to a slow boil, stirring constantly.

5. Add arrowroot that has been mixed with water, simmer for 5 minutes, add chutney and reserved fruit cocktail.

6. Remove ducks from oven, remove breast bones, rib cage and thigh bone. Serve half of duck with 2-3 ladles of sauce over top per person.

Serves: 4
Preparation: 40 minutes
Baking: 2½ hours

This is such an elegant dish and so simple to make.

CORNISH HENS STUFFED WITH ORANGE PECAN STUFFING AND SAUCE BÉCHAMEL

2 Cornish hens, washed and dried

STUFFING:
½ 8-oz. package Pepperidge Farm herb stuffing
1 pippin apple, peeled, cored and chopped, or 1 Granny Smith apple, peeled, cored and chopped
2 Tablespoons raisins
½ orange peeling, zested
¼ cup pecans, chopped
1 Tablespoon Triple Sec or Cointreau*
2 Tablespoons orange marmalade
1 stick of butter, melted

CREAM SAUCE BÉCHAMEL:
4 Tablespoons butter
3 Tablespoons flour
½ cup milk
½ cup Half and Half
2 egg yolks, beaten
½ cup dry white wine
½ teaspoon salt
½ teaspoon dry mustard
Pepper to taste
Parsley sprigs (garnish)
Paprika (garnish)

*See page 309.

Serves: 4
Preparation: 35 minutes
Cooking and Baking: 1 hour

1. Mix all stuffing ingredients until well blended and moist.

2. Stuff Cornish hens with stuffing, bake in shallow baking dish uncovered in preheated 350° oven for 1 hour. Baste hens with butter.

3. Melt butter for cream sauce, add flour and make a roux over medium heat.

4. Gradually add milk and Half and Half, stirring constantly until lightly thickened. Do not boil. Cream in egg yolks, wine, mustard, salt and pepper.

5. Remove Cornish hens from oven when done and split down the center.

6. Place half of stuffing for each half of hen on dinner plate. Top with half of hen and spoon sauce over top. Sprinkle with paprika and garnish with parsley sprig. Serve.

I created this for our 1982 Christmas dinner. The results were outstanding.

101

CHICKEN ENCHILADAS OR CRÊPES

FLORENCE HENNINGSEN
Tempe, Arizona

1 onion, finely chopped
2 Tablespoons butter
4 cups cooked chicken or turkey, chopped (can use canned)
1 4-oz. can green chilies, drained and chopped
1 10-oz. can condensed cream of chicken soup
12 corn tortillas or crêpes*
1 10-oz. can condensed cream of celery soup
1½ cups sour cream
1 lb. Monterey Jack cheese, shredded
Sour cream and guacamole* to garnish (optional)

1. Sauté onions in butter until limp. Mix in chicken, chilies, and chicken soup. Remove from heat.

2. Place 3 Tablespoons of chicken mixture in middle of tortillas or crêpes. Fold side over side. Lay sides down on well-buttered 9" x 13" baking pan.

3. In a small bowl blend sour cream and celery soup. Pour over enchiladas or crêpes.

4. Sprinkle Monterey Jack cheese over all and bake for 30 minutes in a 350° oven.

5. Or you can cover with Saran Wrap and microwave for 10 to 15 minutes on high, rotating dish halfway through cooking.

*See pages 17 and 293.

Serves: 8-12
Preparation: 25 minutes
Baking: 30 minutes or 10-12 minutes

Compliments galore, and always a favorite.

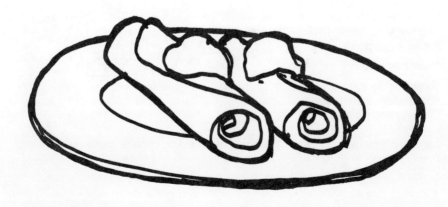

Veal Beef & Pork

VEAL
Veal Scaloppine 104
Veal Oscar 105
Veal in Morel Sauce 106
Veal with Tarragon Sauce 107
Medallions de Veau au Cognac . . 108
BEEF
Filet Mignon in Mustard Sauce . . 109
Steak Diane 110
Victorian Fillet 111
Beef Rouladen 112
Russian Meat Rolls 113
Peppersteak a la Chef Norbert . . 114
Beef en Brochette 115
Prime Rib Gourmet 116
Roth's Nevada Strip Steak 117
Chimichanga 118
Élégante Steak in Marinade 119
Swiss Austrian Steak 120
Cantonese Toss 121
Onion Beef Roast 122
Marion's Beef Burgundy 123
Bertie's Beef Stroganoff 124
Liver, Apples and Onions 125
Chris's Meat Loaf 126
Roxy's Meat Loaf 127
Corned Beef Croquettes 128

Fettucini Ala Bolognese 129
Mom's Spaghetti Sauce
 with Meat 130
Beef Braicole 132
Meat Balls Supreme 133
Don's Super Burgers 134
White Hastle Hamburgers 135
Yummy Sloppy Joes 136
Beer Salami 137
Bologna 138
Fred's Beef Jerky 139
PORK
Sausage, Vegies and
 Hard Rolls 140
Homemade Pizza 141
Homemade Sausage 142
Baked Beans and Kielbasa 143
Baked Pork Chops with
 Barbecued Beans 144
Pigs in a Blanket 145
Hungarian Pork Chops 146
Sweet and Sour Pork 147
Pork Chops with White Wine . . . 148
Crown Roast of Pork with Apricot
 Brandy Sauce 149
Ham Loaf 150

VEAL SCALOPPINE

1½ lbs. veal steak sliced thin
½ cup olive oil
½ lb. mushrooms, washed
  and sliced
1 medium onion, chopped
1 clove garlic, minced
½ teaspoon oregano
1 16-oz. can of tomatoes,
  crushed
3 small tomatoes, chopped
½ cup white wine, or
½ cup Marsala wine
1 teaspoon salt
¼ teaspoon pepper
1 cup Parmesan cheese,
  freshly grated
1 Tablespoon Bovril beef
  extract

Serves: 4-6
Preparation: 30 minutes
Cooking and Baking: 1 hour

1. Brown meat in oil. Remove and set aside. Sauté mushrooms and onions until limp.

2. Add remaining ingredients, including meat and mix well.

3. Place in casserole and bake uncovered in preheated 400° oven for 30 to 40 minutes or until mixture is bubbling. Serve.

Another northern Italian recipe that was taught to me and always requested.

CHEF NORBERT RUEGG
Basin Street Restaurant
Palm Bay, Florida

VEAL OSCAR
—For one (1)—

VEAL:
5 oz. thinly sliced veal
(scaloppine)
1 cup flour (about)
Salt and pepper to taste
4 oz. butter
1½ oz. brandy
½ oz. beef stock

ASPARAGUS:
5 green asparagus spears

CRABMEAT:
3 oz. crabmeat
1 teaspoon lemon juice
1 Tablespoon butter

BÉARNAISE SAUCE:
1 egg yolk
½ teaspoon water
1 oz. butter, melted and cooled
¼ teaspoon Worcestershire
sauce
½ teaspoon lemon juice
4 drops Tabasco sauce
Salt to taste
Pinch tarragon leaves
Pinch dried parsley
Dash tarragon vinegar

Serves: 1
Preparation: 20 minutes
Cooking: 10 to 15 minutes

1. Season veal with salt and pepper. Coat both sides of veal with flour. Sauté in four ounces of butter about 10 minutes. Remove to heated platter. (Place platter in low, preheated oven to keep hot.)

2. Deglaze sauté pan with brandy, add the beef stock, mix and pour over veal.

3. Cook fresh asparagus spears about 4 minutes, drain and lay over veal.

4. Sauté crabmeat in lemon and butter about 3 to 4 minutes, strain and place over asparagus.

5. Put egg yolk and water in double boiler over medium heat. Whisk until mixture doubles in volume. Remove from heat. Add remaining ingredients, blending well, and pour over crab and serve.

You can cook asparagus and sauté crab the last 5 minutes that you are sautéing the veal.

One of the easiest to prepare and one of the most elegant, delicious dinners to serve.

CHEF VINCENT GUERITHAULT
Vincents French Cuisine
Scottsdale, Arizona

VEAL IN MOREL SAUCE

12 morels, or
12 mushrooms
¼ cup water
4 ½-inch thick slices of veal
   steaks
Clarified butter
Flour
Salt
White pepper
4 shallots, chopped
2 Tablespoons clarified butter
1 cup white wine
2 cups heavy cream
1 teaspoon chicken granules
1 teaspoon morel liquid
12 mushrooms, sliced
1 bunch of spinach, washed
   and cleaned
1 clove of garlic, minced
Salt
Pepper

1. Soak morels or mushrooms in ¼ cup water.

2. Pound veal thin (but not too thin). Season with salt and white pepper, dust lightly with flour. Sauté immediately in very hot clarified butter. Sauté 1 minute on each side. Remove and keep warm. Pour out excess butter.

3. Sauté shallots in 2 Tablespoons butter for 1 minute. Add 1 cup white wine. Reduce to nothing and add cream, 1 teaspoon chicken granules and 1 teaspoon morel liquid. Add morels and mushrooms, boil down to serving consistency, stirring constantly. Add veal.

4. Blanch spinach for 2 minutes, refresh in ice water. Reduce some cream and garlic in another pan, add spinach and season with salt and pepper.

5. Serve veal with morel sauce on bed of creamed spinach.

Serves: 4
Preparation: 20 to 30 minutes
Cooking: 15 minutes

A ten plus—very, very elegant.

CHEF VINCENT GUERITHAULT
Vincent's French Cuisine
Scottsdale, Arizona

VEAL WITH TARRAGON SAUCE

4 ¾" veal loin slices
Salt
Pepper
Flour
3 Tablespoons clarified butter

SAUCE:
4 Tablespoons shallots, chopped
2 Tablespoons butter
1 cup white wine
1 chicken cube, or
1 teaspoon chicken granules
½ Tablespoon tarragon (let sit in 1 Tablespoon water 10 minutes)
2 cups cream
2 Tablespoons softened butter

Serves: 4
Preparation: 20 minutes
Cooking: 15 to 20 minutes

The sauce is sensational—a 10 plus.

1. Pound veal slices to ½" thick, dust with flour and seasoning and brown on each side in hot clarified butter. Keep warm in butter.

2. Remove excess butter from pan. Brown shallots in 2 Tablespoons butter, add wine and reduce to nothing.

3. Add chicken cube, tarragon and cream, reduce slightly.

4. Add 2 Tablespoons softened butter and juice from veal. Mix well, pour sauce over veal and serve.

CHEF PATRICK TOMBELAINE
Golden Eagle Restaurant
Phoenix, Arizona

MÉDALLIONS de VEAU au COGNAC

(Medallions of Veal with Cognac)

1½ lbs. veal loin
Flour
Butter
1 Tablespoon shallots,
   chopped
1 lb. mushrooms, sliced thin
Salt and pepper to taste
2 oz. cognac
1½ cups brown sauce (1 Knorr
   Swiss-Hunter Sauce)
3 oz. heavy cream
16 halved artichoke hearts,
   canned
Cooked fettuccine

1. Have butcher cut veal loin into medallions about ⅜" thick and 2" in diameter.

2. Pound them with a mallet between sheets of waxed paper.

3. Flour them lightly and sauté them in butter on both sides. Prepare brown sauce and set aside.

4. When veal is bright brown, add shallots, mushrooms, salt and pepper.

5. Sauté for a few minutes, add cognac and sauté a few minutes longer. Remove veal from pan.

6. Add cream and brown sauce; reduce until sauce is smooth.

7. Put the veal back in the pan with the artichoke hearts and cook for a few minutes.

8. To serve, place three medallions on a plate, top with artichoke halves and finish with the sauce. Serve with freshly made fettuccine.

Serves: 6
Preparation: 20 minutes
Cooking: 15 to 20 minutes

Very, very elegant—a ten plus.

CHEF VINCENT GUERITHAULT
Vincent's French Cuisine
Scottsdale, Arizona

FILLET MIGNON IN MUSTARD SAUCE

6 1¼" fillets
Salt
Pepper
¼ cup clarified butter

SAUCE:
4 Tablespoons shallots,
  chopped
1 cup white wine
1 cup duck stock, or
1 cup chicken stock
⅓ cup Dijon mustard
⅓ cup unsalted butter

Serves: 6
Preparation: 20 to 25 minutes
Baking: 10 to 20 minutes

1. Trim tenderloin of all fat. Sauté quickly over high heat in clarified butter and season with salt and pepper. Place in preheated 475° oven for 5 minutes.

2. Make sauce. Sauté shallots, throwing out excess butter. Add 1 cup wine and reduce. Add 1 cup stock, reducing slightly. Add ⅓ cup Dijon mustard. Do not boil at this point. Beat in juices from beef and ⅓ cup of unsalted butter. Place fillets on individual plates with sauce on top and serve.

The rich mustard sauce makes this so elegant and scrumptious.

CHEF PATRICK TOMBELAINE
Golden Eagle Restaurant
Phoenix, Arizona

STEAK DIANE

1½ lbs. center cut tenderloin
1 cup mushrooms, sliced
8 shallots, chopped fine
1 cup brown sauce (1 Knorr
  Swiss-Hunter Sauce)
¼ cup heavy cream
1 teaspoon Dijon mustard
1 Tablespoon Worcestershire
  sauce
1½ oz. cognac
Rice pilaf

1. Make brown sauce and set aside.

2. Cut tenderloin ½" thick and pound flat with the palm of the hand.

3. In a heated skillet melt enough clarified butter to cover bottom of pan.

4. Sauté the steak very quickly over high heat. (The steak should be seared on both sides, then sautéed slowly over medium heat until done to your liking.)

5. Remove the steaks from pan and put the heat on low.

6. Put mushrooms and shallots in pan and sauté lightly, add cognac and reduce slightly.

7. Add remaining ingredients plus brown sauce and stir until sauce is well blended.

8. Place steaks back into pan just long enough to heat. Serve with rice pilaf.

Serves: 4
Preparation: 20 to 30 minutes
Cooking: 10 to 20 minutes

Always complimented as a 10 plus.

VICTORIAN FILLET

CHEF PETE WYNKOOP
Strawberry Mansion
Melbourne, Florida

4 8-oz. fillets
8 medium shrimp, cleaned, deveined and cooked
1 8½-oz. can artichoke hearts, drained and quartered
½ lb. fresh sliced mushrooms sautéed in butter
1 cup Béarnaise Sauce*

1. Broil fillets to desired taste.

2. Steam the shrimp and artichoke hearts a few minutes (or drop in boiling water to heat thoroughly).

3. Put fillet on plate with 2 shrimps on each fillet. Arrange quartered artichokes around fillet, top with ¼ cup Béarnaise Sauce* over each dish and then top with the drained, sautéed mushrooms. Serve with a salad and baked potato.

*See page 293.

Serves: 4
Preparation: 25 minutes
Broiling: To your desire

Ahh—Bon appétit.

111

BEEF ROULADEN

JUDY CASEY
Tempe, Arizona

1½ to 2 lbs. round steak cut
   into 4 to 5 steaks
2 teaspoons Dijon mustard
2 large dill pickles, cut into
   thin strips
2 slices bacon, cut into
   thin strips
1 onion, chopped
4 Tablespoons butter
1½ cups beef broth
½ cup Rhine wine
1 clove garlic, minced
1 bay leaf
Salt and pepper to taste
1 Tablespoon cornstarch mixed
   with 1 Tablespoon water

1. Spread each steak with mustard. Season with salt and pepper.

2. Divide pickles, onion and bacon among steaks.

3. Roll steaks up jelly roll style and secure with toothpicks.

4. Sauté meat rolls in butter, add broth, wine, garlic, bay leaf, salt and pepper. Cover and simmer 1½ hours in an electric skillet.

5. When ready to serve, blend cornstarch and water, add into pan juices to make gravy. Serve with German Potato Salad.*

*See page 157.

Serves: 4
Preparation: 45 minutes
Cooking: 1½ hours

A wonderful authentic German dish.

NICHOLAS HULYK
KATHERINE HULYK
Kiev, Russia

RUSSIAN MEAT ROLLS

3 lb. beef chuck roast
½ stick butter
1 large package onion
    soup mix
1 small onion, sliced
2 lbs. ground round hamburger
1 large onion, chopped
1 Tablespoon parsley, chopped
1 teaspoon garlic powder
1 teaspoon pepper
1 Tablespoon onion, chopped
    fine
1 teaspoon dill
1 teaspoon salt
2 cups mashed potatoes
1½ cups carrots, chopped
    very fine
5 stalks of celery, chopped
    very fine
½ cup sour cream

1. In a roaster, place roast, with butter cubed on top. Sprinkle on onion soup mix and sliced onion. Bake covered in preheated 350° oven for 2½ hours. Cool, shred and chop meat. Mix in with baked onion mix.

2. In the meantime, sauté the ground round and the large chopped onion until brown. Add beef roast mixture into ground round mixture, 1 Tablespoon onion, spices, potatoes, carrots, celery and sour cream (and add more seasoning if desired).

3. Make your own biscuits* or buy 6 packages of Pillsbury Biscuits. Roll out on a floured bread board to a diameter of 4" and place 1 Tablespoon of mixture in center of dough. Fold over and press edges with a fork, dampening edges with water so that they don't open. Place on buttered baking pan. You will have about 60 total.

4. Or you can use puff pastry. Use 4 layers. Roll out each about 10" x 12." Lay two on a buttered baking pan, divide mixture between each. Place tops on each, fold over edges, press with fork. Bake in preheated 400° oven for 20 to 30 minutes until golden. Serve hot.

5. You can serve the individual ones as an appetizer or both individual and large ones as a main entrée. Serve with a green salad.

Yield: 60 individual or 2 large
Preparation: 1 hour 30 minutes
Baking: 2-3 hours

*See page 193.

A Russian gourmet appetizer or entrée.

CHEF NORBERT RUEGG
Basin Street Restaurant
Palm Bay, Florida

PEPPERSTEAK
À LA CHEF NORBERT

2 8-oz. New York strip steaks
1 Tablespoon black
peppercorns, crushed
1 Tablespoon olive oil
2 Tablespoons butter
1 Tablespoon paprika
2 Tablespoons onion, chopped
1 cup fresh mushrooms, sliced
2 garlic cloves, minced
2 oz. brandy
½ cup heavy cream
3 fresh scallions, chopped
Salt to taste

1. Pound the crushed peppercorns into one side of steaks. (Cover meat with wax paper while pounding.) Heat oil in skillet to very hot. Sauté steaks on each side to desired taste. Remove, set aside and keep warm.

2. Add butter and paprika, simmer 1 minute, stirring constantly. Add onion and mushrooms, stirring constantly for 2 more minutes.

3. Add garlic and brandy, reduce heat, add cream and scallions. Simmer sauce for 5 minutes. Add juice from steak to sauce, add salt, pour sauce over steaks and serve.

Serves: 2
Preparation: 15 minutes
Cooking: 10 to 15 minutes

Men really enjoy this tasty dish.

CHEF DON SCHUBERT
Torrance, California

BEEF EN BROCHETTE

1½ lbs. top sirloin
1 onion
1 bell pepper
10 mushrooms
Cherry tomatoes
Celery
Zucchini
Carrots
Bacon
(Anything more that you desire)

MARINADE:
1 cup salad oil
½ cup olive oil
⅓ cup cider vinegar
2 Tablespoons lemon juice
1 to 2 cloves of garlic, minced
1½ teaspoons salt
Pepper, freshly ground, to taste
¼ teaspoon oregano
¼ teaspoon marjoram

Serves: 5-6
Preparation: 1 hour
Baking: 8 to 10 minutes

Always a hit with family and friends.

1. Cut beef into 1" cubes and cut vegetables, when necessary, into pieces close in size to the 1" beef cubes.

2. Place meat and vegetables alternately on skewers. (Do not crowd.) Allow 4 to 5 cubes of meat to skewer.

3. Mix all marinade ingredients.

4. Place skewers in a pan and surround with marinade and cover. Marinate 24 to 48 hours, turning skewers occasionally.

5. Drain well and place under broiler, 4 to 5 minutes on each side or until at desired doneness.

6. Serve on a bed of Risotto Rice.*

*See page 162.

PRIME RIB GOURMET

1 5-lb. standing prime rib
1½ cups dry red wine
½ teaspoon bay leaf powder
1 clove garlic, minced
1 teaspoon salt
½ teaspoon pepper

GRAVY:
Drippings from roast
4 Tablespoons flour
2 cups water
½ cup white wine
½ Tablespoon Bovril
   meat base
Salt and pepper to taste

1. In a large shallow roaster lay the prime rib on side of meat.

2. Mix wine, bay leaf powder, garlic, salt and pepper together and pour over prime rib.

3. This is very important—marinate uncovered at room temperature for 6 to 12 hours or overnight. Turn meat from side to side often, about every hour, if possible, so that the flavors can get into the meat.

4. Preheat oven at 11:30 A.M. to 325.° Remove prime rib from roaster, pat dry with paper towel, discard marinade and place prime rib back into the roaster. Stand roast up (fat side on top and ribs on bottom).

5. Place roaster in oven uncovered and bake 1 hour. Turn off oven and let roast sit in oven 3 to 6 hours. Do not open the oven door at any time until completely finished roasting. (This is the secret of this marvelous roast.)

6. Time your dinner and turn on oven to 325° again. Bake to your choice of preparation: 1½ hours (well done), 45 minutes (medium), ½ hour (rare).

7. The times given above are in addition to the 1 hour at noon.

8. Remove prime rib to heated platter and put roaster on burner. Make a roux with the drippings and flour. Gradually add remaining ingredients and serve gravy in separate bowl. Serve with mashed potatoes also.

Serves: 4-6
Preparation: 12 to 18 hours
Baking: ½ to 3 hours

This prime rib recipe is magnificent. If you want to impress people, make this never fail prime rib.

116

ROTH'S NEVADA STRIP STEAK

BARBARA ROTH
Las Vegas, Nevada

**2½ to 3 lbs. New York Strip
(have butcher slice it thin)
6 Tablespoons butter
1 medium onion, chopped
½ lb. fresh mushrooms, sliced
1 garlic clove, minced
1 cup pale dry sherry
1 5¾-oz. can mushroom and
  steak sauce
½ cup water
1 package Hunter Sauce Mix
  (by Knorr-Swiss)
Season to taste**

1. Trim any fat that is on steaks. Sauté quickly on each side in hot butter. Remove from skillet and set aside.

2. Sauté onions and mushrooms until limp. Add garlic and cook a few minutes. Add sherry.

3. Combine steak sauce, water and Hunter Sauce in a small container until well blended and stir into wine mixture.

4. Heat thoroughly. Add the thin steaks and heat only until steaks are heated through. Serve on a platter.

Serves: 4-6
Preparation: 20 minutes
Cooking: 15 to 20 minutes

This entrée gets rave reviews from everyone. Men love it! Thanks, Barb.

CHIMICHANGA

JUDY CASEY
Tempe, Arizona

MEAT:
2 lbs. stew meat (beef or pork or both)
1 Tablespoon oil
Water
Dash of garlic powder

FILLING:
2 onions, chopped
2 cloves garlic, chopped
2 Tablespoons oil
1 large fresh tomato, diced
½ teaspoon oregano
1 teaspoon salt
1 Tablespoon cilantro or parsley
1 4-oz. can green chilies, diced
2 Tablespoons to ¾ cup beef broth, depending on dryness
Large flour tortillas
Sour Cream
Guacamole*

Serves: 4-8
Preparation: 1 hour
Baking: 4 hours (approximately)

1. Brown stew meat in oil, cover with water and add garlic powder. Simmer 3 to 4 hours until tender. Shred and save broth.

2. Brown onion and garlic in oil. Add remaining ingredients and meat. Simmer until flavors blend.

3. Place some meat filling (to your desired amount) on large tortilla, roll up burrito style and secure with toothpicks.

4. Deep fry until crisp at 375.° Keep warm in 275° oven. Serve with sour cream and guacamole*

*See page 17.

You will never be satisfied with any other chimichanga after these.

ÉLÉGANTE STEAK IN MARINADE

PEGGY HUGHES
Tempe, Arizona

1 cup Kikkoman soy sauce
½ teaspoon ginger
½ to 1 teaspoon garlic powder
5 Tablespoons brown sugar
½ cup vodka or whiskey
½ cup water
6 steaks of your choice

1. Stir all ingredients and pour over steaks. Marinate from ½ hour to 3 hours.

2. Either broil or charcoal and baste often with marinade. Cook to your taste.

3. If you have less steaks and don't need to use all the marinade over the steaks, bottle unused marinade on shelf. It keeps well. (Can use chicken also, but only marinate for ½ hour.)

Serves: 6
Preparation: 20 minutes
Baking: 10-20 minutes

This is so superb and special.

SWISS AUSTRIAN STEAK

1 cup flour
2 Tablespoons oil
¼ cup butter
1½ lbs. round steak
1 large can tomatoes, mashed
1 small can tomato juice
  and water
1 large onion, sliced
2 cloves of garlic, minced
2 stalks of celery, chopped
1 Tablespoon Bovril meat
  sauce
1 teaspoon salt
¼ teaspoon pepper

1. Melt butter with oil in electric skillet.

2. Pound steak (or have butcher put it through the tenderizer). Cut steak into 1″ x 4″ strips.

3. Coat steak with flour in a bag (discard any leftover flour). Brown steak on medium-low temperature.

4. Remove steak from skillet and set aside.

5. Add tomato juice to skillet to blend in the juices from steak.

6. Add remaining ingredients plus steak, cover and simmer over low heat 1½ hours. Stir occasionally.

Serves: 6-8
Preparation: 45 minutes
Cooking: 1½ hours

This transforms round steak into something special.

"CORNELIUS"
Corning Ware
Corning, New York

CANTONESE TOSS

1 lb. flank steak, or
1 lb. lean boneless pork
*1½" square piece fresh
   ginger, minced
2 large cloves of garlic, finely
   minced
3 Tablespoons soy sauce
½ cup juice drained from
   pineapple
3 Tablespoons oil
1 cup celery in ½" diagonal
   slices
1 small can water chestnuts,
   sliced
1 green bell pepper, cut in
   thin wedges
2 medium onions, cut into very
   thin wedges
1 bunch green onions (and
   tops) in diagonal 1" slices
1 cup pineapple chunks
2 Tablespoons cornstarch
3 Tablespoons dry sherry

*If fresh ginger is unavailable,
   substitute 1 teaspoon (to
   taste) ground ginger

Serves: 4-5
Preparation: 20 minutes
Cooking: 10-12 minutes

1. Lay the meat flat on plate and place in freezer until firm but not frozen. Cut meat into very thin slices across the grain. Place the meat in a shallow dish and pour over a mixture of ginger, garlic, soy and pineapple juice. Marinate the meat for 2 hours.

2. Heat oil in 10" Rangetoppers skillet over high heat. Drain the meat, reserving the marinade, and add to the skillet. Toss for 2 minutes or until meat is no longer red. Add the celery, water chestnuts, bell pepper, onions, green onions and pineapple. Cover and cook over medium high heat for 5 minutes, stirring occasionally.

3. Combine the cornstarch with the reserved marinade and sherry, stirring until dissolved.

4. Pour liquid into skillet and cook, uncovered, for 2 minutes, stirring. Taste for seasoning (you might need more soy sauce). Serve over rice or thin noodles.

Cornelius says, "This is an incredible dish! It's easy to do at the last minute provided you've planned ahead," and I agree!

DONALD MILLER
Tempe, Arizona

ONION BEEF ROAST

2½ to 3 lb. chuck roast
1 large package dry onion
soup mix
1 large onion, sliced
1 stick of butter
1 bay leaf
¼ teaspoon garlic powder
¼ cup corn starch
¼ cup water
2 cups water

1. Place roast in a roaster and place ingredients on top of roast in order given, except the corn starch and water.

2. Bake covered in preheated 350° oven for 2½ to 3 hours.

3. Scrape onion topping off into roaster for gravy and remove roast to platter.

4. Mix ¼ cup water and ¼ cup corn starch together. Add this to onion topping and mix thoroughly. Add the 2 cups of water slowly to blend well. Bring gravy mixture to slight boil and then serve. (You could use 2 cups of potato water if making potatoes).

Serves: 6
Preparation: 15 minutes
Baking: 2½-3 hours

This is the tastiest and the most tender beef roast—the gravy is superb over mashed potatoes.

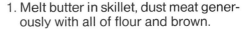

MARION CARDONES
Warren, Ohio

MARION'S BEEF BURGUNDY

6 Tablespoons butter
3 lbs. beef cubes
⅓ cup flour
1 can tomato soup
1 can beef broth
½ Tablespoon Bovril beef base
1 cup burgundy wine
2 bay leaves
1 clove garlic, minced
1 teaspoon salt
⅛ teaspoon pepper
½ lb. fresh mushrooms, sliced
1 20-oz. bag of small frozen onions
2 carrots, diced
Serve with noodles, rice or mashed potatoes

1. Melt butter in skillet, dust meat generously with all of flour and brown.

2. Add soup and broth in skillet to collect all the drippings from beef. Add remaining ingredients, except last 3, and mix thoroughly.

3. Pour in a buttered casserole, cover and bake in preheated 350° oven for 1 hour.

4. Add onions, mushrooms and carrots for one more hour. Uncover and bake another 15 minutes.

Serves: 8
Preparation: 40 minutes
Cooking and Baking: 2 hours, 30 minutes

Splendid version of a classic.

BERTHA BEACH
Niles, Ohio

BERTIE'S BEEF STROGANOFF

1 lb. sirloin steak, cut into
   1" x 4" strips
4 Tablespoons flour
6 Tablespoons butter
1 teaspoon salt
¼ teaspoon pepper
1 medium onion, chopped
1 clove garlic, minced
1 lb. mushrooms, washed and
   sliced
1 can chicken broth
1 teaspoon chicken bouillon
   granules
1 cup sour cream
Serve with noodles, rice
   or potatoes

Serves: 4-5
Preparation: 30 minutes
Cooking: 1 hour 45 minutes

A rich delicious dish for anyone.

1. Pound meat, dust generously and brown on both sides in electric skillet. Remove meat and set aside.

2. Sauté onions, garlic and mushrooms until limp. Add meat and remaining ingredients except sour cream.

3. Cover and simmer at a low temperature for 1 hour, stirring often. Thicken more if necessary.

4. When ready to serve, stir in sour cream and serve.

LIVER, APPLES AND ONIONS

1 large onion, sliced vertical
1 large apple, cleaned, peeled, cored and sliced thin
1 stick of butter
1 lb. of calves liver
Flour
Salt and pepper to taste
1 cup white wine
1 cup sweet apple cider
1 teaspoon Bovril meat base
½ cup water
2 Tablespoons flour

1. Sauté onion and apple slices in 4 Tablespoons butter until limp. Remove and set aside.

2. Dust calves liver in flour, season to taste and brown in remaining 4 Tablespoons butter for 4 minutes on each side. Remove and set aside.

3. Add wine and apple cider. Reduce to half, add flour to water and meat base. Mix well. Add onions and apples, heat thoroughly.

4. Add liver and heat until meat is heated through. Serve immediately. Can serve with rice or mashed potatoes.

Serves: 4
Preparation: 20 minutes
Cooking: 25 minutes (approx.)

This is a recipe that has been a part of our family since I can remember.

CHEF HENRI LABAZEE
CHRIS WEBSTER
Melbourne, Florida

CHRIS'S MEAT LOAF

1½ lbs. ground beef
2 medium onions, chopped
1 small green pepper, chopped
2 Tablespoons butter
¼ cup parsley, chopped
1 clove garlic, chopped
½ teaspoon celery salt
½ teaspoon Lawry's seasoned
  salt
⅓ large package Pepperidge
  Farm bread stuffing
¼ teaspoon pepper
2 eggs
1 cup beef bouillon
Parmesan cheese, grated
¼ cup ketchup or (optional)
1 Tablespoon tomato paste

1. Sauté green pepper and onion in 2 Tablespoons butter.

2. Mix all ingredients and shape into 2 meat loaves.

3. Place in shallow baking dish. Place on tomato paste or ketchup. Grate cheese on top of meat loaves.

4. Bake at 375° for 1 hour.

Serves: 6-8
Preparation: 30 to 40 minutes
Cooking: 1 hour 10 minutes (including sautéing of onion and pepper)

Chef Henri Labazee created this meat loaf recipe for his daughter, Chris. It is outstanding.

MARY MACIAS
South Pasadena, California

ROXY'S MEAT LOAF

MEAT LOAF:
1 ½ lbs. ground beef
1 ¼ cups bread crumbs
1 large egg, beaten
1 small onion, minced
1 clove garlic, minced
1 teaspoon salt
1 teaspoon Italian seasoning
¼ teaspoon pepper
1 8-oz. can tomato sauce

TOPPING:
2 Tablespoons butter, melted
¼ cup bread crumbs
2 Tablespoons Parmesan
   cheese, freshly grated
2 Tablespoons parsley, freshly
   chopped

*See page 154.

Serves: 4-6
Preparation: 30 minutes
Baking: 45-50 minutes

Very Italian in flavor and great with Italian browns.*

1. Mix all meat loaf ingredients, shape and bake in preheated 350° oven for 40 minutes.

2. Meanwhile melt butter, toss in crumbs, cheese and parsley.

3. Remove meatloaf from oven, spread topping on top of meat loaf and bake another 5 to 10 minutes or until golden.

CORNED BEEF CROQUETTES

2 Tablespoon butter
1 small onion, chopped fine
1 Tablespoon raw carrot,
    chopped fine
2 Tablespoons celery, chopped
    fine
1 small clove garlic, minced
2 large potatoes, cooked,
    peeled and cooled
1 1-lb. can corned beef
1 Tablespoon onion greens,
    chopped fine, or
1 Tablespoon chives, chopped
    fine
1/8 teaspoon nutmeg
1 teaspoon salt
1/4 teaspoon fresh ground
    black pepper
2 egg whites
Hot oil (350° to 375°)

Yield: About 9
Preparation: 30 minutes
Frying: About 3 minutes

1. Sauté onion, carrot, and celery in 2 Tablespoons butter until limp. Add garlic the last 2 minutes.

2. Mash the potatoes with a fork, mash corned beef and add to potatoes with all ingredients except for egg whites.

3. Shape mixture into 2" balls and set aside until you have shaped them all.

4. Dip each ball in egg white before frying to prevent sticking together. Fry until golden, drain on paper towel and keep warm in the oven until ready to serve. Serve with a salad.

A poor man's delight with a taste of satisfaction.

FETTUCINI ALA BOLOGNESE

CHEF NORBERT RUEGG
Basin Street Restaurant
Palm Bay, Florida

1 Tablespoon olive oil
4 oz. salt pork, chopped fine
1 large onion, chopped
2 celery stalks, chopped
3 to 5 garlic cloves, chopped
¼ lb. hot Italian sausage
2 lbs. ground beef
¼ teaspoon oregano
¼ teaspoon basil
Salt to taste
Pepper, freshly ground, to taste
2 cups red wine
½ lb. fresh mushrooms, sliced
2 teaspoons sugar
4 medium tomatoes, peeled
   and diced
2 lbs. fettucini spinach
   noodles, or
2 lbs. fettucini regular noodles
½ cup Parmesan cheese,
   grated
2 cups heavy cream

Serves: 8-10
Preparation: 30 minutes
Cooking: 35 to 45 minutes

1. Heat oil in a large saucepan over medium heat, add salt pork and brown lightly. Add onion, celery and garlic and simmer for 3 minutes. Add sausage and beef and cook for 15 minutes or until meat is cooked.

2. Stir in oregano, basil, salt, pepper, wine and mushrooms. Cook for another 15 minutes.

3. Add diced tomatoes and sugar last; simmer a few minutes.

4. Cook fettucini al dente, rinse under cold water for 2 minutes and add to sauce. Also add the cream and Parmesan cheese, heat thoroughly and serve immediately. (Can add more cheese, if desired.) Serve with a green salad, a rosé wine and a hard crusted bread.

Ah—what a magnificent meal, and so quick and easy.

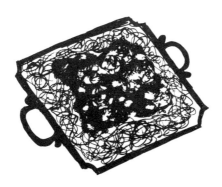

MOM'S SPAGHETTI SAUCE WITH MEAT

¼ cup pure olive oil
½ lb. medium hot sausage*
1 ½ lbs. beef or pork neck
  bones or both
2 lbs. ground beef
3 eggs
½ cup fine bread crumbs
2 Tablespoons fresh Romano
  cheese, grated
1 Tablespoon fresh parsley,
  chopped
½ teaspoon garlic powder

SAUCE:
1 46-oz. can tomato juice
1 32-oz. jar Clamato juice
1 6-oz. can tomato paste
1 16-oz. can tomatoes, crushed
1 29-oz. can tomato sauce
1 large onion, chopped
2 Tablespoons fresh parsley,
  chopped
1 large bay leaf or 2 small
1 teaspoon anise seed
½ Tablespoon crushed
  oregano (crush in palm
  of hand)
1 teaspoon basil
1 teaspoon marjoram
2 Tablespoons fresh Romano
  cheese, grated

1. Put oil in large kettle and brown neck bones and sausage (either homemade or store bought) over medium heat.

2. While that is cooking, mix ground beef, eggs, bread crumbs, cheese, parsley and garlic powder. Make meat balls about 2" wide and brown on all sides, carefully turning them with a fork so that they don't break apart.

3. Remove meat from kettle and set aside.

4. Add ½ can of tomato juice, stirring and scraping sides of the pan with a wooden spoon to collect all the juices that are on bottom of pan. Add remaining juice and remaining ingredients (except for the garnish and spaghetti). Stir well and add all the meat.

5. Cover and simmer over low heat for 2½ hours, stirring occasionally.

6. When ready to serve, place about 3 Tablespoons grated Romano on the bottom of large bowl, about 1 cup of sauce over this, then cooked spaghetti, about 2 cups of sauce over spaghetti noodles with more cheese on top. Mix all together.

Mom's Spaghetti Sauce w/Meat (continued)

1 ½ teaspoons salt
1 Tablespoon sugar
½ teaspoon tarragon
1 large garlic clove, minced
1 lb. mushrooms, sliced
More Romano cheese, grated
   (garnish)
2 lbs. spaghetti cooked
   al dente

Serves: 6-8
Preparation: 45 minutes
Cooking: 3 hours

7. Remove meat to a platter and serve separately.

8. Serve side dishes of sauce and cheese for those who desire more.

   *See page 142.

This sauce is outstanding on pizza also. I was taught to make this by two people from northern Italy. My husband says "no restaurant could ever beat it."

BEEF BRAICOLE

1 large round steak
Garlic powder
Salt
Pepper
Romano or Parmesan cheese,
    grated
Chopped fresh parsley
Oil
String

1. Pound meat thin, remove all fat and cut into 4" x 8" strips.

2. Sprinkle with garlic powder, salt and pepper.

3. Generously sprinkle top with cheese and parsley.

4. Roll (wide end) lengthwise facing you, rolling away from you. Tie string securely around braicole several times.

5. Brown on all sides in oil, add to Spaghetti Sauce,* and cook in sauce.

6. When ready to serve, cut off string carefully and cut into 2" pieces.

*See page 130.

Serves: 4-6
Preparation: 1 hour
Cooking: 2 hours

This Braicole recipe was from Italy and our favorite over other Braicole recipes.

MEAT BALLS SUPREME

2 Tablespoons oil
¼ cup butter
2 lbs. ground beef
1 large onion, chopped
2 eggs
1 stalk celery, chopped
½ cup fine bread crumbs
1 lb. mushrooms, cleaned
  and sliced
1 can cream of mushroom soup
  and water
1 13-oz. can Pet evaporated
  milk
1 teaspoon salt
½ teaspoon pepper
¼ teaspoon garlic powder
1 Tablespoon Bovril meat
  sauce

Serves: 6-8
Preparation: 40 minutes
Cooking: 1 hour

Sensational.

1. Mix ground beef, onions, eggs, celery and bread crumbs. Make into about 2″ meat balls.

2. Brown in oil and butter in skillet using care in turning as not to break them.

3. Remove meat balls from skillet and set aside.

4. Sauté mushrooms until limp.

5. Add mushroom soup and water to blend up the juices from meat.

6. Add remaining ingredients, blend well and add meat balls.

7. Simmer over low heat for 45 minutes.

DONALD MILLER
Tempe, Arizona

DON'S SUPER BURGERS

1 lb. lean ground beef
Sweet pickle relish
Dijon mustard
4 slices American cheese
A-1 Sauce or steak sauce
Sliced onions
Onion Rolls*

1. One-half hour before making Super Burgers, light charcoal grill.

2. Divide hamburger into fourths and shape into <u>even</u>, round patties. (Use a tuna fish can for a mold, with both ends removed.)

3. Apply A-1 sauce on top and bottom of all patties, brush in with a pastry brush. (Use about 1 Tablespoon on each side.)

4. On one side only of <u>two patties</u> apply mustard, relish and onions generously.

5. Apply 2 slices of cheese on each filled patty, then apply plain patty on top of each filled patty. Place many toothpicks in each Super Burger to hold in place.

6. Place on Pam sprayed grill and charcoal until done, about 10 minutes on each side. Serve on Onion Rolls* or buns.

*See page 192.

Serves: 2
Preparation: 15 minutes
Charcoal: 20 minutes

McDonald's, eat your heart out!

GLORIA PITZER
Secret Recipes
P.O. Box 152
St Clair, Michigan 48079

WHITE HASTLE HAMBURGERS

2½ lbs. ground beef
1 3½-oz. jar strained veal baby food
⅔ cup beef broth
Onion salt
Pepper
Chopped onions
Onion Rolls* or hamburger buns

1. In mixing bowl combine meat, veal baby food and beef broth.

2. Mix well and shape into ¼" thin square patties about 3" x 3" and dust liberally with onion salt and pepper.

3. Fry briskly on lightly oiled, very hot grill or skillet. Do not crowd patties.

4. Make 3 or 4 holes in each patty with handle of table knife.

5. Brown the one side and turn onto a few Tablespoons chopped onions, browning in same skillet.

6. When patties have been turned, place bottom half of onion roll or hamburger bun cut side down over patty and place cut side down of top half over that, letting buns steam in the heat of patties until patties are tender.

*See page 192.

Serves: 10 patties
Preparation: 45 minutes
Cooking: 20 to 30 minutes

Affectionately referred to as Gut Busters or Belly Bombers. People crave these from coast to coast!

135

MARION CARDONES
Warren, Ohio

YUMMY SLOPPY JOES

2 lbs. ground beef
1 medium onion, chopped
½ green pepper, chopped
  (optional)
1 teaspoon salt
2 Tablespoons brown sugar
1 can tomato soup
1 teaspoon mustard
½ cup catsup
Onion buns* or hamburger
  buns

Serves: 6-8
Preparation: 15 minutes
Cooking: 30 minutes

1. Brown beef, onion and pepper. Drain grease, add remaining ingredients and heat thoroughly and serve on buns.

   *See page 192.

They are so easy to make and so yummy.

136

BEER SALAMI

GLORIA PITZER
Secret Recipes
Box 152
St. Clair, Michigan 48079

4 lbs. ground beef
1 envelope Good Seasons Italian Salad Dressing Mix
1 Tablespoon Durkees Hickory Smoked Salt
3 Tablespoons Morton Tender Quick Curing Salt
1 teaspoon ground pepper, ground by pepper mill
½ teaspoon anise extract
1 teaspoon cumin powder
1 teaspoon garlic salt
1 Tablespoon Worcestershire sauce
1 8-oz. can of light beer or ale
1 Tablespoon dill seeds
½ teaspoon anise seeds
1 Tablespoon mustard seeds

Serves: 4 1-lb. rolls
Preparation: 30 minutes
Baking: 3 hours

1. In a 4-quart bowl combine all ingredients, knead well, cover and refrigerate for 24 hours.

2. Knead 5 minutes, divide into 2 equal portions, cover and refrigerate another 24 hours.

3. Repeat this kneading method every 24 hours for 3 days, keeping mixture covered and refrigerated during storage.

4. Roll into 4 rolls of equal size, place on broiler pan and bake in preheated 225° oven for 3 hours, turning every 30 minutes. Cool completely. Freeze until needed.

This is so good for parties, or anytime.

137

BOLOGNA

GLORIA PITZER
Secret Recipes
Box 152
St. Clair, Michigan 48079

5 lbs. ground beef
5 rounded teaspoons Morton Tender Quick Salt
2 teaspoons mustard seeds
2 Tablespoons coarse pepper
2 teaspoons garlic <u>salt</u>
1 Tablespoon Hickory smoke salt or
2 Tablespoons liquid smoke

1. In a large bowl mix well, cover and keep in refrigerator for 24 hours.

2. Once a day for the next 4 days, knead mixture as you would bread dough, blending the mixture thoroughly for about 5 minutes each day.

3. On 5th day shape into 5 rolls of equal size (like salami).

4. Place on rack in shallow roasting pan on lowest shelf of oven and bake at 275° for 6 hours, turning rolls quarter turns every 30 minutes.

5. Sausage makes its own casing during baking. Keep refrigerated. Slice like lunchmeat when it is well chilled. Use in one week or freeze any that you want for later.

*See page 143.

Serves: 5 1-lb. rolls
Preparation: 30 minutes
Baking: 6 hours

Gloria has had repeated requests for this recipe. We love it crumbled in the Baked Bean and Kielbasa Casserole. It does add to the bean mixture flavor.*

FRED'S BEEF JERKY

FRED DAILY
Winter Garden, Florida

1½ lbs. flank steak
2 teaspoons Liquid Smoke
¾ teaspoon garlic powder
¼ teaspoon pepper
½ Tablespoon MSG
1 teaspoon onion powder
¾ cup soy sauce
¼ cup Worcestershire sauce
¼ cup barbecue sauce

1. Trim off all fat. It is important to trim off all possible fat. Semi-freeze chunks for easier slicing. Slice ⅛" thick. Put marinade in quart jar, add meat as it is sliced, making sure each piece is coated.

2. Lay jar on side in refrigerator at least 12 hours, turning often.

3. Drain on paper towels. Lay pieces on cake racks. Pieces may touch each other, but do not overlap. Each piece will shrink as it dries, so do not stretch piece out, but push it into as small a piece as possible (lengthwise).

4. Will drip some as drying, so place foil or cookie sheet under cake racks. Set oven at 150° and leave oven door slightly ajar (use a clothespin to keep door open about an inch). Roast 8-12 hours (overnight). Taste to find when it is as chewy or crisp as desired.

5. When dried and cooled, store in mason jar in refrigerator.

Yield: 1½ lbs.
Preparation: 1 hour
Baking: 8-12 hours

Marvelous for camping. Great tasting.

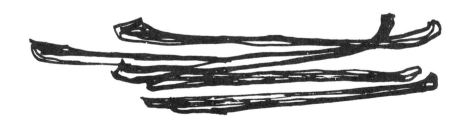

SAUSAGE, VEGIES AND HARD ROLLS

PAUL RUSH
Temple City, California

1½ lbs. pork sausage*
1 large onion, sliced
½ lb. mushrooms, sliced
1 large green pepper, seeded
  and sliced
½ teaspoon basil
½ teaspoon oregano
½ teaspoon rosemary
¼ teaspoon garlic powder
½ teaspoon marjoram
1½ teaspoons sugar
2 large tomatoes, diced
4 hard rolls, medium size
½ cup Mozzarella or Jack
  cheese, grated (optional)

*See page 142.

1. Sauté sausage until done. Remove and set aside.

2. Discard all grease except 3 Tablespoons and add remaining ingredients except tomatoes and hard rolls. Cook covered for about 7 minutes.

3. In the meantime cut and butter the inside of the rolls. Sprinkle ⅛ cup of cheese on both sides of roll and place on a cookie sheet in a preheated 350° oven for about 5 to 7 minutes.

4. Add diced tomatoes and sausage to vegie mixture and cook another 3-4 minutes uncovered.

5. Serve sausage and vegie mixture over rolls with cheese (dividing into 4 parts) as an open face sandwich. Serve with small salad.

Serves: 4
Preparation: 35 minutes
Cooking: 15-30 minutes

Yummy—they are so good!

140

HOMEMADE PIZZA

PIZZA DOUGH:
1 package dry yeast
¼ cup warm water
2 teaspoons sugar
¾ cup warm water
3 cups flour
1½ teaspoons salt
2 Tablespoons oil

SAUCE:
1 15½-oz. jar of Ragu Spaghetti
Sauce or leftover homemade
spaghetti sauce
½ teaspoon basil
1 teaspoon oregano

TOPPING:
2 Tablespoons oil
½ cup Parmesan cheese,
freshly grated, or
½ cup Romano cheese, freshly
grated
½ lb. Mozzarella cheese,
grated
1½ lbs. pork sausage*
½ lb. mushrooms, sliced
1 green pepper, seeded and
sliced thin
1 medium onion, sliced
Oil
Chopped black olives
Pepperoni, sliced thin

*See page 142.

Yield: 1 18" x 24" pizza
Preparation: 1 hour, 30 minutes
Baking: 20-30 minutes

1. In a small dish dissolve yeast and 2 teaspoons sugar in ¼ cup warm water. Let set until yeast bubbles.

2. Put flour, salt into processor or heavy duty mixer. Gradually add yeast mixture, oil and remaining water, mix thoroughly until well blended. Cover and let rise for about 1 hour.

3. In the meantime, mix Ragu sauce with oregano and basil and set aside. (If you have any leftover spaghetti sauce, use it instead.)

4. In a skillet sauté the mushrooms, pepper and onion until limp and set aside.

5. Take pizza out after one hour, knead a little on floured board. Roll out to fit an 18" x 24" cookie sheet. Oil cookie sheet well and lay the dough inside cookie sheet.

6. Oil top of dough lightly and sprinkle with ¼ cup Parmesan cheese. Spread top of cheese with Ragu sauce.

7. Sprinkle remaining ¼ cup Parmesan cheese on top of Ragu sauce.

8. Sprinkle the sautéed sausage over this, then sprinkle vegetables and olives over all, ending with Mozzarella cheese on the very top.

9. Bake in preheated 400° oven for 20 to 30 minutes, or until crust is lightly golden brown. Serve hot. Cut into 8 9" x 6" pieces.

You could use pepperoni, salami, meatballs or seafood instead of sausage. Whatever, you will have the best pizza in town.

141

HOMEMADE SAUSAGE

1½ lbs. pork, ground
2 teaspoons oregano
Pinch of cayenne pepper
Pinch of black pepper
2 teaspoons anise seeds
1 teaspoon salt
1½ teaspoons chili powder
1 clove of garlic, minced
¼ teaspoon basil
1 teaspoon paprika

1. Mix all together by hand and use for spaghetti, sandwiches, pizza or as desired.

Serves: 4
Preparation: 30 minutes

Much cheaper than regular Italian mild sweet sausage. Try grinding your own pork in a processor and go from there in mixing.

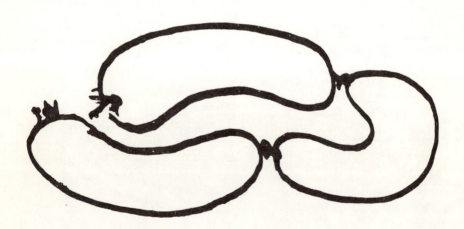

BAKED BEANS AND KIELBASA

1½ lbs. Polish Kielbasa
1 2-or 3-lb. can baked beans
6 slices bacon, chopped
1 large onion, chopped
1 cup ketchup
½ cup water
¼ cup brown sugar
(or more to taste)
1 heaping teaspoon Dijon
mustard
1 homemade Bologna Roll*
crumbled (optional)

1. Cut Kielbasa into 2″ pieces. Boil in water for about 15 minutes, drain and set aside.

2. Sauté bacon and onion together until bacon is about half cooked and onion is limp; set aside.

3. Grease 2½ quart casserole.

4. Mix baked beans, Kielbasa, cooked onion, bacon, ketchup, water, brown sugar, crumbled bologna and mustard. Blend well and pour into casserole.

5. Bake in preheated 350° oven for 1 hour uncovered. Serve with Italian Browns* and Uncle Johnie's Cole Slaw.*

*See pages 55, 138 and 154.

Serves: 4-6
Preparation: 30 minutes
Baking: 1 hour

Fred's favorite.

143

BAKED PORK CHOPS WITH BARBECUED BEANS

4 Tablespoons butter
6 large pork chops
Dash of sage
1 medium onion, chopped
1 clove garlic, minced
2 Tablespoons brown sugar,
  or more if needed
1 teaspoon dry mustard
2 Tablespoons white vinegar
1 cup ketchup
1 teaspoon salt
¼ teaspoon pepper
1 15-oz. can kidney beans,
  undrained
1 box frozen fork hook
  lima beans

1. Brown chops on each side in butter with sage sprinkled lightly over chops.

2. Sauté onions until limp, about 5 minutes. Add remaining ingredients, mixing well together. Cook about 5 minutes over low heat.

3. Place pork chops in a deep, buttered casserole. Pour bean-barbecue mixture over the chops. Bake uncovered in preheated 350° oven for 1 hour.

Serves: 4-6
Preparation: 35 minutes
Cooking and Baking: 1 hour, 35 minutes

This is another old, old family recipe that we love. Serve with mashed potatoes and rye bread.

PIGS IN A BLANKET

STELLA VOSS
Toledo, Ohio

2 lb. cabbage head
2-3 lbs. pork spare ribs, or
1½ lbs. Hungarian sausage

FILLING:
½ cup long grain rice
1 lb. lean, fresh ground pork
1 lb. lean ground beef
1 small onion, chopped fine
1 egg, beaten
½ cup water
Salt, pepper and paprika
  to taste

STEWING SAUCE:
1 large can sauerkraut, washed
  and drained
1 2-lb. can whole tomatoes
1 small onion, chopped fine
2 Tablespoons sugar
Salt, pepper and paprika
  to taste

1. Remove core from cabbage head and put in boiling water until outer leaves begin to wilt.

2. Scald rice in boiling water for 5 minutes. Rinse in cold water. Mix rice with the remaining filling ingredients.

3. Place 1 large heaping Tablespoon of filling on each cabbage leaf. Fold one end of leaf over, then each side and roll tightly. Secure with a toothpick. Set them aside.

4. Chop the remaining cabbage that is left, add remaining stewing sauce ingredients and mix well. Set aside.

5. Lightly brown spareribs that have been cut into individual ribs or sausage that has been cut into 4″ pieces.

6. Pour a little sauce in the bottom of a large kettle, then place cabbage rolls and meat together. Repeat with layers of sauce, meat and cabbage rolls until all are in the kettle. Fill with water to cover the top of all ingredients.

7. Put lid on kettle and cook over low heat for about 1½ hours. (Water may need to be added during cooking to keep rolls completely covered.)

Serves: 6-8
Preparation: 1 hour, 30 minutes
Cooking: 1 hour, 30 minutes

These surpass all the pigs in a blanket recipes that I have made in my lifetime. Serve with potatoes and refrigerator rolls and you have a complete dinner.

HUNGARIAN PORK CHOPS

LIBBY LAFFERTY
La Canada, California

4 large pork chops
1 to 2 Tablespoons oil
½ onion, chopped
1½ teaspoons sweet
  Hungarian paprika, or
1½ teaspoons regular paprika
½ bell pepper, chopped
1¾ cups chicken broth
¼ cup flour
1 cup Half and Half
Salt and pepper to taste

1. Brown pork chops in oil. Salt and pepper them and set aside.

2. Drain off any excess fat, reserving about 2 Tablespoons.

3. Sauté onions until transparent; add paprika and sauté briefly. Add pork chops, green pepper and chicken broth, cover and simmer slowly in electric skillet until tender, about 40 minutes or longer if needed, or blend juices from the pan, place chops in an 8" x 8" baking dish, place broth mixture over chops and cover with tin foil. Bake in preheated 350° oven for 1 hour.

4. Blend flour with Half and Half until smooth (can use blender). Add to juices.

5. Remove chops. Stir in juices and cook on top of stove until thickened, stirring constantly. Do not boil. Add chops and serve.

Serves: 4
Preparation: 20 minutes
Cooking: 40-55 minutes

Sensational!

146

SWEET AND SOUR PORK

FRED DAILY
Winter Garden, Florida

1½ lbs. pork loin cut into
2" strips
3 Tablespoons oil
2 cloves garlic, minced
1 large green pepper, seeded
and cut into ½" strips
4 medium carrots cut into
match sticks
½ lb. snow peas or
1 box frozen snow peas,
thawed
1 can water chestnuts, drained
and sliced
1 20-oz. can pineapple chunks
4 Tablespoons cornstarch
¼ cup water
½ cup brown sugar, firmly
packed
¼ cup soy sauce
3 Tablespoons wine vinegar
2 Tablespoons sherry
1 teaspoon ginger
4 cups cooked rice

Serves: 4-6
Preparation: 30 minutes
Cooking: 20-30 minutes

Really crisp, crunchy and a superb taste.

1. Heat oil in large skillet, add pork and cook until lightly brown, about 10 to 15 minutes.

2. Add garlic, carrots, pepper, snow peas and water chestnuts. Cook 5 minutes.

3. Drain pineapple; save juice.

4. Blend cornstarch, water, brown sugar, pineapple juice, soy sauce, vinegar, sherry and ginger and bring to a light boil, stirring constantly until thickened. Add pineapple chunks then add this to meat mixture. Serve over rice.

5. Try this sauce for sweet and sour chicken or shrimp.

147

PORK CHOPS
WITH WHITE WINE

6 1" loin pork chops
⅛ teaspoon rosemary
⅛ teaspoon sage
4 Tablespoons butter
2 large onions, sliced thin
½ lb. mushrooms, sliced thin
Salt and pepper to taste
½ cup white wine (optional)
½ cup chicken broth
2 teaspoons chicken granules
1 cup heavy cream
**½ Tablespoon Bovril (brown
  meat base)**
Cooked rice

1. Brown pork chops in 4 Tablespoons butter.

2. Place in well buttered 9" x 13" baking pan. Save juices for sauce.

3. Place onions and mushrooms on top of pork chops, cover with lid or foil and bake in preheated 350° oven for 1 hour.

4. Remove chops from pan, add wine and sauté about 3 minutes. Add remaining ingredients and cook until slightly thickened.

5. Add pork chops and juices from chops. Cook only a few minutes or until pork chops are heated through.

6. Serve on a bed of cooked rice or with mashed potatoes.

Serves: 6
Preparation: 30 minutes
Cooking and Baking: 1 hour, 15 minutes

Another old family favorite.

CROWN ROAST OF PORK WITH APRICOT BRANDY SAUCE

JUDY CASEY
Tempe, Arizona

8 to 9 lb. rib crown roast (14 to 16 ribs)

STUFFING:
1 lb. pork sausage, unseasoned
½ cup butter
1 large onion, chopped
⅓ cup celery, chopped
1 red delicious apple, cored and chopped with skin on
1 cup yellow raisins, cut up
½ cup apricots, cut up
½ cup brandy or sherry
3 cups whole wheat bread crumbs
¼ teaspoon cinnamon
¼ teaspoon mace
1 teaspoon salt
¼ teaspoon pepper
½ cup chicken broth
Pinch of sage
Pinch of thyme
Pinch of nutmeg

APRICOT BRANDY SAUCE:
1 12-oz. jar apricot jam
2 Tablespoons lemon juice
⅓ cup kirsch
2 Tablespoons butter
2 to 3 Tablespoons of pan drippings from roast

Serves: 10-12
Preparation: 1 hour
Baking: 3-4 hours

Elegant—Elegant—Elegant!

1. Cook sausage and drain. Set aside. Sauté onion and celery in butter until limp. Combine all ingredients in a large bowl with sausage and mix well.

2. Season roast with salt and pepper. Mound stuffing high in the center of roast. Cover top of stuffing with tin foil to prevent burning. Bake uncovered in preheated 400° oven or until internal temperature reads 170° with meat thermometer (about 3½ hours). You could also do a crown leg of lamb the same way.

3. Mix all ingredients in saucepan for Apricot Brandy Sauce. Bring to a boil and serve in separate bowl.

4. Around the roast garnish with peach and pear halves. Top each with a spoon of cranberry sauce.

SENATOR JOHN GLENN
ANNIE GLENN
Washington, D.C.

HAM LOAF

1 lb. ham, ground
½ lb. fresh ham, ground, or
½ lb. pork, ground
1½ cups bread crumbs
2 eggs, beaten
¾ cup milk
Salt and pepper to taste

GLAZE:
¼ cup vinegar
½ cup brown sugar
¼ cup water
1 Tablespoon Dijon mustard

Serves: 6-8
Preparation: 20 minutes
Baking: 1 hour, 30 minutes

1. Mix all ingredients for ham loaf and mold into two loaves. Place in a well-buttered baking pan.

2. Mix all ingredients for glaze and pour over the ham loaf.

3. Bake in a preheated 350° oven for 1½ hours, basting every 15 minutes.

4. Remove from oven, slice and serve with glaze.

This was Senator Glenn's mother's recipe, and thank you, Annie, for sharing this marvelous recipe.

POTATOES
Brenda's Irish Potato
Casserole................152
Walker's Au Gratin Potatoes....153
Bacon Almond Potatoes......154
Italian Browns..............154
Bear Claws Potatoes.........155
Baked Creamed Dumplings....156
German Potato Salad.........157
Sweet Potato Delight.........158
Fettucini Alfredo............159
RICE
Lemon Rice................160
Peking Oriental Rice.........161
Risotto Rice...............162

STUFFING
Mushroom Sage Dressing.....163
Green Pepper Noodle
Stuffing...................163
CHEESE & EGGS
Mom's Pierogi..............164
Greek Cheese Gourmet......166
Macaroni and Cheese
Gourmet.................167
Swedish Onion Quiche.......168
Chilie Rellenos..............169
Quiche Roma...............170

BRENDA LETSON
Warren, Ohio

BRENDA'S IRISH POTATO CASSEROLE

8-10 medium potatoes, peeled, cooked and drained
1 8-oz. package cream cheese
1 8-oz. carton sour cream
½ cup butter, melted
¼ cup chopped chives or onion greens
1 clove garlic, minced
1 teaspoon salt
Paprika

1. Mash potatoes. Add all the following ingredients except the paprika.

2. Beat until smooth and creamy.

3. Place potato mixture in a well-buttered, 2 quart casserole, sprinkle on paprika.

4. Cover and refrigerate overnight.

5. Remove from refrigerator, uncover and let sit at least 15 to 30 minutes before baking.

6. Bake at 350° for 30 minutes.

Serves: 8-10
Preparation: 30 minutes
Cooking and Baking: 1 hour

These are the tastiest mashed potatoes you will ever have. They are so yummy.

WALKER'S AU GRATIN POTATOES

MARY WALKER
McDonald, Pennsylvania

6 large potatoes, scrubbed and boiled first, then peeled
1 large onion, chopped
6 Tablespoons butter
4 Tablespoons flour
3 cups milk
12 oz. Velveeta cheese, cubed
1 teaspoon salt
¼ teaspoon ground pepper

Serves: 6-8
Preparation: 30 minutes
Baking: 1 hour

So good with ham or pork.

1. Preheat oven to 350°.

2. Cut potatoes in 1" cubes and set aside.

3. Sauté onions in butter until limp. Add flour and stir until smooth. Add milk, cheese and seasoning, stirring constantly until melted.

4. Generously butter a 9" x 13" baking pan, place in cut potatoes, pour on milk mixture and bake 1 hour at 350°.

153

BACON ALMOND POTATOES

5 slices bacon, fried and crumbled
2 large potatoes, peeled, cooked and mashed
¼ cup butter, melted and cooled
3 green onions, chopped (use green onion stems only)
½ teaspoon salt
Flour
1 egg, beaten
Sliced almonds
Oil (deep frying)

Serves: 4
Preparation: 45 minutes

A wonderful combination.

1. Mix hot mashed potatoes with bacon, butter, onion greens and salt. Blend well. Set in refrigerator for at least 1 to 2 hours.

2. Make potato mixture into size of golf balls. Roll in flour, dip in beaten egg, then roll in sliced almonds.

3. Deep fry at 375° until golden. Remove and drain on paper towel. Serve immediately (2 per person).

FRED DAILY
Winter Garden, Florida

ITALIAN BROWNS

¼ cup oil
8 large potatoes (cut into 1″ cubes
4 medium onions, sliced vertical
2 Tablespoons fresh parsley, chopped
1 teaspoon garlic powder
1 teaspoon salt
½ teaspoon pepper
1 stick of butter, cubed

Serves: 6
Preparation: 30 minutes
Baking: 1 hour, 30 minutes

1. Preheat oven to 400.° Place oil in shallow baking pan and all ingredients. Mix well.

2. Bake uncovered for 1½ hours, turning potatoes over about every 10 minutes.

Super with steak, hamburgers and breaded fish.

154

BEAR CLAWS POTATOES

DR. KATIE SPANGERBERG
Laguna Beach, California

4 medium potatoes
4 Tablespoons butter, melted
2 teaspoons beef bouillon
  granules
1 heaping teaspoon basil
Garlic powder
Freshly ground pepper

1. Wash potatoes, slice lengthwise ½" thick and make slits at one end of slice to resemble a bear foot.

2. Put butter in a 9" x 13" baking pan; coat both sides of potatoes with butter.

3. Sprinkle bouillon granules, basil, garlic powder and pepper evenly over top of potatoes (do not overlap potatoes in baking pan).

4. Bake in preheated 350° oven for ½ hour, turn over and bake another ½ hour. Serve hot. Super with steak or fish.

Serves: 4-6
Preparation: 15 minutes
Baking: 1 hour

Absolutely fantastic; always a hit!

BAKED CREAMED DUMPLINGS

DUMPLINGS:
¼ cup yellow cornmeal
½ cup water
1 cup flour
2 Tablespoons Parmesan cheese, fresh grated
1 cup water
½ cup butter
¼ teaspoon salt
4 eggs

SAUCE:
4 Tablespoons butter
4 Tablespoons flour
1 10¾ -oz. can chicken broth
1 13-oz. can evaporated milk
2 teaspoons chicken granules
½ cup Swiss cheese (grated)

1. Boil ½ cup water. Add ¼ cup cornmeal and cook until thick. Set aside.

2. Boil 1 cup water. Add ½ cup butter. Keep to a boil and add flour, salt and cheese. Mix well until mixture leaves sides of pan. Remove from heat and add one egg at a time, beating well with electric beater until smooth.

3. Beat cornmeal into mixture and beat again until smooth.

4. Drop by Tablespoonful into boiling water and boil for about 10 minutes, turning over. Remove with a slotted spoon onto a well-buttered, deep baking pan.

5. Melt butter in skillet. Add flour to make a roux. Add broth and chicken granules. Mix until well blended. Add milk and pour over dumplings. (Can prepare up to this point and refrigerate.)

6. Bake in preheated 350° oven for 20 minutes. Remove from oven. Sprinkle with Swiss cheese and bake another 10 minutes or until golden on top. Serve hot.

Serves: 6-8
Preparation: 1 hour
Baking: 30 minutes

Splendid. Everyone's favorite.

156

GERMAN POTATO SALAD

JUDY CASEY
Tempe, Arizona

½ lb. bacon, diced
1 onion, sliced
8 small red potatoes, cooked
   and sliced
½ cup vinegar
1 cup water
½ teaspoon dry mustard
½ teaspoon celery seed
⅓ cup sugar
½ teaspoon salt
½ teaspoon Lawry's
   Seasoned Salt
Fresh ground pepper to taste
2 Tablespoons flour
Fresh parsley, chopped
   (garnish)

Serves: 4
Preparation: 1 hour

1. Brown bacon. Remove from grease, add to onion and potatoes in a large bowl.

2. Stir flour into bacon grease.

3. Add remaining ingredients and cook until thick.

4. Pour over potatoes and mix. Serve warm.

There are many recipes for German Potato Salad, but we feel this is the best.

SWEET POTATO DELIGHT

2 Tablespoons brown sugar
1 16-oz. can yams, drained
1 heaping Tablespoon orange
  peel, grated
¼ cup pecans, chopped
½ cup graham cracker crumbs
1½ Tablespoons butter,
  softened
5 large marshmallows, halved
Cornflakes, crushed lightly

Yield: 10
Preparation: 30 minutes
Baking: 15 minutes

Delicious!

1. Mix all ingredients except marshmallows and cornflakes.

2. Shape mixture around a half marshmallow about the size of golf ball, roll in cornflakes and place on greased baking dish. (Place them close together.) Bake in preheated 350° oven for 15 minutes.

3. You can make these in the morning and refrigerate until time to bake.

FETTUCCINE ALFREDO

CHEF PATRICK TOMBELAINE
Golden Eagle Restaurant
Phoenix, Arizona

8 oz. fettuccine, cooked
4 Tablespoons butter
1 shallot, chopped fine
2 cloves garlic, minced
2 Tablespoons fresh parsley, chopped
½ pint cream (and Half and Half, if needed)
½ cup Parmesan cheese, fresh grated
Dash of nutmeg

Serves: 4
Preparation: 30 minutes

The Best.

1. Sauté shallot and garlic in butter about 3 minutes. Add to hot, cooked fettuccine. Mix well and add remaining ingredients. Heat if necessary and add more cream, if necessary. Serve as side dish. (I sometimes like to sauté 1 clove of garlic and put the other in raw when I'm mixing in the butter and fettuccine.)

LEMON RICE

CHEF BILL MALDONADO
Maldonado's Restaurant
Pasadena, California

4 cups cooked rice
½ pint whipping cream,
heated to simmer
½ stick butter
Juice and grated rind of
1 lemon
Parsley sprigs

1. If rice is "sticky" this won't work. If this is the case, rinse rice in cold water before beginning the recipe.

2. Melt butter, sauté lemon rind for about 3 minutes, remove rind and set aside.

3. Add lemon butter and juice to rice, tossing gently. Add heated cream and rind and toss gently again. Pour into oven-proof dish and keep warm in 150° oven for 1 hour before serving time.

4. If ½ pint of cream is absorbed too quickly, add a little canned milk or Half and Half.

5. Garnish with parsley sprigs and serve.

Serves: 6-8
Preparation: 35 minutes

Sensational and definitely a ten plus.

PEKING ORIENTAL RICE

3 Tablespoons butter
1 small onion, chopped fine
1 celery stalk, chopped fine
Juice of 1 large orange
1 Tablespoon orange zest
1½ cups water
½ cup rice
½ teaspoon thyme
1 large carrot, chopped
1½ teaspoons chicken
  granules
Salt to taste
Pepper to taste
1 6-oz. box frozen snow peas
2 Tablespoons Cointreau*
  (optional), or
2 Tablespoons Grand Marnier
  (optional)

Serves: 4-6
Preparation: 20 minutes
Cooking: 25 minutes

1. Sauté onion and celery in Teflon skillet until limp, about 5 minutes. Add juice of orange, orange zest and water. Bring to a boil, add rice, thyme, chopped carrot and seasonings. Cover and simmer over low heat for 20 minutes. Do not remove the lid.

2. Add snow peas, stir well, cover and simmer another 5 minutes.

3. Add Cointreau* or Grand Marnier. Stir well and serve with fowl, ham or pork.

*See page 309.

Voilá—I finally came up with this marvelous tasting rice and vegetable complement.

RISOTTO RICE

CHEF DON SCHUBERT
Torrance, California

½ cup onion, chopped fine
3 Tablespoons butter
1 cup long grain rice, or
1 cup converted rice
2 cups chicken stock
Pinch of saffron
½ bay leaf
1 teaspoon seasoned salt
2 Tablespoons Parmesan
cheese (optional)

Serves: 6
Preparation: 15 minutes
Baking: 30-35 minutes

Super tasting and will go with anything.

1. Sauté onion in butter until transparent. Add rice and sauté briefly. Add liquid and seasonings and bring to a boil.

2. Pour into a buttered casserole, cover and bake in preheated 400° oven for 30 to 35 minutes without stirring.

3. Fluff rice with two forks, remove bay leaf, arrange on platter and sprinkle with Parmesan cheese, if desired.

MUSHROOM SAGE DRESSING

FRED DAILY
Winter Garden, Florida

1 lb. butter
2 stalks of celery, chopped
2 medium onions, chopped
½ lb. mushrooms, sliced
6 large eggs
1 16-oz. and 1 8-oz. package
   Pepperidge Farm Herb
   Stuffing
1½ Tablespoons sage
Salt to taste

Serves: 8-10
Preparation: 45 minutes

1. Sauté celery, onions and mushrooms in butter until limp.

2. Mix stuffing, sage and salt with eggs. Add butter and mix well. Sit in refrigerator until ready to use. This will stuff a 14 to 18 lb. turkey.

If you like the taste of sage, you'll love this dressing.

GREEN PEPPER NOODLE STUFFING

MARY WALKER
McDonald, Pennsylvania

1 8-oz. package medium width
   egg noodles, cooked and
   drained
1 stick of butter (no substitute)
3 egg yolks
½ green pepper, chopped
½ teaspoon black pepper
   (or more if desired)
Salt to taste

Serves: 6
Preparation: 20 minutes
Cooking (of noodles): 25 minutes

1. Cook noodles al dente, add butter and mix until melted.

2. Stir in egg yolks and remaining ingredients. Mix well and refrigerate overnight.

3. Stuff chicken or any desired fowl and bake.

Mary has so many outstanding recipes, and this is certainly one of them.

NICK HULYK
KATHERINE HULYK
Kiev, Russia

MOM'S PIEROGI

DOUGH:
3 cups flour
3 eggs
¼ cup water
½ Tablespoon salt

FILLING:
4 medium potatoes, peeled,
　boiled tender and drained
½ stick butter, softened
6 oz. very sharp Cheddar
　cheese, grated
¼ teaspoon freshly
　ground pepper

TOPPING:
3 large onions, chopped
1 lb. butter
2 cups sour cream

1. In a large bowl place 2½ cups flour. Make a well in center, add eggs, water and salt. Mix and knead to consistency of bread dough. May need more flour; if so, add gradually. Cover for ½ hour.

2. Mash potatoes, adding butter, cheese and pepper. Set aside to cool.

3. Make dough into balls about 1″ round, making about 1 dozen at a time. Keep doughs in bowl and board covered. Roll each ball on a well floured board to about 2½″ diameter.

4. Fill center with 1 heaping teaspoon filling, fold in half and pinch edges all around opened edges. Repeat until all dough is used.

5. Boil in large pot of boiling water to which 3 Tablespoons oil have been added. Boil about 7 minutes. They will rise to the top. Turn over and boil another 7 minutes. Remove to a well buttered platter. Keep warm in oven.

6. Sauté onions in butter until limp. Place butter and onions in a separate bowl and serve with the platter of dumplings. In another bowl place sour cream. Spoon a ladle full of butter and onions over individual servings with a dollop of sour cream on each.

(continued)

Mom's Pierogi (continued)

a. These can be frozen uncooked on a cookie sheet (don't overlap). When frozen, place in plastic bag until ready to use.
b. Leftovers can be fried the next day in butter until golden brown. They are so good this way, also.
c. Try making these with a pitted prune and 1 teaspoon sugar. Cook as regular pierogi and serve with a dollop of sour cream or 1 part sour cream and 1 part whipped cream mixed together.

Yields: 30-35 3" x 2" pierogi
Preparation: 3 hours
Cooking: 15 minutes

Well worth the time and effort—truly a treat!

GREEK Á LA CHEESE GOURMET

MARION CARDONES
Warren, Ohio

1 lb. ground beef
1 medium onion, chopped
¼ lb. butter
1 (4-oz.) can tomato sauce
¼ cup water
Dash cinnamon and nutmeg
1 Tablespoon salt
½ teaspoon pepper
½ lb. macaroni
5 eggs
¼ lb. butter
1 cup Cheddar cheese, grated

CREAM SAUCE:
½ quart milk
1 Tablespoon butter
1½ Tablespoons flour
Salt to taste
½ cup Cheddar cheese, grated

1. Brown onion in ¼ lb. butter. Add beef, tomato sauce, water, cinnamon, salt and pepper and cook 15 minutes. Simmer while making cream sauce.

2. Boil milk. Melt butter in saucepan, add flour and stir until smooth. Add hot milk and salt to taste, cook over medium heat until thick and creamy, stirring constantly. Add grated cheese and cook a little longer.

3. In 1 quart salted boiling water, cook macaroni until tender. Drain macaroni and put in large pan, adding immediately 4 beaten eggs, butter, 1 cup grated cheese. Mix together and pour ½ macaroni mix in buttered pan, 9" x 13."

4. Cover with meat sauce and spread evenly. Cover with remaining macaroni mix and spread evenly. Spread cream sauce on top. Beat remaining egg and spread over cream sauce on top to give color. Sprinkle top with grated cheese. Bake 350° uncovered for 30 minutes. Cut in squares and serve.

Serves: 8-10
Preparation: 1 hour
Cooking and Baking: 1 hour

This is a marvelous Greek dish.

MACARONI AND CHEESE GOURMET

MACRINA SUDIMACK
San Rafael, California

½ lb. macaroni
¼ cup butter
1 medium onion, chopped
3 Tablespoons flour
1 cup Half and Half or milk
½ cup white wine
2¼ cups Cheddar cheese, grated
Salt and pepper to taste
4 drops Tabasco sauce
1 Tablespoon chopped pimentos

1. Cook macaroni al dente, strain and set aside.

2. Melt butter, saute onion until limp, add flour, salt, pepper and Tabasco sauce. Make a roux.

3. Gradually add Half and Half and wine. Stir until the consistency of gravy. Add cheese and stir constantly until cheese is melted. Add pimento, stir lightly.

4. Pour cheese sauce over macaroni and pour mixture in a well buttered casserole.

5. Bake in preheated 350° oven for 30 minutes.

Serves: 4-6
Preparation: 30 minutes
Cooking and Baking: 1 hour

A hearty vegetarian delight.

167

SWEDISH ONION QUICHE

1 pastry shell*
5 Tablespoons butter
¼ cup water
1 large onion, chopped
3 cups green onions, chopped
4 eggs, beaten
1½ cups Half and Half
1 teaspoon salt
⅛ teaspoon pepper
⅛ teaspoon nutmeg
**½ cup Parmesan cheese,
   freshly grated**

*****See page 294.**

Serves: 4-6
Preparation: 45 minutes
Cooking and Baking: 40 minutes

An excellent one-dish meal.

1. Make pie shell (omit the sugar).

2. Sauté onions in butter and water until limp over medium heat, about 10 minutes.

3. Combine eggs, Half and Half, salt, pepper, nutmeg, onion mixture and half of the Parmesan cheese. Pour into pastry shell.

4. Sprinkle remaining cheese on top of mixture.

5. Bake in preheated oven 375° for 30 minutes or until knife comes out clean.

CHILIE RELLENOS

CHEF MIKE ZYLA
Paradise Valley Country Club
Paradise Valley, Arizona

8 oz. Velveeta cheese
12 oz. Monterey Jack cheese
1 (10-oz.) can green chilies, Ortega brand
1 (2-oz.) can pimentos, chopped
1 cup milk
10 eggs
4 Tablespoons flour
Salt to taste
Jack cheese, grated

1. In a blender add ½ cup milk, eggs, flour and salt. Beat well.

2. Spoon on buttered griddle or skillet to just cover bottom and brown on each side as a pancake. Do this until all batter is used. You will have about 8 to 10 pancakes.

3. Remove seeds in chilies, lay one in center of each pancake, cut Jack cheese in ½" wide by 2" long strips and lay on top of chilie, roll up pancake and place in a well buttered, 9" x 13" baking pan.

4. In a saucepan melt Velveeta cheese with ½ cup milk, chopped pimentos and 1 chopped green chilie.

5. Pour over rellenos, top with grated Jack cheese and bake in preheated 350° oven for 20 to 30 minutes or until it bubbles.

Serves: 4-6
Preparation: 1 hour
Baking: 20-30 minutes

There are rellenos and rellenos and rellenos, but never will you have better rellenos than these.

169

QUICHE ROMA

1½ lbs. homemade sausage*
1 Tablespoon oil
1 Tablespoon butter
1 bunch green onions,
  chopped
½ lb. mushrooms, sliced
1 celery stalk, chopped
1 large tomato, chopped
Pinch of cayenne pepper
½ teaspoon salt
⅛ teaspoon oregano
½ teaspoon basil
½ lb. Monterey Jack cheese,
  grated
½ cup Half and Half
½ cup milk
13 eggs, beaten

*See page 139.

Serves: 6-8
Preparation: 1 hour
Baking: 35-45 minutes

1. Crumble sausage in large skillet and brown until cooked. Remove with slotted spoon and set aside.

2. Drain grease, add oil, butter, onions, mushrooms and celery, and cook until limp. Remove from heat, set aside and stir in chopped tomatoes.

3. Combine remaining ingredients in a large bowl and beat with electric mixer until well blended. Add sausage and vegetables mixture; mix well.

4. Pour into a well-buttered 13" x 9" baking dish and bake in a preheated 400° oven for 35 minutes or until knife comes out clean. Serve as an entrée. Can even eat cold as an appetizer.

Another dish that is a long time family favorite.

VEGETABLES

Barbecue Beans. 172
Creamy Sweet Corn. 173
Lemon Apple Sauce. 173
Carrots Brittany. 174
Carrots del Turco. 174

Stuffed Mushrooms with
   Bechamel Sauce. 175
Broccoli Fettucini Alfredo. 176
Broccoli Charmaine. 177
Creamy Cheese Onions. 178

BARBECUE BEANS

SANDRA NICHOLAS
California, Maryland

1 box frozen lima beans
1 can kidney beans, drained
1 can pork and beans
6 strips bacon, chopped
¼ teaspoon dry mustard
¾ cup ketchup
1 large onion, chopped
½ cup brown sugar,
  firmly packed
½ cup green pepper, chopped

1. Mix all ingredients together and bake covered in 300° oven for 1 hour.

2. Uncover and bake at 375° for 1 hour and serve.

Serves: 6-8
Preparation: 15 minutes
Baking: 2 hours

Great for picnics.

CREAMY SWEET CORN

OLGA RUSH
Temple City, California

1 package frozen corn or
2 ears fresh corn
½ cup whipping cream
½ cup milk
1 Tablespoon sugar
½ teaspoon salt
1 Tablespoon butter
1 Tablespoon flour

1. Crush ¼ package of frozen corn. If using fresh ears of corn, you need only to chop corn off ear.

2. Boil corn, cream, milk, sugar and salt lightly, stirring occasionally.

3. Melt butter, add flour, make a roux, add to corn mixture and serve.

4. Can add chunks of left-over ham if desired.

Serves: 4-6
Preparation: 15 minutes
Cooking: 10 minutes

You will never taste a better creamed corn.

LEMON APPLESAUCE

4 Granny apples, peeled, cleaned and cored
½ cup sugar
¼ cup water
The zest of 1 medium lemon
1 teaspoon cinnamon
¼ teaspoon nutmeg

1. Cut apples into 1″ cubes, add the remaining ingredients. Cook over medium heat for about 15 minutes or until apples are cooked through and tender. Stir every couple of minutes.

Serves: 4
Preparation: 15 minutes
Cooking: 15-20 minutes

The lemon zest gives this applesauce a marvelous taste. I feel you will enjoy it as we do.

CARROTS BRITTANY

BOBBIE LANGER
McDonald, Pennsylvania

8 medium carrots, sliced
2 teaspoons chicken bouillon
   granules
1 ½ cups water
¼ cup butter
3 Tablespoons flour
6 small onions, cleaned
   and quartered
Salt and pepper to taste

1. In a saucepan combine carrots, bouillon granules and water. Cook about 15 minutes.

2. Melt butter in frying pan, add onions and cook until limp and tender. Be careful not to brown or break onions apart.

3. Remove onions and set aside.

4. Add flour to butter and make a roux. Add onions, carrots and liquid. Cook until thickened and serve.

Serves: 4-6
Preparation: 25 minutes
Cooking: 20-30 minutes

The chicken flavor accents the carrots and onions.

CARROTS DEL TURCO

BARBARA ROTH
Las Vegas, Nevada

1 lb. carrots, grated
¾ cup water
½ teaspoon salt
½ teaspoon sugar
¼ cup butter
2 Tablespoons amaretto*
   or Grand Marnier
2 Tablespoon slivered almonds
1 teaspoon lemon juice

*See page 308.

Serves: 4-6
Preparation: 20 minutes
Cooking: 10-13 minutes

1. Place carrots, water, salt and sugar in a skillet, bring to a boil, cover and cook over low heat for 10 minutes. Stir occasionally and be careful that carrots don't burn.

2. Add remaining ingredients, heat gently and serve.

STUFFED MUSHROOMS WITH BÉCHAMEL SAUCE

JUDY CASEY
Tempe, Arizona

18 large mushrooms, washed
   and patted dry with stems
   removed

BÉCHAMEL SAUCE:
2 Tablespoons butter
3 Tablespoons flour
1/2 teaspoon salt
Pepper
Pinch cayenne
Generous pinch nutmeg
1 bay leaf
1 cup cream, or
1 cup Half and Half

STUFFING:
3 Tablespoons butter
18 stems of mushrooms,
   chopped fine (from above)
1 medium onion, chopped fine
1 clove garlic, minced
1 10-oz. package frozen
   spinach, thawed and
   drained well
Salt, pepper and seasoned
   salt to taste
3/4 cup ham, or
3/4 cup bacon, fried and
   drained, or
3/4 cup crab, chopped fine, or
3/4 cup shrimp, chopped fine
1 cup Béchamel sauce
Parmesan cheese, fresh grated

Yield: 18 mushrooms
Preparation: 35 minutes
Baking: 10-15 minutes

1. Make Béchamel sauce. In a skillet melt butter, stir in flour and cook until bubbly. Remove from heat, add cream slowly and seasonings. Return to heat, stir constantly and cook until thickened.

2. Place mushroom caps on a cookie sheet in a 350° oven for 5 to 10 minutes to sweat them. Remove and set aside.

3. Stuffing. Sauté onion, garlic and mushroom stems in butter. Add spinach (squeezed dry) and simmer 3 minutes while stirring. Remove from heat and stir in ham and Béchamel sauce. Stuff mushroom caps, sprinkle with Parmesan cheese and bake in a preheated 350° oven for 10 to 15 minutes. Serve as an appetizer or as a vegetable with main course.

Either way of being served, your guests will enjoy them.

BOBBIE LANGER
McDonald, Pennsylvania

BROCCOLI FETTUCINE ALFREDO

4 oz. medium noodles
4 oz. spinach noodles
1 stick butter
1 medium onion, chopped
1 box frozen broccoli, or fresh broccoli
1 garlic clove, minced
1 cup dry cottage cheese
¼ cup Parmesan cheese, fresh grated
Salt to taste
Pepper to taste

Serves: 4
Preparation: 30 minutes
Cooking: 20 minutes

1. Cook noodles. While they are cooking, sauté the onion in butter until limp.

2. Cook broccoli and drain. Drain the noodles and add the broccoli, sautéed butter and onion, garlic, cottage cheese and Parmesan cheese. Mix well and serve.

What a marvelous combination to serve.

176

BROCCOLI CHARMAINE

CHARMAINE WILSON
Scottsdale, Arizona

**2 packages frozen or large
bunch of broccoli cooked
and drained
³/₄ cup sour cream
1 can mushroom soup
2 Tablespoons pimentos,
chopped
½ cup sharp Cheddar cheese,
shredded
½ cup celery, chopped
1 teaspoon salt
½ teaspoon ground
black pepper**

1. Combine all ingredients and pour in buttered 1½-quart casserole. Bake in preheated 350° oven 30 minutes.

Serves: 4-6
Preparation: 20 minutes
Baking: 30 minutes

Very tasty.

177

CREAMY CHEESE ONIONS

ANNETTE CAMPBELL
West Farmington, Ohio

6 to 8 medium onions
¼ lb. bacon, fried and chopped
1 8-oz. jar Cheez Whiz

1. Peel, boil, drain and cool onions. (Cook in water about 10 to 15 minutes, just until tender.)

2. Carefully take center out of onions leaving only 3 layers around outside edge.

3. Chop centers, mix with fried, chopped bacon and cheese, spoon into the outer 3 layers of onion and stand up in flat pan.

4. Place under broiler until brown on top, about 5 to 10 minutes.

Serves: 6-8
Preparation: 45 minutes
Cooking: 20-30 minutes

These are magnificent.

178

Bread
&Sweet Breads

BREADS & DINNER ROLLS
Alligator Bread 180
Pepperoni Bread 182
French Bread Brioche 184
Bacon Bread 185
Don's Onion Bread 186
Merry Callender Corn Bread
   (California) 187
Walnut Cheddar Loaf 188
Mom's Cheese and Raisin
   Dinner Rolls 189
Potato Refrigerator Rolls 190
Mom's Orange Pecan Dinner
   Rolls 191
Onion Buns 192
Cheese Poppy Seed Garlic
   Toast 193
Angel Biscuits 193
Spicy Cheese Crisps 194

SWEET BREADS & SWEET ROLLS
Griswold's Bran Muffins 195
Finn Nisu Bread
   (Sweet Bread) 196
Grandma Campana's Easter Bread
   (Sweet Bread) 197
Raisin Cinnamon Bread 198
Cherry Nibble Bread 199
Zucchini Bread 200
Banana Bread Supreme 201
Caramel Nut Roll 202
Powdered Orange Puffs 203
Bubba's Kolachy Rolls 204
Danish Rolls 205
PANCAKES
Mom's Apple Pancakes 206
Blueberry Buttermilk
   Pancakes 207
Pumpkin Puff Pancakes 208

JUDY CASEY
Tempe, Arizona

ALLIGATOR BREAD

1½ batches homemade French or Italian
   pepperoni bread dough,* or
1½ loaves Brigford French Bread dough
   (3 loaves will make <u>2 alligator-breads</u>)

*See page 182.

Foil, approximately 12 inches by 6 inches
Toothpicks
1 egg, beaten
2 candied cherries, or 2 raisins

1. (a) To prepare foil used to hold mouth open during baking, fold piece several times until it measures about 2″ wide by 6″ long.

1. (c) Lightly flour working surface and flour dough until it can be handled. Use 1¼ loaves for body and save remaining ¼ for legs. Cut the ½ loaf in a diagonal from large end to opposite end.

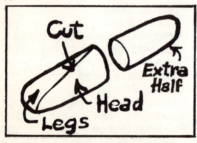

2. (a) Cut corners of large, pointed end for mouth and flour inside the mouth.
2. (b) Then brush inside mouth with beaten egg.

1. (b) Fold over in shape of a V and grease foil well. Make 4 to 6 holes in foil for the toothpicks used to hold dough on top of foil.

1. (d) Attach wide end to regular loaf end, the pointed end for mouth. With hands elongate dough for body, making tail end very narrow, making dough a length of 18″ to 20″ long. Smooth out dough to break air bubbles. Place on a greased cookie sheet. Stretch out body in curved form or desired shape.

2. (c) Slip in foil V and stretch out mouth to form a wide open shape.
2. (d) Stick toothpicks through holes in foil to hold dough in place and 1 toothpick in mouth to hold open during baking.

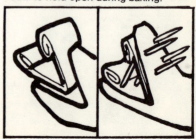

(continued)

Alligator Bread (continued)

3. With scissors snip dough along upper and lower mouth and on top of snout. Snip along top of head for a "prickly" look. Snip out dough on either side of head for eyes. Remove dough and lift up to form eyebrows.

4. Use remaining dough for legs. Cut in four equal parts. Shape each leg and attach to body by pinching dough together. It is important that legs be securely attached so as not to separate from body during baking. The back legs should be in the opposite direction from the front legs.

5. Use a candied cherry (or raisin) for each eye. Flour and roll removed pieces of dough to flatten into strips. Wrap a strip around each cherry, dip in egg and put in place, securing each with a toothpick.

6. Make cuts ½" deep and ½" apart, snipping, pinching, and lifting dough to form ridges down the back and then along the sides of the body in the opposite direction.

7. Make 4 cuts on legs for paws. Next make cuts on legs in the opposite direction from paws.

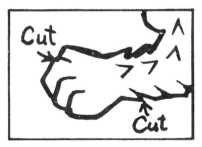

8. Bake at 350° for 30 to 35 minutes. About 10 minutes before removing from oven glaze entire body with beaten egg. Return to oven for remainder of baking.

9. Remove from oven, cool completely. Tie a ribbon around his neck then into a bow. Great for gifts, centerpieces, also to eat.

10. Use your imagination. Make Christmas wreaths, a turkey, Easter bunny, etc.

PEPPERONI BREAD

ANGIE PORRINI
Warren, Ohio

DOUGH:
2 packages dry yeast
½ cup warm water
1 Tablespoon sugar
Pinch of ginger
6 cups flour
1½ cups warm water
¼ cup dry powdered milk
½ Tablespoon salt
2 Tablespoons sugar
¼ cup oil

FILLING:
1 medium green pepper, chopped
1 medium onion, chopped
2 Tablespoons oil
½ lb. pepperoni, coarsely ground
¼ lb. Mozzarella cheese, grated
¼ cup Romano cheese, grated, or
¼ cup Parmesan cheese, grated

1. In a small bowl place ½ cup warm water, yeast, 1 Tablespoon sugar and ginger. Set aside until bubbly.

2. In a small saucepan put 1½ cups warm water, powdered milk, salt, 2 Tablespoons sugar and oil. Heat only to lukewarm.

3. Place the 6 cups of flour in a large bowl and make a well in the center. Pour in milk mixture and yeast mixture. Mix until well blended. (You can also mix it in food processor or a heavy duty mixer with a dough hook.) Place dough on a well-floured bread board and knead until smooth and elastic, about 10 to 15 minutes. (If dough is mixed by heavy duty mixer or processor, you only need to knead about 3-5 minutes.) (May add more flour, if needed.)

4. Place dough in a greased bowl, turn once and cover with a towel. Let rise 1 hour in a warm place.

5. Punch down, cover and let rise 1 hour again.

6. Sauté green pepper and onion in oil until soft and limp. Remove from heat, cool, then add pepperoni and cheeses. Mix well and set aside.

7. Divide dough into 2 parts. Roll each part on a floured board 14" x 12" x ½" and spread ½ of pepperoni mixture onto within 1" of edge. Roll up lengthwise like a jelly roll, stretching dough lengthwise and place seam side down on a well greased cookie sheet. Repeat with the 1 remaining dough and mixture.

(continued)

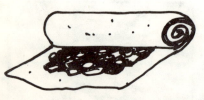

Pepperoni Bread *(continued)*

8. Cut deep slits (with scissors) across the top at 2″ intervals. Cover with towel and let rise again ½ hour. Bake in preheated 350° oven for 30 minutes or until golden brown. Remove from oven, brush tops with melted butter.

9. Can be served warm or cold, and these can be frozen by cooling first, wrap in foil, freeze and bake again in foil at 350° for 30 minutes. this dough can also be used for 1 12″ x 18″ pizza or 2 Italian breads. Bake 2 Italian breads or pizza at same temperature. Great for Alligator Bread* also.

*See pages 42 and 180.

Yield: 2 long loaves
Preparation: 1 hour
Baking: 30 minutes

WOW! *This is so good! Try it with Grandpa's Antipasto Salad* and a glass of red wine. Raves, Raves, Raves! A 10 plus.*

CHEF VINCENT GUERITHAULT
Vincent's French Cuisine
Scottsdale, Arizona

FRENCH BREAD BRIOCHE

3³/₄ cups all purpose flour
6 eggs
¹/₂ Tablespoon salt
2¹/₂ Tablespoons sugar
1 package yeast
¹/₄ cup water
³/₄ lb. cold butter

1. You must use a heavy duty mixer or a food processor (and use the steel blade). A hand mixer <u>will not work</u>. In a small bowl mix yeast and ¹/₄ cup water and set aside.

2. In the mixing bowl place flour, eggs, salt, sugar and yeast mixture and beat for about <u>5 to 10 minutes</u> at <u>medium</u> speed with the dough hook (or 4 minutes with processor).

3. Add butter and beat until well blended throughout, about 5 minutes.

4. Cover and let rise 1 hour in a warm place.

5. Punch down and let rise 1 hour again.

6. Dust hands lightly with flour and place dough in 18 well buttered brioche pans, 2 (2-qt.) brioche pans or 2 (5" x 9") bread pans. Cover and let rise 1 hour again. (This dough is so light, you may think that there isn't enough flour in it, but believe me, there is.)

7. Bake individual brioche in a preheated 375° oven for 10 to 12 minutes. For the larger loaves, bake at 375° for 20 to 25 minutes or until bread is deep golden. Remove from oven, take from pans and put on a bread rack to cool.

Yield: 18 individual or 2 loaves
Preparation: 45 minutes
Baking: According to pans used

This bread is as light and fluffy as a cloud and equally as delicious. A ten plus, plus.

184

BACON BREAD

GRACE GARD
Kissimmee, Florida

**5 slices of bacon, fried crisp
and crumbled (reserve
grease)
1½ cups scalded milk
2 teaspoons salt
4 Tablespoons brown sugar
2 teaspoons bacon grease
2 packages dry yeast
½ cup warm water
1 egg, beaten
4 cups all purpose flour
1 cup whole wheat flour**

1. Combine milk, salt, 2 Tablespoons brown sugar and bacon grease. Cool.

2. Mix yeast, remaining 2 Tablespoons brown sugar and water and let rest about 5 minutes.

3. Combine cooled milk mixture and yeast mixture. Add egg and flours. Knead to elastic feeling, smooth and satiny.

4. Cover and let rise in a warm place about 1 hour.

5. Work in bacon, shape into two loaves and put into two well-greased 9″ x 5″ loaf pans. Let rise again for 30 minutes.

6. Bake in preheated 350° oven for 30 minutes. Rub top with butter when removed from oven.

Yield: 2 loaves
Preparation: 45 minutes
Baking: 30 minutes

Grace's mother's creation, and a marvelous one.

DON'S ONION BREAD
(No Kneading)

1 cup milk, scalded
3 Tablespoons sugar
½ Tablespoon salt
1½ Tablespoons butter
2 packages yeast
¾ cup warm water
½ cup <u>fresh</u> onion, minced
  very fine
1 2.75-oz. envelope of Lipton
  Onion Soup
1 cup whole wheat flour
3½ cups all purpose flour

1. Stir in sugar, salt and butter into scalded milk. Cool to lukewarm.

2. Dissolve yeast in warm water.

3. Place cooled milk mixture, yeast mixture and remaining ingredients into mixing bowl and beat with heavy duty mixer or food processor until well blended. (Dough will still be sticky.)

4. Place Saran Wrap on top of bowl. Cover with towel and let rise for 1 hour in a warm place.

5. Stir down batter, divide into two well-buttered 5″ x 9″ bread pans. (Cover and let rise for 30 minutes.)

6. Bake in preheated 350° oven for 35 to 45 minutes, until deep brown and bread sounds hollow when tapped. Remove from oven and brush butter on tops of bread. (For a slight change of taste try putting 2 Tablespoons caraway seed in also.)

Yield: 2 loaves
Preparation: 25 minutes
Baking: 40-45 minutes

I created this for Don.

GLORIA PITZER
Secret Recipes
P.O. Box 152
St. Clair, Michigan 48079

MERRY CALLENDER CORN BREAD (CALIFORNIA)

1 9-oz. package Jiffy corn
   muffin mix
1 9-oz. package Jiffy yellow
   cake mix
2 slices bacon
¼ lb. butter
½ cup honey

1. Prepare corn muffin mix as directed on the package and set as directed on the package and set aside.

2. Prepare yellow cake mix in another container as directed on the package and set aside.

3. Fry bacon until crisp. Remove bacon from pan and set aside.

4. Pour drippings from bacon into cake batter, beating well.

5. Beat the two batters together for about 3 minutes. Pour into a 9" x 12" well greased baking pan.

6. Bake in a preheated 400° oven for 20 minutes or until tooth pick inserted comes out clean.

7. Mix crispy bacon, butter and honey, beating on medium speed for about 3 minutes until fluffy.

8. Serve at room temperature with warm corn bread squares. Refrigerate butter when not in use.

Serves: 8
Preparation: 25 minutes
Baking: 20 minutes

Gloria—It melts in your mouth—Yummy!

DEANNA MATTHEWS
Matthews 1812 House
Cornwall Bridge, Connecticut 06754

WALNUT CHEDDAR LOAF

2½ cups flour
2 Tablespoons granulated sugar
2 teaspoons baking powder
¼ teaspoon salt
½ teaspoon dry mustard
½ teaspoon baking soda
¼ cup shortening
1 cup sharp Cheddar cheese, grated
½ teaspoon Worcestershire sauce
1 egg, lightly beaten
1 cup buttermilk
1 cup walnuts, chopped

1. Sift flour, sugar, baking powder, salt, dry mustard and baking soda.

2. With a pastry blender or with fingertips work shortening as though making pastry. Stir in the grated Cheddar cheese.

3. Combine the Worcestershire sauce, egg and buttermilk. Stir into the flour mixture until just moistened. Mix in the chopped nuts.

4. Bake in well-buttered 9" x 5" pan (smooth top of dough) in preheated 350° oven for 55 minutes. Remove from oven and cool on a rack. Serve warm or cold.

Yield: 1 loaf
Preparation: 45 minutes
Baking: 55 minutes

Great for luncheons and brunches, and super with ham, cheese or pork.

MOM'S CHEESE AND RAISIN DINNER ROLLS

ROLL MIXTURE:
1 cup milk, scalded
¼ cup sugar
¼ cup butter
1 teaspoon salt
1 package yeast
¼ cup lukewarm water
1 egg, beaten
4 cups flour

FILLING:
¼ cup sugar
1 cup dry cottage cheese
1 egg, beaten
½ cup raisins

1. Add sugar, butter and salt to scalded milk. Cool to lukewarm.

2. Mix yeast into warm water. Let sit for 5 minutes.

3. Add milk mixture to beaten egg and yeast mixture. Stir well.

4. Add 4 cups of flour, mix until blended and smooth.

5. Cover bowl with a towel and let rise in a warm place for 2 hours.

6. Punch down and let rise again for 45 minutes.

7. Knead on a floured board until smooth and satiny.

8. Roll out in a rectangle 12" x 24." Cut into 12 squares placing each square separately in well greased muffin tin of 12.

9. Mix filling together and place into middle of each piece of dough in the tin. Use all the filling. Pinch the four corners of dough together.

10. Bake in preheated 375° oven to 20 to 25 minutes until golden brown. Remove to wire rack. Serve hot or cold.

Yield: 12
Preparation: 40 minutes
Baking: 20-25 minutes

These are special—a plus—plus—plus!

MARY RUSH
Temple City, California

POTATO REFRIGERATOR ROLLS

POUR:
1½ cups warm water

OVER:
1 package dry yeast

STIR IN:
1½ teaspoons salt
⅔ cup sugar
⅔ cup shortening, or
⅔ cup margarine
1 cup mashed potatoes
2 eggs

MIX WELL AND ADD:
7-7½ cups flour, gradually
starting only with 3 cups and
mix until well blended. Then:

Yield: 40 rolls
Preparation: 35 minutes
Baking: 10-12 minutes

1. Mix remaining 4-4½ cups flour. Knead on a floured board until it is no longer sticky.

2. Wrap in plastic wrap loosely because it will rise, or place in large plastic food bag. Place in the refrigerator for 4 to 24 hours.

3. When ready to use, take out of refrigerator, punch down and shape into dinner rolls. Place on a well-buttered baking pan. Cover and let rise about 2 hours, but not until doubled in size.

4. Bake in preheated 400° oven for 10 to 12 minutes. Makes about 40 rolls. Serve hot, or they even taste sweeter when cold.

A family favorite. So light and tasty, you'll not stop with just one or two.

MOM'S ORANGE PECAN DINNER ROLLS

ROLL MIXTURE:
1 cup milk, scalded
¼ cup sugar
¼ cup butter
1 teaspoon salt
1 package yeast
¼ cup lukewarm water
1 egg, beaten
4 cups flour

FILLING:
½ cup sugar
¼ cup butter, melted
1 orange, grated
1 Tablespoon orange juice
1 cup pecans, chopped

1. Add sugar, butter and salt to scalded milk. Cool to lukewarm.

2. Mix yeast into warm water. Let sit for 5 minutes.

3. Add milk mixture to beaten egg, add yeast mixture and stir well.

4. Add 4 cups of flour and mix well.

5. Cover bowl with a towel and let rise in a warm place for 2 hours.

6. Punch down and let rise again for 45 minutes.

7. Knead dough on floured area until smooth and satiny.

8. Roll out into a rectangle 16" x 8" about ⅓" thick.

9. Mix filling, put in center length of the dough and spread out.

10. Roll dough up like a jelly roll and pinch edge to conceal filling.

11. Spray muffin tins with Pam (1 12-muffin tin and 1 6-muffin tin.)

12. Cut roll in half then fourths. Cut the fourths into 1" pieces. Place cut side down in tins.

13. Bake in preheated oven at 375° for 20 minutes until golden. Remove from pan to wire rack to cool.

Yield: 18
Preparation: 45 minutes
Baking: 20 minutes

Super tasting. Good with poultry or ham. Great for brunches, also.

ONION BUNS

SHERRY BURDETTE
Temple City, CA.

2 packages yeast
1 teaspoon sugar
½ cup warm water
½ cup sugar
3 eggs
1 teaspoon salt
1 cup scalded milk, cooled
½ cup butter or margarine
5-5½ cups flour
1 package dry onion soup mix
¼ cup minced dried onion
flakes

1. Dissolve yeast in warm water with 1 teaspoon sugar.

2. Scald milk and add butter.

3. Mix eggs, sugar, salt, milk and butter in large bowl.

4. Mix in yeast mixture.

5. Blend in flour, onion soup and onion flakes, mixing thoroughly. (This is a soft dough.)

6. Cover, let rise 2 hours.

7. Beat down dough. Roll out on well floured board to about ½" thick.

8. Cut with round cookie cutter and place on greased cookie sheet.

9. Cover and let rise again ½ hour.

10. Bake in preheated oven to 350° 10 to 12 minutes until golden. Brush tops with butter while still hot.

*See pages 135 and 136.

Yield: 24 buns
Preparation: 1 hour (not including rising)
Baking: 10-12 minutes

These are so light. Marvelous with "White Hastle Hamburgers*" or sloppy joes or as a dinner roll.

CHEESE POPPY SEED GARLIC TOAST

Butter, softened
French bread, sliced 1″ thick
Garlic powder
Poppy seeds
Parmesan cheese, freshly
grated

1. Butter both sides of bread and arrange slices on baking sheet.

2. Sprinkle tops <u>only</u> with garlic powder, poppy seeds and cheese.

3. Bake in preheated 350° oven for 5 to 10 minutes or until golden brown, being careful not to burn. Turn once.

Yield: 10 slices
Preparation: 15 minutes
Baking: 5-10 minutes

Quick, easy and tasty with steaks and Italian dishes.

BOB NICHOLAS
California, Maryland

ANGEL BISCUITS

2 cups Bisquick
1 cup whipping cream

1. Mix Bisquick and cream in mixing bowl until well blended.

2. Knead lightly on a floured board, about 8 turns by folding over edges to center.

3. Roll out to about ½″ thick, cut with biscuit cutter.

4. Bake in a preheated 450° oven on an <u>ungreased</u> baking sheet for 10 minutes.

Yield: 14 biscuits
Preparation: 15 minutes
Baking: 10 minutes

So light, so flaky, so quick and so easy.

193

PATRICIA R. ELDREDGE
Melbourne, Florida

SPICY CHEESE CRISPS
(Crackers)

1/2 lb. sharp Cheddar cheese,
  grated
1 stick margarine, soft
1 cup flour
1/2 teaspoon cayenne pepper
  (to your taste)
1/4 teaspoon salt

1. Put all ingredients in food processor or mix by hand with a pastry blender until well blended and smooth.

2. Divide dough into 8 parts and spread evenly on an ungreased 11" x 17" jelly roll pan. With the palm of your hand, press and pat dough evenly over the whole pan.

3. Gently run a fork over the top of dough from end to end till you have done the whole tray. Cut with a knife into 2" squares before baking.

4. Bake in preheated 400° oven 10 minutes.

5. You could use the various combinations on top or mixed in before baking. (You could section off the jelly roll pan into thirds and sprinkle to your taste the following combinations or just eat them plain:)
   a. Sprinkle dill seeds, onion flakes and dust lightly with onion powder.
   b. Bacon bits.
   c. Sprinkle on basil, oregano and a little Parmesan cheese.
   d. Sesame seeds.
   e. Chopped walnuts and poppy seeds.
   f. Dust lightly with dry mustard and sprinkle on caraway seeds.
   g. Chopped dried apple.

Yield: 42 squares
Preparation: 35 minutes
Baking: 10 minutes

6. When baked, recut the squares, cool completely, remove to a serving platter and serve.

No matter what way you serve these, they are easy to make and addictive. You'll never want any other crackers! Thanks, Pat.

GRISWOLD'S BRAN MUFFINS

GRISWOLD'S RESTAURANT
Claremont, California

MUFFIN SPREAD:
¼ cup butter, or
¼ cup margarine
6 Tablespoons brown sugar
6 Tablespoons granulated
  sugar
2 Tablespoons honey
1 Tablespoon water

MUFFIN BATTER:
½ cup whole wheat flour
¾ cup cake flour
6 Tablespoons sugar
½ teaspoon salt
½ teaspoon cinnamon
½ teaspoon soda
½ cup raisins
2 eggs
¼ cup honey
¼ cup oil
¼ cup crushed pineapple,
  drained
3 cups whole bran cereal
1½ cups buttermilk

Yield: 18 muffins
Preparation: 35 minutes
Baking: 18-20 minutes

1. Cream butter. Gradually beat in sugar. Blend in honey and water and whip until fluffy.

2. Coat muffin pans liberally and evenly with mixture, using about 2 teaspoons per tin. Now prepare batter.

3. Combine flours, salt, cinnamon, sugar, and soda. Stir in raisins, eggs, honey, oil, and pineapple. Stir in bran and buttermilk and mix until batter is smooth.

4. Fill coated muffin tins ¾ full.

5. Bake at 400° for 18-20 minutes.

6. Remove from tins immediately by turning upside down on cooling racks.

Griswolds are famous in California for their bran muffins, and I'm happy to say they want everyone in the U.S.A. to enjoy them, also.

195

FINN NISU BREAD

IDA HINTSA
Karstula, Finland

(Sweet Bread)

2 packages dry yeast
½ cup warm water
2 cups milk, scalded and
** cooled**
1 cup sugar
1 teaspoon salt
1 or 2 teaspoons cardamom
4 eggs, beaten
8-9 cups flour
½ cup butter, melted
Glaze top with 1 beaten egg
Sprinkle with sugar

1. Dissolve yeast in water; set aside until bubbly.

2. Mix yeast mixture, milk, sugar, salt, cardamom, eggs and ¼ of flour. Beat well with mixer. Add 3 cups of flour and butter and beat again until well blended.

3. Add remaining flour and mix well. Let set for 15 minutes on a floured board.

4. Knead until smooth and elastic, place in a well-buttered bowl, cover and let rise in a warm place for 1 hour. Punch down, cover and let rise again for 30 minutes.

5. Divide dough in half. Then divide each half into 3 balls, rolling and stretching each ball into 18" to 20" strips. Braid the 3 strips, pinching ends underneath. Place on greased cookie sheet and repeat with second half. Cover and let rise for 30 minutes.

6. Glaze with beaten egg and sprinkle top with sugar. Bake in preheated 400° oven for 30 minutes. (This makes 2 large sweet breads, or you can cut ingredients in half and make 1 large or 2 small loaves. Bake small loaves for 20 minutes and large loaves for 30 minutes, or until deep golden. Try placing candied fruit of your choice in this (nice for the Holiday season) and then glaze with confectioners icing after baked.

Yield: 2 large braids
Preparation: 1 hour
Baking: 30 minutes

Very light, delicate taste and super for breakfast or any meal. You'll enjoy them, also. This bread is a 100-year-old family bread recipe, handed down from Bob Hintsa's mother.

ADELA C. BRUTZ
Warren, Ohio

GRANDMA CAMPANA'S
EASTER BREAD (Sweet Bread)

2 packages dry yeast
½ cup warm water
6 large eggs
12 rounded Tablespoons sugar
2 rounded Tablespoons Crisco
5½-6 cups flour
1 teaspoon vanilia
2 rounded teaspoons anise
   seeds

1. Dissolve 2 packages of yeast in ½ cup warm water with 1 Tablespoon of sugar and set aside.

2. In a small bowl beat eggs, remaining 11 Tablespoons sugar and Crisco until well blended.

3. Place 5 cups of flour in a large bowl. Make a well in the center, add vanilla, anise seeds, egg and yeast mixture.

4. Mix by hand until well blended and knead in remaining ½ to 1 cup of flour as you would with bread. Knead unitl it springs back and doesn't stick to hands.

5. Cover and let rise 1 hour in warm place. Pound down and divide into 4 parts. Place in 4 well-buttered 3½" x 7½" pans. Slit with sharp knife deep across the middle, lengthwise. Cover and let rise again 1 more hour. Don't use larger bread pans, they must be this size or they will not bake properly.

6. Bake in preheated 325° oven for 45 minutes. Glaze with confectioners icing when cooled and sprinkle top with candy sprinkles and serve.

Yield: 4 loaves
Preparation: 30 minutes
Baking: 45 minutes

The bread has body, and the anise seeds give it a marvelous taste.

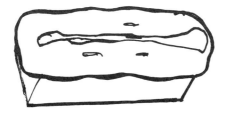

197

MACRINA SUDIMACK
San Rafael, California

RAISIN CINNAMON BREAD
(No Kneading)

1¾ cups milk
5½ Tablespoons butter or margarine
½ cup sugar
2 packages yeast
1 generous Tablespoon cinnamon
½ cup chopped dried apples
1 cup dark raisins
1½ teaspoons salt
5¼ cups flour

1. Warm milk and butter in a saucepan to lukewarm (not hot) and set aside.

2. Place sugar and yeast into heavy duty mixing bowl. Pour warm milk over sugar and yeast and let sit for 3 minutes. Use a dough hook and blend milk mixture, yeast and sugar.

3. Add cinnamon, salt and 3 cups of flour. Blend for 3 minutes.

4. Add the chopped apples, raisins and remaining 2¼ cups of flour. Mix on medium speed for 5 minutes.

5. Place in a well-buttered bowl. Turn over once, cover and let rise 1 hour in a warm place.

6. Punch down, divide in half, place into two well-buttered 9" x 5" bread pans and bake in a preheated 350° oven for 30 minutes.

7. Remove from oven and rub butter over tops. Let sit for 10 minutes and remove from pans onto wire rack to cool. (Could also ice them with confectioners glaze if desired.)

Yield: 2 loaves
Preparation: 30 minutes
Baking: 30 minutes

Mom's recipe, and we have always enjoyed this homemade raisin bread with breakfast.

198

CHERRY NIBBLE BREAD

BRENDA LETSON
Warren, Ohio

CHEESE FILLING:
2 3-oz. packages cream cheese
⅓ cup sugar
1 Tablespoon flour
1 egg, beaten
1 teaspoon almond extract

NUTBREAD:
1 16.6-oz. package cherry
   nutbread (Pillsbury mix)
½ cup maraschino cherry juice
½ cup water
1 egg, beaten

1. Mix cream cheese mixture until smooth and set aside.

2. Mix bread mixture and put two-thirds of batter into a well greased 9" x 5" x 3" loaf pan.

3. Put cheese filling over batter.

4. Put remaining batter on top of cheese batter.

5. Bake in preheated 350° oven for 1 hour.

6. Cool for 10 minutes in pan. Cool on wire rack completely.

7. Wrap in foil and refrigerate. Will keep for 3 to 4 days, if it lasts that long.

Serves: 6-8
Preparation: 25 minutes
Baking: 1 hour

You cannot stop nibbling on this!

199

ZUCCHINI BREAD

AUDREY MOORE
Minneapolis, Minnesota

3 eggs
2 cups sugar
1 cup oil
1 teaspoon nutmeg
1 teaspoon cinnamon
1 teaspoon vanilla
1 (8-oz.) can crushed pineapple
8 oz. dried apricots, chopped, or
8 oz. dried nectarines, chopped
1 teaspoon baking soda
1 teaspoon salt
1/4 teaspoon baking powder
3 cups flour
2 cups zucchini, chopped fine
1 cup almonds, chopped

1. Beat eggs and sugar until thick. Add remaining ingredients and blend well.

2. Pour into 2 well-buttered 9" x 5" bread pans and bake in preheated 350° oven for 1 hour, 5 to 10 minutes. Cool completely. Cut and serve plain or with cream cheese.

Yield: 2 loaves
Preparation: 45 minutes
Baking: 1 hour, 5 to 10 minutes

Very moist and light.

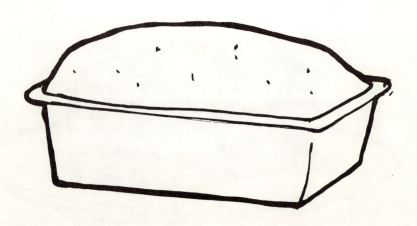

good!

BANANA BREAD SUPREME

FRED DAILY
Winter Garden, Florida

BREAD:
1 cup oil
1 cup brown sugar
1 cup white sugar
2 eggs
2 cups mashed bananas
(3 large)
3 cups regular flour
1 teaspoon salt
½ teaspoon vanilla
1½ cups whole pecans
2 teaspoons soda
2 Tablespoons hot water

TOPPING:
6 Tablespoons Half and Half
1 cup brown sugar
2 cups chopped pecans
¾ cup coconut

Yield: 2 large or 3 small loaves
Preparation: 30 minutes
Baking: 45 minutes to 1 hour

1. Mix bread ingredients in order. Grease pans well. Bake in a 350° oven 1 hour for 2 large loaf pans or 45 minutes for 3 small loaf pans.

2. Combine Half and Half, nuts and sugar. Bring to a boil and add coconut. Blend well.

3. Spread on top of baked bread and put under broiler until lightly browned, about 2-3 minutes.

This recipe will be the only one you will make, after once making.

201

CARAMEL NUT LOAF

GRISWOLD'S RESTAURANT
Claremont, California

EGG BREAD DOUGH:
1½ cups milk
1 egg plus 1 egg white
1½ teaspoons salt
3 Tablespoons sugar
3 Tablespoons cold butter
3 Tablespoons dry yeast
4½ cups all purpose flour

FILLING:
2 cups brown sugar, firmly
    packed
2 Tablespoons cinnamon
½ cup whole eggs
    (2 large eggs)
1 Tablespoons salad oil
¾ cup walnuts or pecans

PAN SMEAR:
½ cup brown sugar, firmly
    packed
¼ cup white sugar
1 cup cold butter
½ cup honey
3 Tablespoons raspberry jam
¼ cup hot water

Yield: 3 loaves
Preparation: 40 minutes
Baking: 35 minutes

1. Use a heavy duty mixer with dough hook to mix egg bread dough. Beat 6 minutes. (I found that my Food Processor worked best, beating 4 minutes with chopping blade.) Cover dough and let rise in a warm place for 1 hour.

2. Mix the filling ingredients in another bowl with an electric mixer for 3 minutes.

3. In another bowl mix the pan smear. Combine the brown and granulated sugars with butter and beat with hand mixer or processor for 3 minutes. Gradually add honey and jam and beat 4 more minutes, adding the hot water at the end.

4. Generously butter 3 (5" x 9") bread loaf pans and coat pan smear evenly in the 3 pans. Set aside.

5. After dough has risen, dust hands in flour, tear off pieces about the size of an egg and stir into the filling mixture. Divide the filling mixture between the 3 pans over the pan smear.

6. Cover and let rise again for 1 hour. Bake in a preheated 350° oven for 35 minutes.

7. After loaves are baked let them sit in pans for 10 minutes, then quickly turn over onto a jelly roll pan with sides and let pans sit on top for about 10 minutes. Remove pans.

8. Let them sit for about an hour and then transfer to tin foil, or serve cold or reheat in microwave on high for 20 seconds.

Now, these are caramel nut rolls! A lot of delicious, gooey nut caramel. Ten stars plus for this one! I am the first to get this marvelous recipe.

POWDERED ORANGE PUFFS

½ cup flour
½ cup water
¼ cup butter
⅛ teaspoon salt
1 teaspoon orange extract
1 Tablespoon sugar
2 eggs
½ orange, grated
Powdered sugar

1. Boil water; add butter, keeping to a boil, and add flour, salt and sugar. Stir until batter leaves sides of pan. Remove from heat. Add extract and grated orange skin and beat well.

2. Beat in one egg at a time with mixer until batter is very smooth.

3. Drop by tablespoonful into 350° oil and deep fry until golden brown (they will split open), turning once. Remove and drain on paper towel.

4. Dust with powdered sugar and serve hot. (Try them with lemon zest and extract instead of orange.)

Yield: 10-12
Preparation: 1 hour
Cooking: 30-40 minutes

They melt in your mouth.

PATTY DAVIS
Warren, Ohio

BUBBA'S KOLACHY ROLLS

DOUGH:
1 package dry yeast
¼ cup warm water
5 cups flour
½ cup sugar
¼ teaspoon salt
1 stick of butter, softened
  (no substitute)
2 egg yolks
½ cup sour cream
1 cup warm milk

FILLING:
1½ Tablespoons cinnamon
2 egg whites, beaten until stiff
1 lb. nuts, chopped
¼ cup sugar
2 Tablespoons milk (or enough
  to make mixture easy to
  spread)
Butter, melted for top of rolls

Yield: 4 rolls
Preparation: 1 hour
Baking: 30-35 minutes

1. Dissolve yeast in warm water. While yeast is dissolving, place 2½ cups flour, sugar, salt, butter, egg yolks, sour cream and warm milk in heavy duty mixer. Mix in yeast mixture. Mix well until all is blended thoroughly.

2. Gradually add 1 more cup of flour until all flour is blended in.

3. Dump out on a board and knead in remaining 1½ cups of flour by hand for 10 minutes.

4. Place back in the bowl, cover with Saran wrap and refrigerate overnight to rise.

5. The next day take out dough and let sit for 1 hour in a warm place. In the meantime mix nut filling mixture and set aside.

6. Divide dough into 4 parts. On a floured board add 2 Tablespoons granulated sugar into flour (repeat sugar with flour each time when needed in rolling out dough).

7. Roll dough out in a circle about 16" wide. Place ¼ nut mixture to within 1" of edge. Roll up and place lengthwise, seam underneath, on a well buttered cookie sheet. Brush with melted butter. Repeat with remaining dough and mixture.

8. Bake in preheated 350° oven for 30 to 35 minutes or until golden.

Patty is a dear friend of 35 years, and over this period of time, people have always commented that these were the best kolachy of all kolachy recipes. So will you!

DANISH ROLLS

PHYLLIS SHORTS
Ravenna, Ohio

2 packages yeast
1/4 cup warm water
2 large eggs, beaten
1 cup shortening
1/2 cup sugar
1/2 teaspoon salt
1 cup lukewarm milk
4 cups flour

FILLING:
1/2 lb. butter, melted
1 cup nuts, chopped
1 cup brown sugar
Cinnamon

ICING:
1 1/2 cups confectioners sugar
1/4 cup butter
2 Tablespoons milk
1 teaspoon maple extract

1. Dissolve yeast in water and let sit until dissolved.

2. Add yeast mixture and remaining ingredients together in large bowl and mix well by mixer. (Dough will be sticky.)

3. Divide dough in half and place on wax paper. Wrap loosely to give dough room to rise. Place dough in the refrigerator overnight.

4. The next day divide the dough in half again, rolling each on a well floured board to about 15" diameter.

5. Brush dough with butter, sprinkle with nuts, sugar and cinnamon.

6. Cut into 12 wedges as a pie, roll as a crescent roll and place on a greased cookie sheet 2" apart.

7. Bake in preheated 350° oven for 15 to 20 minutes or until slightly golden.

8. Remove from cookie sheet to a wax papered counter and cool completely.

9. Make icing and spread over rolls. You could also make a plain confection icing.

Yield: 48 rolls
Preparation: 1 hour
Baking: 15 to 20 minutes

They are ever so light and a family favorite for over 30 years.

205

DR. KATIE SPANGERBERG
Laguna Beach, California

MOM'S
APPLE PANCAKES

PANCAKES:
3 eggs
¾ cup flour
⅛ teaspoon salt
2 teaspoons sugar
1 cup milk
Butter for frying

FILLING:
¼ cup butter
2 Granny Smith apples, peeled,
   cored and sliced thin
Juice and zest of ½ lemon
Cinnamon
Nutmeg
Sugar
Butter
Powdered sugar as garnish

Yield: 4-6 pancakes
Preparation: 35 minutes
Baking: 20-25 minutes

We can never stop with just one.

1. Mix all ingredients for pancakes. Fry on each side in butter and set aside.

2. In a large skillet melt ¼ cup butter, fry apples briefly and place in 500° oven for 15 minutes. When nearly done, sprinkle with cinnamon, nutmeg, sugar and bits of butter on the top. Place back in oven for a few minutes (or until cooked). Remove.

3. Before serving, sprinkle lemon juice and zest of lemon on top of apples.

4. Divide apple mixture between pancakes, roll up and serve individually, sprinkled heavily with powdered sugar.

FRED DAILY
Winter Garden, Florida

BLUEBERRY BUTTERMILK PANCAKES

(And Topping)

PANCAKES:
2 cups buttermilk
2 eggs, beaten
2 cups flour
1 teaspoon baking soda
2 teaspoon baking powder
½ teaspoon salt
1 Tablespoon sugar
¼ cup butter, melted
1 cup blueberries, fresh
Topping as garnish
Whipped cream as garnish

TOPPING:
1 cup sugar
2 cups fresh blueberries
1 cup water
2 Tablespoons cornstarch
2 Tablespoons water
2 teaspoons lemon juice

Serves: 6
Preparation: 35 minutes

Sooo light and always asked for.

1. Mix butter, milk and eggs together. Add dry ingredients and beat until smooth. Add butter and blueberries. Mix lightly and bake on lightly buttered skillet or griddle. (Keep warm in warm oven until topping is made.) Serve with topping and whipped cream.

2. For Topping—(You can substitute 1 (1-lb.) can of blueberries for the first three ingredients.) In a saucepan combine sugar, blueberries and water. Cook to a simmer.

3. Mix the cornstarch with 2 Tablespoons water and lemon juice. Add to blueberries, stirring until thickened. Serve with pancakes.

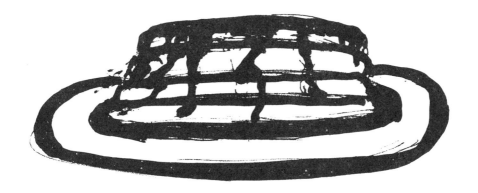

207

LIBBY LAFFERTY
La Canada, California

PUMPKIN PUFF PANCAKES

PANCAKES:
2 eggs
1 cup milk
½ cup canned pumpkin
1¾ cups Bisquick Mix
2 Tablespoons sugar
½ teaspoon cinnamon
½ teaspoon nutmeg
½ teaspoon ginger
¼ cup salad oil
¼ teaspoon orange peel, grated (optional)

RUM FLAVORED SYRUP:
1 cup maple syrup
1 Tablespoon butter
½ teaspoon rum extract

Yield: 40 (2″) pancakes
Preparation: 30 minutes
Baking: 3-6 minutes

1. Beat eggs in a small bowl on high speed for about 5 minutes or until thick and lemon colored.

2. Stir in remaining ingredients. Pour batter by tablespoonsfuls on a medium hot griddle.

3. Bake until puffed and bubbles begin to break. Turn and bake on other side until brown.

4. Heat maple syrup and butter. Remove from heat and add rum extract. Serve over pancakes.

These are the tastiest pancakes ever.

Desserts

CAKES

Hungarian Chocolate Raisin
Cake. 210
Flourless Chocolate Cake. 211
Renie's Chocolate Cheese
Cake. 212
Wesley's Peanut Butter
Cheesecake. 214
Fruit Gateau. 215
Duchess Prune Torte. 216
Hazelnut Chocolate Torte. 217
Creamy Banana Torte. 218
Raspberry, White Chocolate,
Blueberry Mousse Cake. . . . 220
Russian Torte. . . . . 222 good *
Italian Torte. 224
Summer Fruit Cake. 225
Dolly's Carrot Cake. 226
Apple Cake. 227
Orange Pecan Chiffon Cake. . . . 228
Orange Pineapple Dream
Cake. 229
Easter Egg Fruit Cake. 230
Dark Fruit Cake. 231
Festive Pumpkin Log. 232
Grandma's Pound Cake. 233

PIES

Bavarian Cream Pie—Coconut
and Banana. 234
Chocolate Buttercrunch. 235
Creamy Peach Pie. 236
Pecan Rum Pie. 237
Deep Dish Apple Dumplings. . . . 238
Peanut Crunch Apple Pie. 239

DESSERTS

Chocolate Coconut Cream
Puffs. 240
Flan de Queso. 242
Rice Pudding a la Berry. 243
Cold Banana Soup
Montego Bay. 244
Edna's Raisin Pudding. 245
Indian Pudding with
English Custard. 246
Soufflé Rothschild. 248
Cointreau Chantilly Trifle. 249

Lime Tart, Lime Mousse (or Lemon
Tart and Lemon Mousse with
Raspberry Sauce). 250
Amaretto Mousse Tart. 251

ICE CREAM AND POPSICLES

Homemade Ice Cream—
8 Flavors. 253
Chocolate Peanut Pops. 254
Fudgesicles. 255
Popsicles. 256
Orange Dreamsicles. 257

COOKIES

Swedish Nut Horns. 258
Apricot Pecan Dreams. 259
Date and Coconut Balls. 260
Strawberries. 261
Cake, Nuts and Booze. 262
Sesame Cookies. 263
Italian Nevella Cookies. 263
Italian Wedding Cookies. 264
French Bon-Bon Cookies. 265
Hungarian Cookies. 266
Moist Devils Food Cookies. 267
Aunt Clodie's Sugar Cookies. . . 268
Apple, Date and Nut Bars. 269
Apricot Cordial Bars. 270
Polynesian Brunch Bars. 271
Pumpkin Squares. 272
Oatmeal Fudge Bars. 273
Caramel Chocolate Bars. 274
Amaretto Fudge Brownies. 275
Ruth's Coffee Bars. 276
Slate Cookie Bars. 277

CANDY

Chocolate Grand Marnier
Truffles. 278
Chocolate Creams. 279
Marshmallow Creams. 280
Coffee Chocolate Cream
Fudge. 281
Stuffed Chocolate Covered
Fruit. 282
Randy's Amaretto Creams. 283
Ohio "Go Bucks" Buckeyes. . . . 284

CONNIE ZIPPERER
Syracuse, New York

HUNGARIAN CHOCOLATE RAISIN CAKE

2 cups flour, sifted
1½ cups sugar
1½ cups seedless raisins,
  ½ white and ½ dark
½ cup cocoa
1 teaspoon cinnamon
¼ teaspoon cloves
¼ teaspoon nutmeg
1 teaspoon salt
1 heaping teaspoon baking
  soda
1 cup chopped walnuts
1 cup sour cream
2 eggs
3 Tablespoons melted
  shortening
1 teaspoon vanilla extract, or
1 teaspoon rum extract
Powdered sugar, or
Whipped cream—as garnish

Serves: 12
Preparation: 40 minutes
Baking: 65 minutes

A favorite.

1. Put raisins in hot water and set aside.

2. Cream shortening, sugar and ¼ of cream. Add eggs and beat well.

3. Drain raisins <u>thoroughly</u>.

4. Add rest of cream alternately with dry ingredients.

5. Add raisins, nuts and extract.

6. Pour into a well-greased tube pan and bake in a preheated 325° oven for 65 minutes or until done. Remove from oven, cool completely and sprinkle with powdered sugar. Serve as is or with a dollop of whipped cream.

CHEF VINCENT GUERITHAULT
Vincent's French Cuisine
Scottsdale, Arizona

FLOURLESS CHOCOLATE CAKE

14 oz. butter
28 oz bittersweet chocolate
22 oz. sugar
18 eggs, separated

1. In a double boiler place butter and bittersweet chocolate. Stir until melted.

2. Butter and flour 4 10" x 2" round cake pans.

3. Beat egg whites until whipped and add sugar.

4. Beat egg yolks and fold into egg white mixture, then fold in chocolate mixture (may be a little streaky with marble effect).

5. Bake in preheated 450° oven for 5 minutes, then bake at 250° for 25 minutes. (Place pans on a cookie sheet in case it spills over.) Remove from oven.

6. Turn out onto plate and serve plain, dusted with powdered sugar or with mousse or ice cream. Do not try to layer these cakes with icing. They are very rich and are to be eaten alone or with one of the above mentioned. The other three can be frozen for a later time. (White chocolate does not work in this recipe.)

Yield: 4 cakes
Preparation: 35 minutes
Baking: 30 minutes

The texture of these cakes is of mousse-like quality—they melt in your mouth. Rated a 10 plus and then some.

PASTRY CHEF ROBIN MURPHY
Strawberry Mansion
Melbourne, Florida

RENIE'S CHOCOLATE CHEESECAKE
(Dedicated to my Mom)

CRUST:
3 cups chocolate wafers,
   crushed fine
½ cup butter, melted
2 Tablespoons kahlua*

CHEESE MIXTURE:
12 oz. semisweet chocolate
2½ Tablespoons butter
2 lbs. cream cheese, softened
   to room temperature

1 cup sour cream
1 cup whipping cream,
   unwhipped
1 teaspoon vanilla
2 teaspoons kahlua*
1½ cups sugar
5 large eggs
3 Tablespoons cocoa powder,
   sifted

GARNISH:
Whipped cream
Strawberries
Chocolate shavings

1. Add melted butter to crushed wafers. Mix well with fork until well blended. Add kahlua* and mix until thoroughly blended.

2. Press crumb mixture into a lightly buttered 10″ spring form pan on bottom and sides. Chill.

3. In a medium size saucepan, melt semisweet chocolate and butter. Cool, mix in cream cheese and beat until smooth. Add sour cream, whipping cream, vanilla and kahlua* and mix until smooth.

4. Add sugar and beat again until smooth. Add the eggs, <u>one</u> by <u>one</u>. At the end, mix in the cocoa powder until completely incorporated.

5. Pour chocolate mixture into chilled crust and smooth top of any bubbles that form on top.

(continued)

Renie's Chocolate Cheesecake (continued)

6. Bake in preheated 325° oven for 50 minutes. Turn off oven and let cheese-cake sit for 1 hour inside oven. Don't open oven door until the 1 hour is up.

7. Remove from oven and chill for at least 3 hours before serving. Serve with a large dollop of whipped cream on top with a strawberry on top of whipped cream, or with chocolate shavings.

*See page 306.

Serves: 10-12
Preparation: 1 hour
Baking: 50 minutes

Another chocolate lover's delight—so sinfully rich and luscious.

WESLEY'S PEANUT BUTTER CHEESECAKE

WESLEY'S RESTAURANT
Virginia Beach, Virginia

CRUST:
6 oz. vanilla wafers
½ cup sugar
2 Tablespoons butter, melted

FILLING:
1½ lbs. cream cheese, at room temperature
1½ cups sugar
1 6-oz. jar creamy peanut butter (⅔ cup)
4 eggs
1 teaspoon fresh lemon juice (optional)
¾ to 1 cup semisweet chocolate chips (optional)

TOPPING:
1 cup sour cream
¾ cup semisweet chocolate chips, melted
½ cup sugar

Serves: 10-12
Preparation: 1 hour
Baking: 1 hour, 25-30 minutes

1. Place all ingredients for crust in a food processor and mix until well blended. Butter a 9" spring form pan. Press in mixture on sides and bottom and set aside. Preheat oven to 350.°

2. Combine all ingredients for filling except chocolate chips and blend until smooth. Add chocolate chips and mix off and on for about 10 seconds.

3. Pour filling into pan prepared with crust. Bake until center of filling is firm, about 70 to 80 minutes. Let stand at room temperature 15 minutes before adding topping.

4. Meanwhile prepare topping by blending all topping ingredients. Spread over cheesecake and bake for 10 minutes. Let cool completely, then refrigerate at least 3 hours before serving.

Extremely rich and highly pleasing to the peanut butter lover's palate.

CHEF JOSEPH ARCHAZKI
O'Shea's Wharf Restaurant
Marco Island, Florida

FRUIT GATEAU

(Start 1 day before)
SPONGE CAKE:
9 oz. whole eggs
3 oz. egg yolks
6½ oz. sugar
6½ oz. sifted flour
3 Tablespoons butter, melted

GLAZE:
1 cup orange juice
½ cup sugar
2 Tablespoons cornstarch

TOPPING:
3 strawberries, sliced
3 kiwi, sliced
1 peach, sliced
½ banana, sliced

FILLINGS:
6 Tablespoons Cointreau* or
 Triple Sec
6 Tablespoons Grand Marnier
1 12-oz. jar pineapple jam
1 12-oz. jar peach jam
1 12-oz. jar orange marmalade

BUTTERCREAM FROSTING:
8 oz. butter (no substitute)
3¼ cups confectioners sugar
½ Tablespoon vanilla
1 teaspoon lemon juice
½ cup toasted almonds, sliced

Serves: 16
Preparation: 1 hour
Baking: 25-30 minutes

1. Whip eggs, egg yolks and sugar in heavy duty mixer 15 minutes or until peaked. Gradually add flour and fold in butter. Pour in two 10" cake pans that are lined on bottom with paper towels. Bake in preheated 350° oven for 25 to 30 minutes or until cake tester comes out clean. Cool completely and freeze overnight.

2. Remove cakes from pans, remove paper towels and slice cakes horizontally in half, making 4 slices.

3. Mix glaze in a saucepan and cook until thickened, stirring constantly. Set aside to cool in ice water. Slice fruits and set aside in refrigerator.

4. On first layer of cake drizzle 2 Tablespoons each of Cointreau* and Grand Marnier. Spread with one jar of jam. Repeat next 2 layers with liquors, and other 2 jars of jam and marmalade.

5. On the top layer, lay sliced fruit in abstract form. Top the fruit with glaze.

6. Whip the first 4 ingredients for the buttercream frosting. Frost sides only and press toasted almond slices onto the sides.

7. Chill for about 2 hours before serving.

*See page 309.

This torte is so beautiful and out of the ordinary. Time consuming, but with that first bite, you'll be glad you took the time.

215

DUCHESS PRUNE TORTE

OLGA RUSH
Temple City, California

CAKE MIXTURE:
1½ cups oil
1½ teaspoons vanilla
5 eggs
3 cups sugar
1½ teaspoons cinnamon
3 cups flour
⅛ teaspoon nutmeg
1½ teaspoons baking soda
1½ teaspoon salt
1½ cups buttermilk
1½ cups prunes, cooked, cooled and chopped
1½ cups pecans, chopped

CREAM FILLING AND TOPPING:
3 Tablespoons butter
2 Tablespoons flour
3 eggs
¾ cup sour cream
1½ cups prunes, cooked, cooled and chopped
1½ cups sugar
⅛ teaspoon salt
1½ teaspoons vanilla
Pecan halves as garnish
Whipped cream as garnish

Serves: 10-14
Preparation: 1 hour, 30 minutes
Baking and Cooking: 1 hour, 45 minutes

Truly royal to serve.

1. Mix all cake mixture ingredients in order given.

2. Butter and flour 3 cake pans. Pour mixture into pans and bake in preheated 325° oven for 1 hour 15 minutes. Remove from oven and cool completely.

3. In a double boiler melt butter, add flour and mix until smooth. Add remaining ingredients except pecans and whipped cream and cook over low heat until thickened (about 25 to 30 minutes), stirring constantly. Cool and chill before spreading between and on top of layers. Garnish top of cake with pecan halves. Refrigerate until serving.

4. Serve with large dollop of whipped cream with each individual piece.

HAZELNUT CHOCOLATE TORTE

4 eggs
5 egg yolks
½ cup sugar
2 Tablespoons fine bread crumbs
⅓ cup cocoa
2 cups hazelnuts or walnuts, ground
½ cup flour
5 egg whites, beaten stiff

ICING:
½ lb. butter
2 eggs, separated
2 Tablespoons sugar
8 oz. of Baker's sweet chocolate, melted and cooled
Chopped nuts as garnish

1. Beat the 4 eggs and 5 yolks with ½ cup of sugar for 15 minutes on a heavy duty mixed.

2. Add bread crumbs, nuts, cocoa and flour and beat until well blended.

3. Beat egg whites and add to the mixture by folding in carefully.

4. Cut paper towel to fit bottom of 3 8" cake pans. (You need not grease at all.)

5. Pour batter into the 3 pans, dividing them equally. Bake in a preheated 350° oven for 25 minutes. Remove from oven and cool completely.

6. In a mixing bowl mix butter, sugar, egg yolks, melted chocolate at medium speed until well blended. (If it should separate, heat over a low flame a few minutes.)

7. Add the egg whites that have been beaten stiff. Blend in the icing until well blended.

8. Take one cake pan at a time and remove cake by running a knife around edge of pan. Hit on counter until cake flips out, remove paper on bottom, place on cake platter and ice. Continue with remaining cakes. Ice tops and sides and sprinkle top with additional nuts. Refrigerate until ready to serve.

Yield: 1 3-layer cake
Preparation: 25-30 minutes
Baking: 25 minutes

Don says this is a 'chocolate lover's delight.' I created it for him to over indulge.

217

CLARA ANDERSON
Niles, Ohio

CREAMY BANANA TORTE

CAKE:
3 cups cake flour, sifted
2 teaspoons baking soda
1 cup Crisco
2 cups sugar
¾ cup milk
2 eggs, slightly beaten
1½ cups mashed bananas
(3 large or 4 small)
½ cup pecans, chopped

FILLING I—
CHOCOLATE CREAM:
1 1-oz. square chocolate
⅔ cup sweetened condensed
milk

FILLING II—
PEANUT BUTTER CREAM:
⅔ cup sweetened condensed
milk
2 Tablespoons smooth peanut
butter

ICING—BANANA GLAZE:
½ teaspoon lemon juice
1 large banana, mashed
1 1-lb. box of confectioners
sugar
¼ cup butter, softened
¼ cup shaved Hershey
chocolate bar
¼ cup pecans, chopped

1. Line 3 9" cake pans with paper towel cut to fit bottom of pans. It is not necessary to grease pans as cake never sticks to sides. Cake will flip out and you can peel off paper when cooled.

2. Cream Crisco and sugar until light and fluffy.

3. Add 2 Tablespoons milk, then eggs. Add dry ingredients and remaining milk, beating thoroughly after each addition.

4. Fold in mashed bananas and pecans. Pour into cake pans and bake in preheated 350° oven for 30 minutes or until toothpick comes out clean.

5. Remove from oven and cool completely before putting fillings on layers and final icing.

6. Chocolate Filling—Melt chocolate in double boiler, add milk, cook and stir until well thickened. Cool completely and place on bottom layer of cake.

7. Peanut Butter Filling—Put milk and peanut butter in double boiler and cook until well thickened. Cool completely. Place second layer of cake on top of chocolate filling and spread with peanut butter filling.

(continued)

Creamy Banana Torte *(continued)*

8. Place third layer of cake on top of peanut butter filling.

9. Cream confectioners sugar and butter together. Combine the bananas and lemon juice together and beat in with creamed sugar. Blend well. If too thick, add 1 Tablespoon milk.

10. Glaze top and sides of torte. Place chopped pecans on first and then shaved chocolate. Keep in refrigerator.

Serves: 10
Preparation: 1 hour, 15 minutes
Cooking and Baking: 40-50 minutes

Truly a masterpiece of beauty and taste.

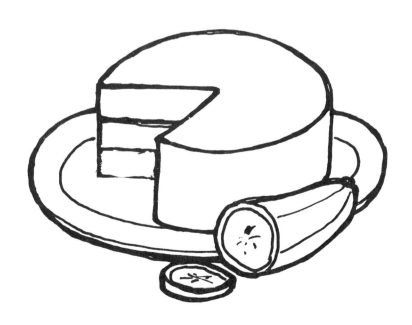

CHEF VINCENT GUERITHAULT
Vincent's French Cuisine
Scottsdale, Arizona

RASPBERRY, WHITE CHOCOLATE, BLUEBERRY MOUSSE CAKE

(Arizona's 1983 Culinary Silver Cup Award)

BLUEBERRY MOUSSE:
2 cups whipping cream, whipped
1 cup blueberry purée (blueberries puréed in blender)
½ cup sugar
½ Tablespoon gelatin

WHITE CHOCOLATE MOUSSE:
2 cups whipping cream
1 lb. white chocolate

RASPBERRY MOUSSE:
2 cups whipping cream, whipped
1 cup raspberry purée (raspberries puréed in blender)
½ cup sugar
½ Tablespoon gelatin

RASPBERRY GLAZE:
1 cup raspberry purée
½ cup sugar
½ Tablespoon gelatin

GARNISH:
Raspberry sauce*
Vanilla sauce*

*See page 295.

1. You need a 10" mold—8" in diameter. Spray lightly with Pam. (You could use a mixing bowl if you don't have a mold this size).

2. Raspberry Mousse. In a small saucepan bring to a boil raspberry purée and sugar. When almost cooled, add gelatin. Let set slightly in the refrigerator. Whip the whipping cream and gently fold in raspberry gel. Pour in prepared mold and put in refrigerator until next step.

3. White Chocolate Mousse. In a small saucepan bring 2 cups whipping cream to a boil. Pour over broken white chocolate pieces and stir until chocolate is melted. Cool completely, whip until thick and stiff and pour over raspberry mousse. Place back in refrigerator until next step.

4. Blueberry Mousse. Repeat raspberry mousse, using blueberries instead of raspberries. Pour over white chocolate mousse. Let set for at least 3 hours or overnight in the refrigerator.

(continued)

Raspberry, White Chocolate, Blueberry Mousse Cake
(continued)

5. Raspberry Glaze. In a saucepan bring to a boil purée and sugar. When almost cooled, add gelatin, cool and then spread by spoonfuls over unmolded mousse, which has been overturned onto a pretty platter. Place back in refrigerator until ready to serve. Serve by cutting into wedges and serve with sauces that are in separate bowls.

Serves: 10-12
Preparation: 1 hour, 30 minutes

Oh, Vincent, thank you for sharing such an excellent, outstanding, masterful achievement!

PATTY DAVIS
Warren, Ohio

RUSSIAN TORTE

4 cups walnuts, chopped
1 cup sugar
1 package dry yeast
¼ cup warm water
3 sticks of butter, softened
  (no substitute)
4 cups flour
4 egg yolks, slightly beaten
¼ cup milk
2 cans of Solo apricot filling
  (or your favorite)
4 egg whites
8 Tablespoons sugar

1. Mix walnuts and 1 cup of sugar in a bowl. Take out ½ cup for topping and set both aside.

2. Dissolve yeast in warm water in a small bowl.

3. In a large bowl place 3 sticks of butter and flour. Work by hand, mixing until crumbly like pie crust dough. Add egg yolks and milk and mix with fork until well blended. Then add yeast mixture, mixing well. Place dough on a <u>well floured</u> board and knead a few minutes.

4. Divide dough into 3 parts. Roll one part into a rectangle that will fit a jelly roll pan with sides. Keep lifting dough and putting flour underneath so it won't stick to the board. After rolling it large enough to fit up the sides of the pan, roll the dough from small end to small end. Lay in a well buttered 12" x 18" jelly roll pan. Spread on large bowl of nut mixture.

5. Roll second layer to fit over nut mixture (without sides). Spread on one can of apricot filling. Repeat with third layer of dough and filling.

6. Bake in a preheated 350° oven for 35 minutes.

7. The last 5 minutes of baking, beat the 4 egg whites very stiff. Add 8 Tablespoons sugar and beat until well blended.

(continued)

Russian Torte *(continued)*

8. Remove torte from oven after 35 minutes. Spread beaten egg white mixture on top and sprinkle remaining ½ cup of nut mixture on top of egg white mixture. Put in the oven for another 12 minutes or until golden on top. Cut into 2" squares and serve warm or cold.

Yield: 28 2" pieces
Preparation: 45 minutes
Baking: 47 minutes

Very different, very special, very appealing and very delicious.

ITALIAN TORTE

JUDY CASEY
Tempe, Arizona

1 large pound cake, frozen*
4 4-oz. squares semisweet
  chocolate gently chopped
1 15-oz. container Ricotta
  cheese
½ cup sugar
1½ teaspoons vanilla
6 Tablespoons Amaretto
  or more*

GLAZE:
1 cup sifted powdered sugar
2 Tablespoons unsweetened
  cocoa powder
1 Tablespoon butter, melted
2 Tablespoons boiling water
2 Tablespoons almonds,
  chopped (garnish)

*See page 233 and 308.

1. Partially defrost cake and slice horizontally into 3 layers. Drizzle 2 Tablespoons Amaretto over each layer.

2. Combine cheese, sugar and vanilla then add chopped chocolate and set aside 2 Tablespoons of cheese mixture.

3. Divide remaining filling in half and spread evenly on the liquored side of two of the cake layers.

4. Stack layers and top with last cake layer.

5. You can use ½ cup citron or candied cherries in cheese mixture, or both, if desired.

6. At this point you can put this in freezer until a later date and then glaze when ready to serve.

7. Mix sugar and cocoa, add melted butter. Stir in water to make a glaze. Spoon over torte.

8. Dollop reserved cheese mixture in 3 dollops on top of cake. Sprinkle with nuts and chill until serving. Slice thin.

Serves: 8
Preparation: 30 minutes
Cooking: 5 minutes

So pretty and so delicious. Great for that special Italian dinner.

SUMMER FRUIT CAKE

DEANNA MATTHEWS
Matthews 1812 House
Cornwall Bridge, Connecticut 06754

CAKE BATTER:
2 cups whole wheat flour
1½ cups sugar
1 teaspoon baking soda
1 teaspoon cinnamon
½ teaspoon salt
3 eggs
¾ cup buttermilk
½ cup oil
2 teaspoons vanilla
2½ cups fresh or frozen
  apricots, nectarines,
  peaches or plums, chopped
  and drained
1 cup walnuts, almonds or
  pecans, chopped
1 cup flaked coconut
1 cup raisins

GLAZE:
⅔ cup sugar
⅓ cup buttermilk
⅓ cup butter
2 Tablespoons light corn syrup
¼ teaspoon baking soda
½ teaspoon vanilla

Serves: 10-12
Preparation: 45 minutes
Baking: 40-45 minutes

1. Combine flour, sugar, baking soda, cinnamon and salt in medium bowl.

2. Beat eggs, buttermilk, oil and vanilla in a large bowl. Add flour mixture to egg mixture and mix until smooth. Stir in remaining ingredients.

3. Pour cake mixture into a well-buttered and floured 9" x 13" baking dish. Bake in preheated 350° oven for 40 to 45 mintues or until tester comes out clean.

4. In the meantime make the glaze by combining all ingredients except vanilla in a 2 quart saucepan. Bring to a boil over medium heat. Stir for 5 minutes and remove from heat, add vanilla and blend thoroughly.

5. After cake has been baked and removed from oven, prick entire surface with a toothpick. Pour glaze over top of cake. Cool completely and serve plain or with a dollop of whipped cream.

We love it made with peaches and nectarines combined.

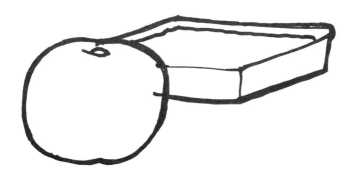

225

DOLLY'S CARROT CAKE

CAKE:
2 teaspoons baking soda
2 cups flour
2 teaspoons cinnamon
¼ teaspoon nutmeg
½ teaspoon salt
2 cups shredded carrots
2 cups sugar
1 cup oil
3 medium eggs, beaten
1 cup chopped pecans
  or walnuts
1 cup shredded coconut
1 small can of crushed
  pineapple, drained
½ cup raisins (optional)

1. Mix oil with beaten eggs, fold in carrots with wooden spoon.

2. Add remaining ingredients.

3. Pour in greased 13" x 9" baking pan and bake in preheated oven at 350° for 1 hour.

FROSTING:
1 8-oz. package cream cheese
½ cup butter, softened
½ package confectioners
  sugar
1 teaspoon vanilla

1. Beat cheese and butter until well blended. Add sugar and vanilla.

2. Spread on cooled cake and refrigerate.

Serves: 8-12
Preparation: 30 minutes
Baking: 1 hour

This carrot cake is the most moist cake you will ever taste.

APPLE CAKE

4 cups apples, diced
2 eggs, beaten
2 cups sugar
½ teaspoon cinnamon
1 teaspoon vanilla
1 cup walnuts, chopped
⅛ teaspoon nutmeg
½ cup raisins
½ cup oil
2 cups flour
¾ teaspoon salt
2 teaspoons baking soda

ICING:
1½ cups confectioners sugar
¼ cup butter, softened
2 Tablespoons cream or milk
1 teaspoon vanilla

Serves: 9
Preparation: 45 minutes
Baking: 1 hour

1. Put apples and eggs in a bowl and mix well with a wooden spoon.

2. Add sugar, cinnamon, nutmeg, vanilla, walnuts, raisins and oil. Mix until well blended.

3. Add flour, salt and baking soda. Mix again until well blended.

4. Pour into a 9" x 13" baking pan that has been well greased and dusted with flour.

5. Bake in preheated 325° oven for 1 hour. Remove from heat.

6. Poke holes in cake. Mix all icing ingredients together. Spread over cake while cake is hot.

Another oldy—super to serve for brunch.

227

SANDY NICHOLAS
California, Maryland

ORANGE PECAN CHIFFON CAKE

2¼ cups cake flour
1½ cups sugar
5 egg yolks, <u>unbeaten</u>
1 teaspoon salt
3 teaspoons baking powder
⅓ cup salad oil
¾ cup orange juice, fresh
1 Tablespoon grated orange peel
7 egg whites
½ cup pecans, chopped
5 Tablespoons Cointreau* drizzled over cake after baked and put on platter

ORANGE COINTREAU* GLAZE:
2 egg yolks
3 Tablespoons Cointreau,* or
3 Tablespoons orange juice
1 teaspoon grated orange rind
2 Tablespoons butter, melted
1½ cups confectioners sugar

1. Mix cake flour, sugar, egg yolks, salt, baking powder, oil, orange juice and orange rind until smooth.

2. In a large bowl beat egg whites until <u>very stiff</u>. <u>Gradually</u> fold egg yolk mixture into beaten egg whites. (Fold in <u>very carefully</u> and <u>easily</u>.) Fold in pecans lightly.

3. Pour into an <u>ungreased</u> 10" tube pan and bake in preheated 325° oven for 55 minutes. Increase heat to 350° and bake another 10 to 15 minutes or until cake springs back when touched. Remove from oven and turn over onto the neck of a pop bottle until cooled completely. Carefully remove turned <u>upside down</u> to cake platter and frost with icing. Drizzle 5 Tablespoons of Cointreau* over cake (optional).

4. Beat egg yolks, add butter, Cointreau,* orange rind, melted butter and confectioners sugar. Spread over cake, let drizzle over sides.

*See page 309.

Yield: 1 10" tube cake
Preparation: 1 hour
Baking: 1 hour, 10-15 minutes

Light, moist and delicate.

PATTY CORCORAN
Niles, Ohio

ORANGE PINEAPPLE DREAM CAKE

CAKE:
1 box Duncan Hines yellow butter cake mix
4 eggs
½ cup oil
1 can mandarin oranges, undrained

TOPPING:
1 20-oz. can crushed pineapple, undrained
1 3¾-oz. package instant vanilla pudding
1 large container Cool Whip
Coconut (garnish)

Serves: 10
Preparation: 30 minutes
Baking: 35-40 minutes

Out of sight!

1. Mix cake mix, eggs, oil and mandarin oranges. Cut paper towel to fit bottoms of two 9" cake pans. (Do not grease pans.) Pour cake mixture in pans.

2. Bake in preheated 325° oven for 35 to 40 minutes or until toothpick comes out clean.

3. Cool completely. Remove paper from bottom of cakes.

4. Mix pineapple with pudding mix and add to Cool Whip. Spread over first layer, add second layer and spread topping over top and sides. Garnish top with coconut. Keep refrigerated.

EASTER EGG FRUIT CAKE
(No baking)

2¾ cups graham cracker
   crumbs
1 10-oz. bag of marshmallows
¾ cup milk
2 cups whole half walnuts
2 cups whole half pecans
1 cup coconut
1 cup chocolate chips
½ cup raisins
¼ cup candied pineapple,
   chopped fine
½ cup mixed candied fruit
   cake mix, chopped

Yield: 2 7½" x 3½" cakes
Preparation: 25 minutes

1. Melt marshmallows with milk until melted, stirring constantly. Place all ingredients in a large kettle and mix by hand.

2. Place fruit cake in <u>wax papered</u> bread tins 7½" x 3½." Press mixture in firm and tightly. Overlap the wax paper to cover top of bread tin completely.

3. Refrigerate for <u>2</u> days before using.

4. Remove wax paper and rewrap in Saran Wrap. Keep refrigerated when not being served. Can freeze.

In creating this I felt there should be a fruit cake that has chocolate chips and coconut and not so much candied fruit. I hope you enjoy it as we do.

DARK FRUIT CAKE
(Big Auntie's)

JUNE ARBOGAST
Melbourne Beach, Florida

1½ cups dark brown sugar, firmly packed
2 sticks of butter, or
2 sticks of margarine
6 eggs, separated
1 cup Taylor's Cream Sherry wine (no substitute)
2 cups flour, sifted
½ teaspoon salt
1 teaspoon baking soda
½ teaspoon cloves
1 heaping teaspoon cinnamon
1 cup flour, sifted
2 cups whole candied cherries
2 cups chopped dates
3 cups pecan halves
2 cups candied pineapple, chopped
1 8-oz. package citron, or
1 heaping cupful citron
2 cups white raisins
More Taylor's Cream Sherry wine (no substitute)

Yield: 3 9" x 5" loaves
Preparation: 35 minutes
Baking: 3½ hours

1. Cream butter and sugar. Add egg yolks (save whites for later) and blend well.

2. Alternate the 1 cup of wine and 2 cups of flour into mixture. Add all spices and mix well.

3. In a separate bowl spread the remaining 1 cup of flour over all the fruit and nuts. Mix well so that all are covered. Set aside.

4. In another separate bowl beat egg whites until stiff. Add to first mixture, blending well.

5. Add the floured candied fruit and nut mixture to batter and stir with a wooden spoon until well blended.

6. Cut 3 pieces of brown paper bags to fit the bottom of 3 9" x 5" loaf pans.

7. Grease the 3 loaf pans generously, lay the brown paper on bottom of pans and divide the cake mixture between the pans.

8. Bake in a preheated 250° oven for 3½ hours. Remove from the oven and pour about ½ cup of wine (or more) on each loaf. Let it sit for about ½ hour. Remove from pan, peel off brown paper, cool at room temperature, wrap in Saran Wrap and store until ready to use.

This fruit cake will be loved by even those who don't care for fruit cakes— A true 10 plus.

231

FESTIVE PUMPKIN LOG

MARION CARDONES
Warren, Ohio

CAKE:
3 eggs
1 cup sugar
2/3 cup pumpkin
1 teaspoon lemon juice
3/4 cup flour
1 teaspoon baking powder
2 teaspoons cinnamon
1 teaspoon ginger
1/2 teaspoon nutmeg
1/2 teaspoon baking soda
1 cup pecans, chopped
1/2 cup powdered sugar

FILLING:
1 cup powdered sugar
4 Tablespoons butter
1/2 teaspoon vanilla
1 8-oz. package cream cheese
10 maraschino cherries,
   drained and halved

Serves: 10
Preparation: 1 hour
Baking: 15 minutes

Great for any occasion.

1. Beat eggs at high speed for 5 minutes and gradually add sugar. Stir in pumpkin and lemon juice. Stir in remaining ingredients, except nuts and powdered sugar.

2. Grease and flour a 10" x 5" jelly roll pan. Pour batter carefully in pan and sprinkle top of batter with the 1 cup nuts.

3. Bake in preheated 375° oven for 15 minutes.

4. Remove from oven, cut all around cookie sheet with a knife and turn onto a towel that has been heavily sprinkled with 1/2 cup powdered sugar. Roll up at narrow end, towel and all. Cool completely. Unroll and spread with filling that has been beaten until smooth. Sprinkle cherries over filling and reroll without towel. Refrigerate until ready to serve.

GRANDMA'S POUND CAKE

JOSEPH SUDIMACK
MACRINA SUDIMACK
San Rafael, California

1 lb. butter (no substitute)
4 cups sifted cake flour
10 large eggs, separated
2 cups sugar
2 teaspoons vanilla
1 teaspoon baking powder

1. In a mixing bowl combine butter and flour, mix with pastry blender as you would a pie crust.

2. In a separate bowl beat egg yolks, sugar and vanilla until thick, fluffy and lemon colored.

3. Add baking powder, butter and flour mixture gradually, beating thoroughly.

4. In a separate bowl beat egg whites until stiff. Add to yolk mixture, beating until well blended, about 3 minutes.

5. Pour into 3 5" x 9" loaf pans that have been generously buttered.

6. Bake in preheated 325° oven for 1 hour, 10 minutes, or until golden brown and toothpick comes out clean.

Yield: 3 loaves
Preparation: 35 minutes
Baking: 1 hour, 10 minutes

One of the best.

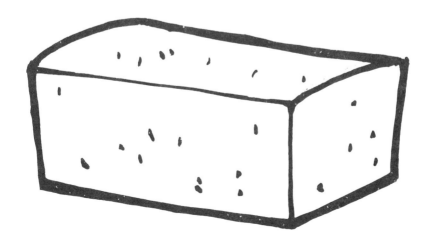

233

MARY WALKER
McDonald, Pennsylvania

BAVARIAN CREAM PIE – COCONUT AND BANANA

2 1-shell pie crusts, baked and cooled*
3 cups milk
2 cups sugar
Dash of salt
6 egg yolks
2 Tablespoons cornstarch
3 Tablespoons milk
2½ Tablespoons gelatin
6 Tablespoons milk
3 cup whipped cream, or
1 small container Cool Whip
1 Tablespoon vanilla
6 egg whites, beaten stiff
¾ cup coconut
1½ banana, sliced
1 medium container Cool Whip

*See page 294.

1. Boil milk, sugar and salt together.

2. Mix egg yolks, cornstarch and 3 Tablespoons milk together. Mix into hot milk mixture, cook until smooth and slightly thickened, <u>stirring constantly</u>. Remove from heat.

3. Dissolve gelatin in 6 Tablespoons milk and add to milk mixture mixing and blending thoroughly. Chill for 2 hours in the refrigerator.

4. Remove from refrigerator and beat well until smooth in texture.

5. Fold in whipped cream, vanilla and egg whites.

6. At this point divide Bavarian cream mixture.

7. Mix ¾ cup coconut in ½ cream mixture and pour into 1 baked pie shell.

8. Slice bananas into second pie shell and pour other half of cream mixture on top of bananas.

9. Spread both pies with Cool Whip and refrigerate until ready to serve.

Yield: 2 pies
Preparation: 1 hour

These pies are absolutely luscious and many 10 plus.

CHOCOLATE BUTTERCRUNCH PIE

BRENDA LETSON
Warren, Ohio

PIE CRUST:
1 oz. unsweetened chocolate
½ of 1 10-oz. package pie
  crust mix
¼ cup light brown sugar,
  firmly packed
¾ cup walnuts, chopped fine
1 teaspoon vanilla
1 Tablespoon cold water

FILLING:
¾ cup light brown sugar,
  firmly packed
½ cup unsalted butter
1 oz. unsweetened chocolate,
  melted and cooled
2 teaspoons instant cofffee
2 large eggs

TOPPING:
1 pint whipping cream or
1 small container Cool Whip
½ cup confectioners sugar
1 Tablespoon instant coffee
Chocolate curls for garnish

1. Grind chocolate, add pie crust mix, sugar, nuts and vanilla extract in large bowl and mix. Drizzle water over mixture and stir. It will be crumbly.

2. Press into a 9″ or 10″ pan. Bake in preheated 375° oven for 15 minutes. Cool.

3. Beat butter until creamy and fluffy (about 3 minutes on high), add sugar, cooled chocolate and coffee and beat together 2 to 3 minutes on high.

4. Add eggs one at a time, beating on high 5 minutes after each egg.

5. Fill cooled crust with filling.

6. Whip cream, sugar and coffee together or stir sugar and coffee into Cool Whip. Let sit in refrigerator for about 10 to 15 minutes.

7. Spread topping on butter cream filling and shave chocolate curls on top of whipped cream mixture as a garnish.

8. Chill pie crust and filling 6 hours or up to 3 days. Can be frozen.

9. Put whipped cream mixture on a couple hours before serving.

Serves: 8
Preparation: 45 minutes
Baking: 15 minutes

There's only one explanation for this pie—sinfully delectable.

235

CREAMY PEACH PIE

CHRIS ZIMMERMAN
Phoenix, Arizona

¾ cup sugar
¼ cup flour
¼ teaspoon salt
¼ teaspoon nutmeg
4 cups fresh peaches, peeled
   and sliced
1 cup heavy cream
1 unbaked 9″ pie shell*

*See page 294.

Yield: 1 pie
Preparation: 30 minutes
Baking: 45 minutes

The name says it all.

1. Combine sugar, flour, salt and nutmeg. Add to the peaches in bowl and toss lightly. Arrange in pie shell. Pour heavy cream over peaches and sprinkle with additional nutmeg if desired.

2. Bake at 400° for 45 minutes or until set. Cool well before serving. Garnish with whipped cream if desired.

PECAN RUM PIE

1 <u>baked</u> Never Fail Pie Shell*
1 cup Half and Half
Dash of salt
4 eggs, separated
¾ cup sugar
1 envelope of unflavored
  Knox gelatin
3 Tablespoons hot water
2 cups whipping cream,
  whipped
1 teaspoon rum extract
1 Tablespoon rum
½ teaspoon nutmeg
½ cup pecans, chopped
Chocolate curls and whipped
  cream as garnish

*See page 294.

Yield: 1 10" pie
Preparation: 45 minutes

1. Heat Half and Half with salt in a sauce-pan. Beat egg yolks with sugar until smooth. Add to Half and Half mixture and scald, stirring constantly. Remove from heat.

2. Dissolve gelatin in hot water and add to Half and Half mixture. Set aside to cool.

3. When <u>completely cooled</u> beat until smooth. Beat egg whites until stiff. Add rum, extract and nutmeg. Blend into Half and Half mixture, blending well.

4. Fold in the whipped cream and pecans and pour into baked pie shell. Refrigerate for at least 1 hour. Serve with a dollop of whipped cream and chocolate curls.

I could eat the whole thing without stopping — soooo yummy.

237

DEEP DISH APPLE DUMPLINGS

Triple pie crust*
7 Granny or Pippin apples,
   peeled and cored
1 teaspoon lemon juice
½ teaspoon cinnamon
⅛ teaspoon nutmeg
½ cup sugar
4 Tablespoons butter
1 cup boiling water
Sugar, cinnamon, milk
   (topping garnish)

*See page 294.

1. Make pie crust, divide in half and roll out to fit a 9" x 13" baking pan, overlapping sides.

2. Slice apples and mix with lemon juice. Lay in pastry lined pan.

3. Put cinnamon, nutmeg, sugar, butter and water in saucepan and bring to a boil. Remove from heat.

4. Roll out the other half of pastry for top of apples.

5. Pour liquid over apples. Lay pastry on top, flute edges and brush with milk. Sprinkle sugar and cinnamon on top of crust.

6. Bake in preheated 375° oven for 35 to 40 minutes or until apples seem tender.

7. Serve in bowl with ice cream or milk.

Serves: 15 pieces
Preparation: 45 minutes
Baking: 35-40 minutes

Another old family recipe. Sometimes I throw in ¼ cup raisins and nuts before baking.

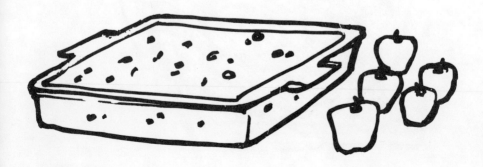

PEANUT CRUNCH APPLE PIE

BOBBIE LANGER
McDonald, Pennsylvania

1 unbaked pie shell*
5 Granny apples, peeled, cored
   and sliced
3 Tablespoons butter, melted
2 Tablespoons flour
2 teaspoons lemon juice
1/4 teaspoon salt
3/4 cup sugar
1/2 teaspoon vanilla
1/4 teaspoon cinnamon

TOPPING:
4 Tablespoons peanut butter
1/2 cup sugar
1 cup corn flakes, crushed

*See page 294.

Yield: 1 pie
Preparation: 30 minutes

1. Place sliced apples in large bowl and set aside.

2. Mix the next 7 ingredients in order given then mix mixture with apples.

3. Put in unbaked pie shell.

4. Mix topping mixture and spread over apple mixture. Bake in preheated 350° oven for 35 minutes.

A different, tasty, crunchy apple delight.

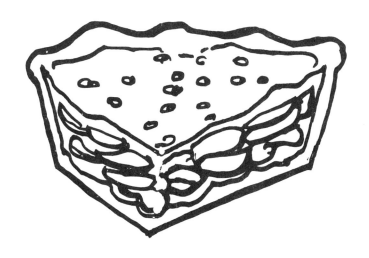

239

CHOCOLATE COCONUT CREAM PUFFS

CREAM PUFFS:
1 cup water
½ cup butter
1 cup flour
¼ teaspoon salt
4 eggs

CREAM COCONUT FILLING:
⅓ cup sugar
¼ cup flour
1 cup milk, scalded
2 egg yolks, well beaten
½ teaspoon vanilla
Pinch of salt
2 cups whipped cream, or
2 cups Cool Whip
½ cup coconut (optional)

CHOCOLATE TOPPING:
2 2-oz. squares unsweetened
 chocolate
1 cup evaporated milk
½ cup sugar
Powdered sugar as garnish

1. Boil water. Add butter, keep to a boil and add flour and salt. Mix well until batter leaves sides of pan. Remove from heat. Beat with electric beater one egg at a time. Beat until smooth.

2. Drop mixture by Tablespoonful (size of a small egg) onto a well-greased cookie sheet about 2" apart.

3. Bake in preheated 450° oven for 10 minutes. Reduce heat to 400° and bake another 15 to 20 minutes or until lightly golden. Remove from oven and cool.

4. Filling—Combine sugar and flour, slowly adding scalded milk, Put in double boiler and cook until thick and creamy. Cover and cook 10 minutes longer. Add a little of hot mixture to beaten egg yolks and then pour into hot mixture. Add salt and cook over hot but not boiling water for about 2 to 3 minutes more. Cool and chill completely.

5. Add vanilla, Cool Whip and coconut.

6. Cut cream puffs horizontally, pull out any excess batter, fill with cream filling mixture and set on tray.

7. In a saucepan combine chocolate squares, milk and sugar. Stir constantly and cook until thickened. Cool slightly (about 3 minutes).

(continued)

240

Chocolate Coconut Cream Puffs *(continued)*

8. Drop chocolate mixture over cream puffs by spoonfuls. Refrigerate until ready to serve. Sprinkle tops of chocolate cream puffs with powdered sugar and serve. (This chocolate topping is super as a dip with fresh fruits. Add 2 Tablespoons Cointreau* or Amaretto* and keep warm in chafing dish.)

*See pages 308 and 309.

Serves: 12-14
Preparation: 1 hour
Baking: 25-30 minutes

Always enjoyed and always complimented.

CARMEN L. PONS
San Juan, Puerto Rico
Submitted by Governor and
Mrs. Rafael Hernández-Colón

FLAN DE QUESO
(Cheese Flan)

1 cup sugar
4 eggs
1 8-oz. package cream cheese
1 13-oz. can evaporated milk
1 can condensed milk
½ teaspoon vanilla

1. Caramelize sugar by melting it in a small 9″ skillet, stirring constantly. Pour into a 2 to 2½-quart well buttered mold and cover sides and bottom with caramel mixture. Set aside.

2. Place eggs, cream cheese, milks and vanilla in a blender. Beat well until liquified and pour into caramelized bowl.

3. Place into a pan of water in a preheated 350° oven for 1 hour or until knife comes out clean. When cooled, place in refrigerator until ready to serve.

4. This can be made up to 3 days ahead.

5. If desired, substitute 3 bananas for the cream cheese, and you will have a banana flan, or if desired, 1 can of Coco Lopez can be substituted to have a coconut flavor. When ready to serve, run a knife around border and unmold onto a plate.

Serves: 8-10
Preparation: 25 minutes
Baking: 1 hour

This cheese flan tastes like a very light cheese cake with a caramel sauce — so elegant.

242

RICE PUDDING À LA BERRY

EDNA ALBION
Point Pleasant, New Jersey

1 cup raw rice cooked as
   directed on package
2 cups milk
¼ cup sugar
⅛ teaspoon salt
1 3-oz. package cream cheese
   at room temperature
1 teaspoon vanilla
2 cups whipping cream
   whipped
Strawberries, or
Blueberries, or
Raspberries
Brown sugar

1. After cooking rice full time, add milk, sugar and salt. Cook until thick and creamy stirring constantly. Remove from heat. Cool, then refrigerate until thoroughly chilled.

2. Beat cream cheese, add vanilla and chilled rice mixture. Fold in whipped cream. Can be eaten this way with a dash of cinnamon and nutmeg on each serving, *or*

3. Place sliced strawberries or whole blueberries or raspberries into individual Pyrex cups, place rice pudding on top and sprinkle about 1 heaping teaspoon of brown sugar on each. Put under broiler for about 2 minutes until bubbly and serve.

Serves: 4-6
Preparation: 40 minutes
Baking: 30-35 minutes

Rich and creamy.

CHEF NORBERT RUEGG
Basin Street Restaurant
Palm Bay, Florida

COLD BANANA SOUP MONTEGO BAY

2 bananas
2 scoops of vanilla ice cream
1 cup Half and Half
1 oz. banana liqueur
2 oz. rum
3 to 4 Tablespoons sugar
Coconut, shredded and toasted
Nutmeg

Serves: 4
Preparation: 5 minutes

Refreshing on hot summer days.

1. In a blender mix 1½ bananas, ice cream, Half and Half, banana liqueur, rum, and sugar, blending well.

2. Serve in a chilled goblet, garnished with ½ of a banana (sliced) and toasted coconut with a dash of nutmeg on the top.

EDNA'S RAISIN PUDDING

OLGA RUSH
Temple City, California

PUDDING MIXTURE:
1⅓ cups flour
¾ cup sugar
1⅔ Tablespoons butter
¾ cup milk
¾ teaspoon nutmeg
1½ teaspoons baking powder
¾ teaspoon baking soda
¾ teaspoon vanilla
1½ cups raisins

CARAMEL SAUCE:
4 Tablespoons butter
1½ cups brown sugar
3½ cups water
Whipped cream as garnish

Serves: 6-8
Preparation: 25 minutes
Baking: 30 minutes

1. Combine all pudding mixture ingredients and place in a well-buttered 2½ quart casserole.

2. Combine caramel sauce ingredients in a saucepan, bring to a boil and pour over pudding mixture.

3. Bake in a preheated 350° oven for 30 minutes.

4. Serve warm or cold with dollops of whipped cream.

The caramel sauce makes this pudding exceptional, a ten plus.

DEANNA MATTHEWS
Matthews 1812 House
Box 15 Whitcomb Hill Road
Cornwall Bridge, Connecticut 06754

INDIAN PUDDING WITH ENGLISH CUSTARD

PUDDING:
5 cups milk
⅔ cup yellow corn meal
Dash of salt
1 cup beef suet (beef fat),
   finely chopped
1 cup molasses
1 cup sugar
1 large egg
1 seedless orange with skin
   and juice, finely chopped
1 cup raisins, finely chopped
½ cup dried currants, finely
   chopped
½ teaspoon cinnamon
½ teaspoon allspice
½ teaspoon cloves
½ teaspoon nutmeg
1 teaspoon baking powder

ENGLISH CUSTARD:
5 egg yolks
⅔ cup sugar
2 cups milk
⅛ teaspoon salt
1 teaspoon vanilla extract

1. Preheat oven to 300.°

2. Bring 4 cups milk to just a boil and put in a large double boiler. Gradually add corn meal, stirring constantly. Add salt and suet stirring constantly for 15 to 20 minutes until thickened.

3. Stir in molasses, sugar and egg.

4. Add chopped orange, raisins and currants (chop in processor) and add spices.

5. Blend remaining cup of milk with baking powder.

6. Bake uncovered in a well-buttered 2 quart casserole for 2 hours. (Can leave in oven until serving time.)

7. For custard, place egg yolks in a saucepan with sugar and beat until thick and lemony.

8. In another saucepan place milk and bring to almost boiling point.

9. Gradually add milk to egg yolk mixture, beating constantly. Add salt and vanilla.

(continued)

Indian Pudding with English Custard (continued)

10. Cook in double boiler and stir constantly until mixture coats the side of the pan and spoon. Remove from heat. Don't let it boil.

11. Remove from burner and set in cold water to stop cooking and chill sauce in refrigerator.

12. Serve chilled custard over warm pudding.

Serves: 8-10
Preparation: 1 hour 15 minutes
Cooking and Baking: 2 hours

Thank you so much, Deanna, for such a marvelous traditional New England recipe.

SOUFFLÉ ROTHSCHILD

CHEF HENRI LABAZEE
Palm Beach, Florida

½ cup candied fruit, minced
¼ cup cognac or brandy
3 Tablespoons butter
¼ cup flour
1½ cups milk
½ cup sugar
5 eggs, separated
Sugar
Strawberries

1. Butter soufflé dish and refrigerate. When dish is chilled, sprinkle and coat with sugar. Put back in refrigerator.

2. In a small bowl place candied fruit and pour cognac or brandy over them. Set aside to marinate.

3. Melt butter, add flour and gradually add milk and sugar. Mix and bring to a boil. Remove from heat and beat in one egg yolk at a time.

4. Beat egg whites separately and blend in souffléd mixture.

5. Strain the candied fruit from brandy and set aside.

6. Pour soufflé mixture into soufflé dish, layering mixture with marinated candied fruit. Top layer should be soufflé mixture.

7. Bake in preheated 375° oven for 25 to 30 minutes.

8. Five minutes before serving, arrange strawberries that have been rolled in sugar on top of the soufflé.

Serves: 8
Preparation: 30 minutes
Baking: 25-30 minutes

Chef Henri created this marvelous soufflé for Baron Edward Rothschild.

COINTREAU CHANTILLY TRIFLE

2 cups <u>whipped</u> cream
1 cup <u>sour</u> cream
5 Tablespoons confectioners
  sugar
4 Tablespoons Cointreau*
1 Tablespoon orange juice
2 teaspoons orange zest
½ teaspoon lemon zest
Pound cake*
Cointreau*
Fresh cut fruit of your choice:
  melon, peaches or kiwi (not
  oranges, grapefruit or
  pineapple

*See pages 233 and 309.

Serves: 6-8
Preparation: 10 minutes

1. Combine whipped cream, sour cream, confectioners sugar, 4 Tablespoons Cointreau, orange and lemon zest. Mix well and refrigerate overnight.

2. Crumble enough pound cake in a long stemmed wine goblet to fill ⅓ of goblet. Drizzle 2 teaspoons or more of Cointreau over each goblet of cake.

3. Place fresh cut fruit over cake to fill the glass ⅔ full.

4. Pile Cointreau Chantilly Crème on top of fruit. Sprinkle a little orange zest on top of crème and a fresh strawberry on very top. Serve.

This is so light and so luscious—Yummy.

CHEF VINCENT GUERITHAULT
Vincent's French Cuisine
Scottsdale, Arizona

LIME TART, LIME MOUSSE.

(or Lemon Tart and Lemon Mousse with Raspberry Sauce*)

CREAM MOUSSE:
Juice of 2 lemons
Juice of 4 limes (save zest of
   limes for lime mousse or pie)
7 oz. sugar
3 eggs
3 egg yolks
10½ Tablespoons butter,
   melted and <u>cooled</u>
A few drops of green food
   coloring

1. Beat sugar, eggs and egg yolks until thick and lemon colored. Cook in a double boiler, whisking constantly until mixture holds a ribbon.

2. Add a bit of cooked egg mixture to the melted butter. Mix until well blended, return to hot mixture and add the juices and most of zest. Whisk constantly and cook until thick.

3. Serve on a plate by spooning mousse in oval shape. Place the remaining zest and Raspberry Sauce* on top.

4. For a lime pie or lemon pie, fold in 1 cup of whipped cream to <u>cooled</u>, cooked mixture and pour into baked pâté brisée.* Top with extra whipped cream and remaining zest. For a lemon pie use all lemons and a few drops of yellow food coloring. Also use zest of 4 lemons from the 6 for the pie or mousse.

*See page 294.

Yield: 1 pie or will serve 8 individual mousse
Preparation: 1 hour
Cooking: Until thick

There is <u>no</u> key lime pie or mousse or lemon pie that could even come near these.

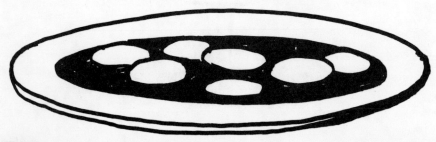

AMARETTO MOUSSE TART

PASTRY:
1¼ cups flour
½ cup butter
2 Tablespoons almonds, chopped
3 Tablespoons sugar
Dash of salt
1 teaspoon amaretto*
¾ Tablespoon water

FILLING:
1 envelope Knox gelatin
¼ cup cold water
1 8-oz. package chocolate chips
¼ cup sugar
½ cup amaretto*
3 eggs, separated
1 cup cream, whipped, or
1 cup Cool Whip
12 teaspons amaretto*
Chopped almonds as garnish
Chocolate shavings as garnish
Whipped cream as garnish

*See page 308.

Serves: 12
Preparation: 1½ hours
Cooking and Baking: 20-30 minutes

1. Mix pastry dough and divide into 12 balls (dough will be a little sticky).

2. Spray a 12-cup muffin tin or 12 small tart tins (3″ size) with Pam.

3. Roll each pastry ball on well-floured board and place into muffin tins. Prick sides and bottom with fork and use fork to flute inside edge of pastry of each tart (or use a 10″ pie pan).

4. Bake in preheated 375° oven for 10 to 12 minutes. Cool completely, about 1 hour.

5. Soften gelatin in cold water.

6. In top of double boiler put chocolate chips, sugar and amaretto. Cook until well blended and remove from water.

7. Beat egg yolks. Add to hot mixture, stirring rapidly. Return to double boiler and cook about 5 minutes until thickened. Stir constantly.

8. Add gelatin and chill completely, about 1 hour.

9. Beat egg whites until stiff. Fold into mousse mixture along with 1 cup of whipped cream. Fill tart shells.

10. When ready to serve, place amaretto mousse tart on dish topped with a teaspoon amaretto, a large dollop of whipped cream, chocolate shavings and chopped almonds.

For a very special dinner party, I created these—Sensational!

HOMEMADE ICE CREAM —8 FLAVORS

(Easy, Basic, No Cooking)

4 eggs
3 cups sugar
½ teaspoon salt
1 quart whipping cream
1 quart Half and Half
4 teaspoons vanilla extract

1. Beat eggs until well beaten. Gradually add sugar and beat until lemon color and very stiff. Add remaining ingredients and mix thoroughly.

2. Put half of mixture into ice cream maker (the other half in refrigerator until ready to make) and make to directions of ice cream maker.

3. This makes 1½ gallons. It can be cut in half.

   French Vanilla—Follow all directions except use 5 Tablespoons vanilla.

   Strawberry—Follow all directions except add 1 quart puréed strawberries.

   Pumpkin Crunch—Follow all directions except add 1 1-lb. can of pumpkin, 1½ teaspoons cinnamon, ½ teaspoon nutmeg, ¼ teaspoon ground cloves, 1 Tablespoon candied ginger (chopped), 1 cup chopped pecans. (I make peanut brittle using pecans instead of peanuts, cool completely and chop into very, very small pieces. Add to ice cream mixture after ice cream is made. Mix in by hand.)

   Piña Colada—Follow all directions except add 2 1-lb. cans crushed pineapple (drained), 2 cups flaked coconut, ½ cup rum and use 2 teaspoons coconut extract instead of 4 teaspoons vanilla.

(continued)

Homemade Ice Cream—8 Flavors (continued)

Kahlua* Chocolate Chip—Follow all directions except add 4 Tablespoons instant coffee, ½ cup Kahlua,* 2 6-oz. packages chocolate chips, 4 crushed Heath toffee candy bars (add crushed toffee bars at the end after ice cream is made).

Peach or Nectarine—Follow all directions except purée fruit and use 2 teaspoons almond extract instead of 4 teaspoons vanilla.

Amaretto*—Follow all directions except add ½ cup amaretto,* 1 cup toasted, chopped almonds and 2 6-oz. packages chocolate chips. Use 2 teaspoons almond extract instead of 4 teaspoons vanilla.

*See pages 306 and 308.

Makes: 1½ gallons
Preparation: 1 hour

So creamy and nothing artificial.

CHOCOLATE PEANUT POPS

1¼ cups peanut butter, chunky
2 8-oz. packages cream
  cheese
2 cups confectioners sugar
1 cup milk
2 9-oz. containers Cool Whip,
  thawed
1 8-oz. package chocolate
  chips
½ cup chopped peanuts
4 oz. paper cups
Popsicle sticks

Makes: 16 4-oz. cups
Preparation: 40 minutes

The kids love 'em!

1. Combine peanut butter, cream cheese and sugar. Beat with electric mixer until smooth.

2. Gradually add milk and beat until well blended.

3. By hand fold in Cool Whip, chocolate chips and peanuts.

4. Spoon into 16 4-oz. paper cups and place in popsicle stick. Put on cookie tray and freeze overnight. The next day put them in a large Baggie and keep frozen.

GLORIA PITZER
Secret Recipes
P.O. Box 152
St. Clair, Michigan 48079

FUDGESICLES

**1 cup Nestles Instant
Chocolate Drink Mix
2 cups dry milk powder
1 3½-oz. package instant
chocolate pudding mix
2½ cups cold water
4 oz. paper cups
Popsicle sticks**

1. Sift Nestles powder drink together with milk powder 3 times. Set aside.

2. Put instant pudding mix with cold water in a bowl and beat with an electric mixer until well blended.

3. Add the drink powder milk mixture to pudding mixture. Beat until smooth.

4. Place into 12 4-oz. paper cups. Freeze for 1 hour and stick in popsicle sticks. Freeze for 24 hours. Peel paper cup off and eat.

5. Store them tightly wrapped in plastic food bags in freezer, up to 1 year.

Makes: 12 4-oz. fudgesicles
Preparation: 30 minutes

Oh, Bill Cosby, you haven't lived until you try these!

POPSICLES

1 6-oz. package cherry Jello
1 small package <u>unsweetened</u>
   cherry Kool-Aid
½ cup sugar (or more to
   your taste)
2 cups hot boiling water
15 3-oz. paper cups
15 popsicle sticks

1. Mix all ingredients in hot water. Stir until Jello is dissolved. Add cold water and pour in paper cups.

2. Place cups on a tray and put in the freezer. After 1 hour place sticks in a freezer until solid (about 4 hours before they are ready to eat).

3. You can make popsicles of your choice. Just make sure the Jello and Kool-Aid match in flavor.

Yield: 15
Preparation: 25 minutes

My children loved these and they are so much better and cheaper than store bought.

GLORIA PITZER
Secret Recipes
P.O. Box 152
St. Clair, Michigan 48079

ORANGE DREAMSICLES

1 3-oz. package cream cheese
1 small can frozen orange juice concentrate (slightly thawed and mushy)
1 teaspoon orange extract
1 envelope Dream Whip powder
1 cup milk
4 oz. Dixie Cups
Popsicle sticks

1. Beat cream cheese and small can of orange concentrate; add extract, Dream Whip powder and milk. Blend thoroughly, pour into 4 oz. Dixie Cups, stick in popsicle stick and place in freezer until firm.

Yield: 12 4-oz. dreamsicles
Preparation: 30 minutes

Ummm—Creamy—Ummm—Oh, thank you, Gloria! It's been a long time since these were made and sold in the stores.

SWEDISH NUT HORNS

COOKIE MIXTURE:
½ lb. butter
2 3-oz. packages cream
   cheese
2 cups flour
Powdered sugar

FILLING:
1 lb. walnuts, chopped fine
2 Tablespoons honey
Sugar to taste, if needed
Milk (if needed to make a paste
   consistency)

1. Cream butter and cream cheese by hand. <u>Cream well</u>. Add flour and work by hand until dough leaves sides of the bowl.

2. Divide dough in half and wrap in wax paper. Chill in refrigerator overnight.

3. Mix nut filling and set aside.

4. Divide dough again (1 part at a time). Roll on powdered sugar into a rectangle about ⅛" thick.

5. Cut into 2" squares and place 1 teaspoon of nut filling in center. Fold opposite corners.

6. Place on a greased cookie sheet 2" apart.

7. Bake in preheated 350° oven for 10 to 15 minutes or until lightly golden. Cool completely.

Yield: 3-4 dozen
Preparation: 1 hour
Baking: 10-15 minutes

For Wayne.

APRICOT PECAN DREAMS

½ lb. butter
½ cup sugar
½ cup confectioners sugar
1 egg yolk
2 cups flour
1 cup apricots, chopped
1 ½ cups pecans, chopped

1. Beat butter until creamy. Add sugars and egg yolk, beating until well blended and creamy.

2. Add flour and continue beating until well blended.

3. Mix in apricots and nuts and let sit in refrigerator for ½ hour.

4. Take about 1 Tablespoon of dough and roll in your hand to the size of a walnut. Place on a greased cookie sheet and bake in preheated 400° oven for 10 to 15 minutes. Remove from oven and cool completely.

5. Dust generously with powdered sugar when completely cooled.

Yield: 5 dozen
Preparation: 45 minutes
Baking: 10-15 minutes

I created these on December 23, 1982, for my beautiful daughter, Suzie.

DATE AND COCONUT BALLS

(For my precious little Ursula)

1 14-oz. can Eagle Brand milk
1½ cups dates, chopped
1 cup pecans, chopped
3¼ lb. coconut
1 teaspoon vanilla
1 8-oz. package chocolate
chips (optional)
Powdered sugar

1. Mix all ingredients by hand. Make into balls about the size of a walnut and place on a greased cookie sheet about 2" apart.

2. Bake in a preheated 350° oven for 15 to 20 minutes. Remove and cool slightly. Re-squeeze to reform the coconut ball more firmly.

3. When completely cooled, dust with powdered sugar. Store in airtight container.

4. (This entire recipe can be cut in half.)

Yield: 10 dozen
Preparation: 1 hour
Baking: 15-20 minutes

Another special favorite, and yes, it does take 3¼ lb. coconut.

STRAWBERRIES

RANDY ZIPPERER
Kissimmee, Florida

¼ lb. butter, melted
1 cup sugar
2 eggs, beaten
½ cup dates, cut up fine
½ cup flour
1 teaspoon vanilla
1 cup nuts
2 cups rice crispies
Red granulated sugar
Large tube of green decorator
** icing**

Yield: 3 dozen
Preparation: 1 hour
Cooking: 10-15 minutes

They are so pretty on a cookie tray and so good.

1. Melt butter, add sugar and 2 beaten eggs. Cook 5 minutes over medium heat, stirring constantly so it doesn't scorch.

2. Add dates and cook 5 minutes more.

3. Lower heat and add flour. Cook until thick and add vanilla. Stir until blended.

4. Add nuts and rice crispies.

5. Shape into strawberries; roll in red sugar; decorate top with green stem.

CAKE, NUTS AND BOOZE

DON MILLER
Tempe, Arizona

1 1-lb. pound cake*
6 oz. chocolate chips
¼ cup sugar
¼ cup water
½ cup chopped pecans
   or walnuts
¼ cup rum, amaretto,* brandy*
   or kahlua*
Granulated sugar, powdered
   sugar or chocolate sprinkles

*See pages 306 and 308.

1. Crumble cake into large bowl.

2. Place chocolate chips, sugar and water in double boiler until chocolate is melted and smooth.

3. Pour over cake, add liquor of choice and nuts. Mix thoroughly and shape into small walnut-size balls.

4. Roll in one of the three, granulated sugar, powdered sugar or chocolate sprinkles.

5. Store in air-tight container. Will keep up to a month on the shelf.

Yield: 48
Preparation: 30 minutes
Cooking: 15 minutes

These are so good, they will never stay in any container for long.

SESAME COOKIES

MACRINA SUDIMACK
San Rafael, California

1 lb. butter
2 cups sugar
2 eggs
2 teaspoons vanilla
6 cups flour
Milk
Sesame seeds

Yield: 6-7 dozen cookies
Preparation: 1 hour 30 minutes
Baking: 10 minutes

1. Mix first 5 ingredients together until well blended.

2. Roll into ½" x 1½" logs, dip in milk then sesame seeds. Place on a greased cookie sheet and bake in preheated 350° oven for 10 minutes or until golden brown.

It's not Christmas at our home without these.

ITALIAN NEVELLA COOKIES

5 cups flour
4 eggs, beaten
½ cup Crisco, melted and cooled
½ cup white wine
½ cup water
1 teaspoon almond or vanilla extract (optional)
Powdered sugar

Yield: 7-8 dozen cookies
Preparation: 1 hour 30 minutes

1. Mix all ingredients. Roll thin and cut into 1" x 4" strips. Tie strips in very loose knots and deep fry in hot oil until slightly golden. Cool on paper towel.

2. Dust well with powdered sugar when completely cooled. Store in airtight container.

An authentic Italian classic and another Christmas favorite.

263

ITALIAN WEDDING COOKIES

3 eggs, beaten
1 cup sugar
½ cup oil
Zest of 1 lemon
4 cups flour
3 teaspoons baking powder
1 teaspoon anise extract
Colored confectioners icing
Coconut

1. Mix all ingredients and make into balls about the size of a nickel.

2. Place about 2″ apart on a greased cookie sheet and bake in preheated 350° oven for 10 minutes. Remove from oven and cool.

3. Mix 1 cup confectioners sugar and 2 drops of food coloring (yellow, green or red) with enough water to make smooth consistency. Dip cookies in icing and then coconut. Let sit for about 2 hours on wax paper and store at room temperature in an airtight container.

Yield: 5-6 dozen
Preparation: 1 hour 30 minutes
Baking: 10 minutes

Another one we always have at Christmas. Very pretty and tasty.

FRENCH BON-BON COOKIES

BON-BON MIXTURE:
1 cup butter softened to room temperature
1½ cups powdered sugar
2½ cups flour
1 Tablespoon vanilla
⅛ teaspoon food coloring
Dash of salt
Dates, or
Pecan halves, or
Maraschino cherries, well drained

ICING:
1 cup confectioners sugar
2 Tablespoons cream
1 teaspoon vanilla

Yield: 2 dozen
Preparation: 1 hour
Baking: 12-15 minutes

Another Christmas favorite.

1. Combine butter, powdered sugar, vanilla and salt. Mix well.

2. Blend in flour and mix thoroughly by hand until well blended.

3. Wrap a level Tablespoon of dough around your choice of dates, pecans or cherries. Place 1″ apart on ungreased cookie sheet.

4. Bake in preheated 350° oven for 15 to 20 minutes until set, but not brown.

5. Mix all ingredients for icing and frost tops of warm cookies. Let set on wax paper.

BETTY MARCZAK
Toledo, Ohio

HUNGARIAN COOKIES

DOUGH:
6½ cups flour
1 lb. butter or margarine
¾ cup sugar
1 pint sour cream
6 egg yolks
1 teaspoon vanilla
3 teaspoons baking powder
¾ teaspoon salt

FILLING I:
1 lb. walnuts, ground
½ cup sugar
Add a little milk to moisten

FILLING II:
1 can of Solo apricot filling
Add a little sugar to suit your
   taste

Yield: 5-6 dozen
Preparation: 1 hour 30 minutes
Baking: 10-15 minutes

Delicious.

1. Work butter into flour until crumbly. Make a well and add sugar. Mix in sour cream, egg yolks, vanilla, baking powder and salt. Blend thoroughly.

2. Divide into 3 balls and refrigerate about 1 hour.

3. Roll out each ball, one at a time, on a floured board. Roll out to about ⅛" thick, cut into 2" squares. Place a teaspoon of your desired filling in center. Fold over opposite corners, leaving each end of square open.

4. Bake on a well-buttered cookie sheet in a preheated 375° oven for 10 to 15 minutes or until golden.

MOIST DEVILSFOOD COOKIES

1/2 cup butter
1 cup brown sugar, firmly
   packed
1 egg
1 teaspoon vanilla
2 1-oz. Hershey's unsweetened
   chocolate squares, melted
   and cooled
2 cups flour, sifted
1/2 teaspoon baking soda
1/4 teaspoon salt
3/4 cup sour cream
1/2 cup walnuts, chopped

FROSTING:
1/4 cup butter
2 Tablespoons cocoa
3 Tablespoons milk
2 cups confectioners sugar
1 1/2 teaspoons vanilla
Dash of salt

Yield: 4 1/2 dozen
Preparation: 1 hour
Baking: 10 minutes

Very moist, a chocolate delight.

1. Cream butter and sugar until fluffy. Beat in egg, vanilla and chocolate.

2. Alternate flour and sour cream. Add in baking soda and salt with flour and mix well.

3. Stir in nuts. Drop by teaspoonful on a greased cookie sheet about 2" apart and bake in a preheated 350° oven for 10 minutes. Remove from cookie sheet to a wax papered area and cool.

4. Mix all ingredients for frosting and ice the cookies. Let the cookies set for about 2 hours so that the icing has a chance to harden. Store in layers with wax paper between layers.

RANDY ZIPPERER
Kissimmee, Florida

AUNT CLODIE'S SUGAR COOKIES

1 cup sugar
½ cup shortening
½ teaspoon vanilla
1 egg
½ cup sour cream
2 cups flour
1 teaspoon nutmeg
½ teaspoon baking soda
2 teaspoons baking powder
½ teaspoon salt
Granulated sugar as topping

Yield: 3½ dozen
Preparation: 20 minutes
Baking: 8-10 minutes

Fred's favorite.

1. In a mixing bowl cream sugar, shortening, vanilla and egg. Add sour cream, then all dry ingredients; blend well.

2. Drop by the teaspoon on a greased cookie sheet about 2" apart. Sprinkle granulated sugar on top and bake in preheated 375° oven for 8 to 10 minutes. Remove from cookie sheet onto wax paper, cool and store in airtight container. You could use colored sprinkles also.

APPLE, DATE AND NUT BARS

CONNIE ZIPPERER
Syracuse, New York

DOUGH:
2 cups flour
10 Tablespoons butter
2 egg yolks, beaten
¼ cup sugar
½ cup sour cream
Juice of ½ lemon

FILLING:
¼ cup Ritz crackers, crushed
4 large cooking apples, sliced thin
¼ cup sugar
10 dates, chopped (optional)
½ cup almonds, chopped
Zest of 1 lemon
Cinnamon, generous amount
Nutmeg, grated (about ¼ teaspoon)
Milk and sugar

1. Dough—Mix flour and butter as for pie dough. Add slightly beaten egg yolks and rest of ingredients.

2. Divide the dough in half. It will be sticky. Dust with enough flour to pat the dough in a well-buttered 9″ x 13″ baking dish.

3. For the filling, place in the sliced apples, crushed crackers, dates and nuts. Sprinkle with the ¼ cup sugar, lemon zest, cinnamon and nutmeg.

4. Dust the remaining half dough with flour, rolling it on wax paper. Lay over top of apple mixture.

5. Brush top with milk and sprinkle generously with sugar. Make slits on the top of the dough.

6. Bake in preheated 350° oven for 30 to 35 minutes until golden. Remove, cool and cut into bars.

Yield: 24 bars
Preparation: 1 hour
Baking: 30-35 minutes

The dates and lemon give them really a special, unique taste.

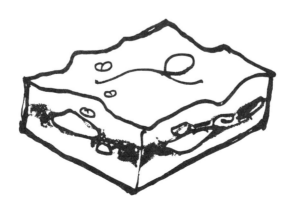

269

EVELYN GREER
Melbourne, Florida

APRICOT CORDIAL BARS

BAR MIXTURE:
1½ cups flour
¼ teaspoon salt
1 cup brown sugar
1 teaspoon baking powder
1¾ cups Mother's Quick Oats
1 cup shortening or
1 cup butter

FILLING:
1 lb. of apricots (from Apricot
  Cordial*), chopped
1 cup water
1 cup brown sugar

*See page 306.

Yield: 24 bars
Preparation: 30 minutes
Baking: 30 minutes

1. Place filling in saucepan and cook until thick, stirring constantly. Cool completely.

2. Mix all ingredients for bar mixture and divide dough in half. Pat one half in a well-buttered 9" x 13" baking pan. Set other one half aside for later.

3. Pour cooled filling mixture over bar mixture in baking pan. Crumble remaining bar mixture over filling and press in lightly.

4. Bake in preheated 350° oven for 30 minutes. Cut into 2" squares while still warm. Let cool in pan, then remove and serve.

Try this crumb mixture with dates instead of the apricots. After the dates have been cooked, place ½ cup chopped nuts on top of date filling. Both are very, very special in their own way. Also substitute the fillings with the apricot filling for the Russian Torte, page 222, and the Apple Date Nut Bars, page 269. Absolutely marvelous.

POLYNESIAN BRUNCH BARS

BAR MIXTURE:
2 eggs
1½ cups sugar
1 1-lb. can fruit cocktail, underlined
underlined
2¼ cups flour
1½ teaspoons baking soda
½ teaspoon salt
1 teaspoon vanilla
½ cup walnuts, chopped
10 maraschino cherries, drained and cut in half
1⅓ cups coconut

GLAZE:
¾ cup sugar
½ cup oleo
¼ cup milk
½ teaspoon vanilla
½ cup walnuts, chopped

Yield: 24 bars
Preparation: 35 minutes
Baking: 35 minutes

A true pleaser for all—brunch or not.

1. Beat eggs and sugar until well blended. Add undrained fruit cocktail and remaining ingredients except coconut.

2. Pour into a well-buttered and floured 9″ x 13″ baking pan. Sprinkle coconut on top.

3. Bake in preheated 350° oven for 35 minutes. Remove from oven.

4. In a saucepan place all ingredients except vanilla and nuts. Bring to a boil and boil hard for 2 minutes stirring constantly. Remove from heat, add vanilla and nuts.

5. Pour over hot cake and spread evenly over cake. Cool completely and cut into 2″ bars.

271

PATTY CORCORAN
Niles, Ohio

PUMPKIN SQUARES

CRUST:
1 ½ cups flour
¾ cup Quick Mothers Oats
¾ cup brown sugar
¾ cup soft butter

FILLING:
1 large can pumpkin
1 13-oz. can evaporated milk
2 medium eggs
¾ cup sugar
1 teaspoon cinnamon
½ teaspoon nutmeg
½ teaspoon ginger
½ teaspoon salt
¼ teaspoon ground cloves or
¼ teaspoon allspice

TOPPING:
¾ cup chopped pecans
½ cup brown sugar
2 Tablespoons butter
Whipped cream and nutmeg
   (optional)

Yield: 24 squares
Preparation: 25 minutes
Baking: 1 hour 15 minutes

1. Mix all ingredients for crust, pat in ungreased pan 9" x 13." Bake at 350° 15 minutes.

2. While still hot, pour mixed filling in and bake 20 minutes more.

3. Mix topping and sprinkle over top of filling and bake until brown and filling is set, about 40 minutes or more.

4. Cut into 2" squares with a dollop of whipped cream and sprinkled nutmeg, or eat plain.

Moist, delicious and hard to stay away from.

LANA HUGO
Tempe, Arizona

OATMEAL FUDGE BARS

CRUST:
½ cup shortening
1 cup brown sugar
1 egg
½ teaspoon vanilla
¾ cup flour
½ teaspoon soda
½ teaspoon salt
2 cups quick-cooking oats

FUDGE CENTER:
1 6-oz. package chocolate chips
1 Tablespoon butter
1 teaspoon vanilla
⅓ cup Eagle Brand milk
¼ teaspoon salt
½ cup nuts, chopped

Yield: 10-12
Preparation: 35 minutes
Cooking: 25 minutes

Yummy!

1. Cream shortening, sugar, beat in eggs and vanilla. Sift flour, soda and salt into sugar mixture. Stir in oats.

2. Remove 1 cup mixture for topping. Press rest of mixture into a 9" x 9" greased baking pan.

3. Cook slowly chips, butter and milk until chips are melted. Add vanilla and nuts.

4. Spread over oatmeal mixture and top with remaining oatmeal mixture.

5. Bake in preheated 350° oven for 25 minutes or until slightly browned. Cool and cut into bars.

273

LYNN L. MILLER
Warren, Ohio

CARAMEL CHOCOLATE BARS

1 16-oz. package caramels
⅓ cup evaporated milk
1 18-oz. box German
  chocolate cake mix
¾ cup butter, softened
⅓ cup evaporated milk
8 oz. chocolate chips
1 cup walnuts, chopped

1. Combine caramels and ⅓ cup evaporated milk in a double boiler. Stir until caramels are completely melted and remove from heat.

2. In a large bowl combine cake mix, butter and ⅓ cup evaporated milk; mix well.

3. Divide cake mixture in half. Press half the dough in a greased 9" x 13" baking pan. Bake in preheated 350° oven for 6 minutes. Remove from oven.

4. Sprinkle chocolate chips and nuts over bottom layer. Then spread caramel mixture over chips and nuts.

5. Crumble remaining cake mixture over caramel mixture and bake for another 15 to 20 minutes. Cool and then chill for at least 2 hours in refrigerator before cutting into bars.

Yield: 30 bars
Preparation: 30 minutes
Baking: 20-30 minutes

Lynn says these are really called 'Over Indulge Bars.' I agree.

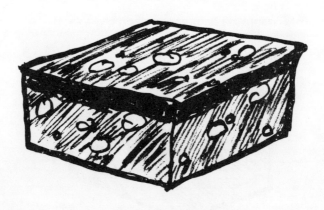

AMARETTO FUDGE BROWNIES

BROWNIES:
⅓ cup butter, oleo or
  shortening
¾ cup sugar
2 Tablespoons water
1 cup chocolate chips
1 teaspoon vanilla
2 eggs
¾ cup flour
¼ teaspoon baking soda
½ teaspoon cinnamon
¼ teaspoon salt
6 oz. chocolate chips
1 cup walnuts, chopped

TOPPING:
6 Tablespoons amaretto*
1 cup confectioners sugar
3 Tablespoons milk
  (more if needed)
¼ teaspoon vanilla
8 oz. chocolate chips

*See pages 306 and 308.

Variations of liquor: kahlua,
  crème de menthe, brandy,
  bourbon, Grand Marnier

1. Mix butter, sugar and water in saucepan. Bring to a boil and remove from heat.

2. Add 1 cup of chocolate chips. Mix until melted; add vanilla.

3. Place chocolate mixture into large bowl and add eggs, one at a time, beating well after each egg.

4. Slowly add flour, baking soda, cinnamon and salt until well blended.

5. Add 6 oz. chocolate chips and nuts.

6. Pour in well greased 12″ x 17″ cookie sheet with sides and bake in preheated 325° oven for 30 to 35 minutes.

7. Remove from oven, pour amaretto over the top and let cool completely.

8. Mix confectioners sugar, milk and vanilla. Ice top of brownies.

9. Melt chocolate chips in double boiler and pour over confectioners glaze. Cool completely until chocolate is set.

10. Cut into 2″ squares.

Yield: 16
Preparation: 1 hour
Baking: 30-35 minutes (including melting chocolate)

Ummmm scrumptious!

RUTH'S COFFEE BARS

BAR MIXTURE:
1 cup raisins
⅔ cup water
1 Tablespoon instant coffee
½ teaspoon cinnamon
Dash of nutmeg
⅔ cup shortening
1 cup sugar
2 eggs
1½ cups flour
½ teaspoon baking powder
½ teaspoon baking soda
¼ teaspoon salt

ICING:
1½ cups confectioners sugar
1 Tablespoon instant coffee
Milk, enough to make a
    spreading consistency

Yield: 35 bars
Preparation: 30 minutes
Baking: 20 minutes

1. Combine raisins, water, instant coffee, cinnamon and nutmeg in a bowl and set aside.

2. Combine remaining bar mixture ingredients in separate bowl. Add in raisin mixture.

3. Pour in well-greased and floured 10" x 15" cookie sheet and bake in 350° oven for 20 minutes.

4. Mix confectioners sugar, instant coffee and enough milk to make icing thin and runny. Ice while still hot. Cool and cut into 2" squares.

Great with a cup of coffee after lunch.

SLATE COOKIE BARS

BETTE RUTTEN
Arcadia, California

1 lb. butter (no substitute)
1¼ cups sugar
5 cups sifted flour

1. Mix until well blended. Pat in 10" x 15" baking pan. Prick with fork tines all over. Bake in preheated 300° oven for 50 to 60 minutes or until lightly golden. Cut into 2" squares while still warm. Leave in pan until cooled completely. Recut and remove to cookie jar.

Note: Try putting in an 8 oz. bag of chocolate chips.

Yield: 3½ dozen bars
Preparation: 15 minutes
Baking: 50-60 minutes

These are the best shortbread cookies that we ever tasted — you will agree.

277

CHEF DEBRA HOLT
Hyatt Regency
Memphis, Tennessee

CHOCOLATE GRAND MARNIER TRUFFLES

CANACHE FILLING:
(Day Before)
1 cup whipping cream
¼ lb. butter
1 lb. 3-oz. semi-sweet
  chocolate, melted

(Next Day)
½ cup Grand Marnier
4 oz. semi-sweet chocolate,
  melted
2-3 large sweet chocolate bars
  (for dipping)

1. For Canache Filling. Put whipping cream and butter in a saucepan. Bring to boiling. Add whipping cream and butter mixture to the semi-sweet chocolate that has been melted over a double boiler. Stir with a wire whip until completely combined. Pour through strainer to remove any unmelted chocolate. Refrigerate overnight.

2. The next day beat the canache filling on medium speed on mixer. Add Grand Marnier and melted semi-sweet chocolate. Beat until well combined.

3. Place mixture into freezer until firm, about 2 hours. Take mixture out and spoon out mixture onto wax paper in 1" balls. Chill again in freezer until firm, about 1 hour.

4. Dip in melted chocolate bar (that has been melted in double boiler). Let harden in the refrigerator and repeat once more. Keep refrigerated until ready to serve.

Yield: About 3 dozen
Preparation: 2 hours (about)

Oh, my, but these are so delicious. You'll think that you died and went to heaven. Thank you, Debra.

CHOCOLATE CREAMS

FONDANT:
2 lbs. powdered sugar
1 can Eagle Brand milk
1 stick of butter, melted
  (no substitute)
Extract

CHOCOLATE COATING:
1 12-oz. package chocolate
  chips
2 1-oz. squares unsweetened
  chocolate
¼ of ¼ lb. block paraffin wax

1. Mix powdered sugar, milk and melted butter until well blended and smooth. Divide into as many parts as desired flavors. Use extract for different flavors.

2. a. You can use coconut and coconut extract.
   b. Chopped nuts and marachino cherries (that have been dried completely by paper towel and chopped), cherry extract.
   c. Chocolate chips, instant coffee, chocolate extract.
   d. Oven dried lemon <u>zest</u>, lemon extract, yellow food dye.
   e. Oven dried orange <u>zest</u>, orange extract, orange food dye.
   f. Strawberry or raspberry extract or dehydrated strawberries and red dye.
   g. Mint extract, green food dye, crushed candy canes.
   h. English walnuts or black walnuts and black walnut extract.
   After mixing the different flavors, place them in individual bowls and in the refrigerator for at least 2 hours.

3. Roll into 1″ balls, refrigerate another 2 hours, and then dip in melted chocolate.

Yield: 10-12 dozen
Preparation: 2-3 hours

Store bought can't compare.

279

MARSHMALLOW CREAMS

1 cup evaporated milk
½ cup sugar
2 2-oz. squares unsweetened
chocolate
15 marshmallows, halved
1 cup pecans, chopped
1 cup coconut

1. In a double boiler place milk, sugar and chocolate, stirring constantly until chocolate is melted. Cook until mixture is thickened.

2. With a fork dip the marshmallows one at a time in the chocolate mixture.

3. Roll in nuts, then coconut and place on wax paper. Refrigerate until the chocolate sets.

Yield: 30
Preparation: 1 hour
Cooking: 10-15 minutes

Soooo good!

COFFEE CHOCOLATE CREAM FUDGE

1³/₄ cups sugar
1 5-oz. can evaporated milk
¹/₄ lb. butter
16 large marshmallows, cut up
1¹/₂ cups chocolate chips
1 teaspoon vanilla
1 Tablespoon instant coffee
1 cup walnuts, chopped

1. Put sugar and milk in a saucepan between low and medium heat. Bring to a slow boil, stirring constantly.

2. Continue to boil for 10 minutes, stirring constantly.

3. Turn off heat and leave pan on burner. Add butter, instant coffee, marshmallows and chocolate chips, beating by hand until all is melted.

4. Add vanilla and nuts.

5. Pour into buttered 9″ x 9″ dish and refrigerate for 24 hours. Cut and serve.

Yield: 36 pieces
Preparation: 30 minutes
Cooking: 10-15 minutes

Ummmmm Yummy Good!

STUFFED CHOCOLATE COVERED FRUIT

¼ cup butter, softened
½ cup graham cracker crumbs
½ cup crunchy peanut butter
1 cup powdered sugar
1 teaspoon vanilla
1 8-oz. package chocolate
   chips
⅛ cake paraffin
24 dried pitted fruits of your
   choice (dates, apricots,
   prunes, peaches, pears
   or figs)
Coconut

1. Combine butter, graham cracker crumbs and peanut butter. Beat until smooth and creamy. Add powdered sugar and vanilla and beat until well blended. Put in the refrigerator for 1 hour.

2. Fill fruits with peanut mixture, about the size of a walnut. Place on a wax papered tray.

3. In a double boiler melt chocolate and paraffin over medium heat.

4. Dip filled fruit with a fork into melted chocolate. Roll in coconut and place on wax papered tray.

5. Place in freezer for about 20 minutes or until set. Place in candy paper cups and serve.

Yield: 24
Preparation: 1 hour

They melt in your mouth.

RANDY'S AMARETTO CREAMS

1 12-oz. package chocolate
   chips
4 egg yolks
¼ cup Amaretto*
⅔ cup butter
¼ cup toasted almonds,
   chopped and cooled
Chocolate sprinkles, or
Chopped almonds
Candy paper cups

1. Melt chocolate in double boiler over medium heat. Remove double boiler when chocolate is melted. Cool to room temperature.

2. Beat in egg yolks, one at a time by hand until well blended. Return double boiler to water and add Amaretto, stirring for about 3 minutes.

3. Pour mixture into a mixing bowl. Using an electric beater, beat in butter, 1 Tablespoon at a time. Beat so that mixture will be fluffy.

4. Add cooled, chopped almonds to mixture. Cover with Saran wrap and refrigerate overnight.

5. Shape into 1″ balls and roll in chocolate sprinkles or almonds. Place in candy paper cups. Keep in refrigerator until ready to use. Try Kahlua* instead of Amaretto.* They both are marvelous.

*See page 306 and 308.

Yield: 3½-4 dozen
Preparation: 1 hour

For Randy.

DON MILLER
Tempe, Arizona

OHIO "GO BUCKS" BUCKEYES

1 cup crunchy peanut butter
1 cup butter, softened
1½ cups graham cracker
  crumbs
1 teaspoon vanilla
1 1-lb. box confectioners sugar
2 8-oz. packages
  chocolate chips
¼ cake of paraffin

1. Beat peanut butter and butter until smooth and creamy. Add graham cracker crumbs and vanilla. Again beat until smooth.

2. Gradually add confectioners sugar and mix until well blended.

3. Shape into 1″ balls, place on wax papered cookie tray and put in freezer for about 1 hour.

4. In the meantime melt chocolate chips and wax over medium heat in a double boiler.

5. With a toothpick dip peanut balls into chocolate mixture, covering <u>only</u> ¾ of peanut butter ball with chocolate mixture, leaving the ¼ uncovered, making it look like a "Buckeye." Store in refrigerator until ready to serve.

Yield: 80 to 100
Preparation: 1 hour 30 minutes

They taste like Reese's Peanut Butter Cups.

MISCELLANEOUS & SAUCES
French Fried Vegetable and
 Meat Batter............286
Aunt Mary's Mayonnaise......287
Butter Blend...............287
Chow Mein Noodles........288
Sea Shell Salad Shells........289
Court Bouillon/Fish Stock.....290
Pumpkin Seeds.............291
Lana's Granola..............292
Mustard...................292
Béarnaise Sauce............293
Crêpes....................293
Never Fail Pie Crust..........294
Pâté Brisée.................294
Raspberry Sauce............295
Vanilla Sauce...............295
JELLY & FRUIT LEATHER
Madeira Pear Butter..........296
Nectarine Jelly..............297
Apple and Banana Leather.....298

BEVERAGES
Bobbie's Spiced Wine........299
Beer Recipe................300
Fruit Wine..................302
Suzie's Hot Apple Cider.......303
Kahlua Coffee...............304
Norwegian Glog.............304
Wassail...................305
Frosty Margaritas............305
Apricot Cordial..............306
Bonnie's Kahlua.............306
Pop's Apricot Brandy.........307
Peach Gin..................307
Homemade Amaretto........308
Galliano Liqueur.............308
Cointreau..................309

FRENCH FRIED VEGETABLE AND MEAT BATTER

Hot grease (350° to 375°)
Vegetables, or
Meat, or
Fish
Flour
1 egg, beaten with
  2 Tablespoons milk
Fine bread crumbs
Salt
Pepper
Garlic powder
MSG (and any herb you may
  wish to include, such as
  oregano or basil)

1. Dip vegetable or meat into water, then flour, then egg, then bread crumbs that have been seasoned as desired. (This is the best coating you'll ever taste.) Deep fry and serve hot.

AUNT MARY'S MAYONNAISE

MARY WALKER
Mcdonald, Pennsylvania

1 Tablespoon butter
1 Tablespoon flour
1 cup sugar
½ cup white vinegar
2 eggs
½ Tablespoon dry mustard

1. Blend flour, sugar, vinegar, eggs and mustard in blender.

2. Melt butter in skillet and add above ingredients. Cook over a <u>low</u> heat (do not stop stirring as it will stick and burn). Cook until thickened. Cool completely. Put in a jar and keep in refrigerator. It will keep up to two weeks.

Makes: 1½ cups
Preparation: 15 minutes
Cooking: 10-20 minutes

A family favorite for potato salad.

BUTTER BLEND

MARION CARDONES
Warren, Ohio

½ lb. butter
½ lb. margarine
½ cup salad oil

1. In a food processor or blender blend all ingredients. Place in plastic container and refrigerate. This will always have a smooth consistency for spreading.

Yield: 1¼ lbs.
Preparation: 10 minutes

Thanks Marion.

287

CHOW MEIN NOODLES

1 package Chinese style <u>fresh</u> noodles
Hot oil

1. You can find the fresh Chinese noodles wrapped in a cellophane package in the <u>produce</u> department in a grocery store. You <u>cannot</u> use any other noodles. They <u>must</u> be the <u>Chinese style fresh noodles</u>.

2. Cut them in 4″ lengths. Deep fry in hot oil at 375° until golden brown.

3. They will be so plump and so much fresher than the ones bought in a can. Keep them in the refrigerator or in a canister that is air tight. You will really enjoy these so much better.

288

SEA SHELL SALAD SHELLS

ANNA LEE SMITH
Warren, Ohio

Egg roll wrappers (large or small)
Flour tortillas (large or small)

1. Use two mesh baskets, where one will fit into the other (use smaller baskets for the small egg roll wrappers and tortillas).

2. Place egg wrapper or tortilla into the larger basket with smaller basket on top.

3. Immerse into hot oil (375°) until lightly golden. Fry as many as you may need. Drain on paper towel.

4. The large ones can be used for salads, the smaller ones for creamed entrées and also for desserts or ice cream. They are easy and pretty, but hard to say!!

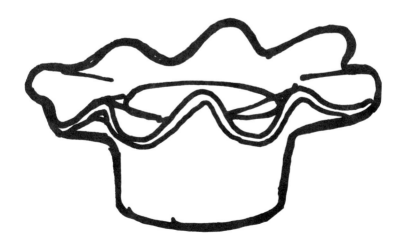

COURT BOUILLON/ FISH STOCK

1 lb. fillet of sole or flounder
1 large chopped onion
2 chopped carrots
1 cup chopped celery
2 Tablespoons chopped
   parsley
1½ cups white wine (optional)
2½ cups water
½ teaspoon basil

1. Cook for 20 to 30 minutes and strain.

2. You can freeze this well.

Yield: 3½ cups
Preparation: 15 minutes
Cooking: 20-30 minutes

I use a fillet of fish because I don't enjoy the thought of cooking fish heads and trimmings.

TOASTED AND SALTED PUMPKIN SEEDS

MACRINA SUDIMACK
San Rafael, California

TOASTED:
1 cup pumpkin seeds (washed
thoroughly)
1 Tablespoon butter (melted)
Onion salt or salt

1. Melt butter on a cookie sheet in a pre-heated 425° oven. Stir the pumpkin around until well coated.

2. Toast about 20 minutes, or until lightly brown, stirring occasionally. Season with salt and store in a covered jar.

SALTED:
2 cups pumpkin seeds
2 Tablespoons salt
¼ cup water

1. Take all stringy fibers from seeds. Wash until slimy coat has been removed. Spread on a cookie sheet.

2. Bake in preheated 225° oven for 10 minutes.

3. Turn off heat and leave in oven until seeds are thoroughly dry.

4. Mix salt and water together and pour over seeds until barely covered.

5. Bake in preheated 425° oven for 20 to 25 minutes or until all water evaporates, leaving a salt film over the seeds.

LANA'S GRANOLA

LANA HUGO
Tempe, Arizona

4 cups uncooked oatmeal
4 cups flaked wheat, from
health food store
1 cup sesame seeds, untoasted
1 cup wheat germ
1 cup sunflower seeds, raw
3 Tablespoons cinnamon
1 cup safflower oil
1 cup honey
1 teaspoon vanilla
½ cup raisins
½ cup dates, chopped
½ cup dried fruits, apples,
apricots, cut up
½ cup chopped nuts
½ cup coconut flakes, toasted

Yield: ½ gallon (approx.)
Preparation: 35 minutes
Cooking and Baking: 20 minutes

1. Mix dry ingredients well. In a small saucepan bring to a rolling boil oil, honey and vanilla.

2. Pour over dry mixture and mix well.

3. Bake for 15 minutes in preheated oven at 350.°

4. Stir well. Bake for 5 minutes more.

5. Stir well. Let cool, then add the following: raisins, nuts, coconut, apples, apricots or any other dried fruits. Mix well and store in tight jar. Keeps a month or so on a shelf. Will keep in refrigerator up to 6 months.

If you like cereal, there is no cereal that could ever beat this. It won't last long.

MUSTARD

BARBARA WATSON
Phoenix, Arizona

10 oz. Dijon prepared mustard
5½ oz. apple jelly
5½ oz. orange marmalade
2 oz. creamed horseradish

Yield: 3 cups
Preparation: 10 minutes

Outstanding.

1. Mix all together and store in a jar in the refrigerator until ready to use.

2. Serve with cheeses of your choice. Super with ham, beef sausage, beer sausage and beef also.

BÉARNAISE SAUCE

CHEF PETE WYNKOOP
Strawberry Mansion
Melbourne, Florida

(2 cups)

6 egg yolks
1 lb. butter, melted
⅓ cup shallots, chopped fine
⅓ cup red wine vinegar
1½ teaspoons tarragon
 leaves, dried
Salt
Cayenne pepper

1. Mix shallots, wine vinegar and tarragon in a small saucepan, simmer and reduce until most of vinegar has evaporated.

2. Place egg yolks in double boiler, whip until thick (do not have heat on any higher than low to medium). Slowly add melted butter and continue whipping until all butter has been added. Add wine vinegar mixture, blend thoroughly and serve.

3. During the blending process, should the egg yolks start to "scramble," remove immediately from heat (your water is too hot). For thinning thick sauce, add a little water.

CRÊPES

2 eggs
1 cup white flour
1 cup milk
2 Tablespoons melted butter

Yield: 8 crêpes
Preparation: 10 minutes
Cooking: 25-30 minutes

1. Mix and refrigerate for at least 2 hours before frying.

2. Can make ahead of time and freeze between sheets of wax paper or keep in refrigerator up to 5 days.

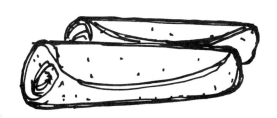

NEVER FAIL PIE CRUST

1 cup flour
2 Tablespoons sugar
½ cup butter or margarine (softened)
1 Tablespoon water (enough to make moist)
¼ teaspoon salt

1. Mix flour, sugar, butter and salt with fork until crumbly, add water and mix until all ingredients are moistened.

2. Roll out on very <u>well</u> floured wax paper, as the dough is <u>very</u> moist. Prick sides and bottom with fork and flute edges with thumb. Bake at 400° for 10 to 15 minutes until lightly brown. Can double recipe for 2 crusted dishes.

Yield: 1 10" pie shell
Preparation: 30 minutes

This is so easy and so light and flaky.

CHEF VINCENT GUERITHAULT
Vincent's French Cuisine
Scottsdale, Arizona

PÂTÉ BRISÉE
(1 bottom pie shell)

9 oz cake flour
5 oz. soft butter
Dash of salt
1 egg, beaten
2 oz. cold water (or less)

1. Blend cake flour, butter and salt with a pastry blender. Add beaten egg.

2. Add cold water slowly. (May not need it if dough is moist enough.) Knead dough slightly, roll out, shape in pan and let rest for 30 minutes.

3. Bake in a 350° oven for 10 minutes.
   a. For a sweet tart dough use 1 oz. sugar.

CHEF VINCENT GUERITHAULT
Vincent's French Cuisine
Scottsdale, Arizona

RASPBERRY SAUCE

1 cup sugar
½ cup water
1 box fresh or frozen
raspberries, puréed and
strained

Yield: 3 cups (approx.)
Preparation: 15 minutes
Cooking: 5-10 minutes

1. Boil sugar and water to a syrup. Cool slightly and add raspberry purée. Refrigerate until thoroughly chilled. Serve on mousse, ice cream, cake, pies, puddings or fruits.

CHEF VINCENT GUERITHAULT
Vincent's French Cuisine
Scottsdale, Arizona

VANILLA SAUCE

8 egg yolks
1¼ cups sugar
1 quart milk

Serves: 8
Preparation: 20 minutes
Cooking: 10-20 minutes

1. Mix sugar and yolk together. Boil milk. Put sugar and yolk into simmering milk for 5 minutes. Do not boil. Chill thoroughly and serve as desired.

MADEIRA PEAR BUTTER

½ cup **Madeira wine**
½ cup **dark raisins**
3½ cups **pears, peeled and cored (about 3 lbs.)**
2 Tablespoons **lemon juice**
⅛ teaspoon **cloves**
½ teaspoon **Allspice**
1¼ teaspoons **cinnamon**
7½ cups **sugar**
2 <u>Certo</u> **liquid pouches**

1. Sterilize jars in dish washer by washing them.

2. Melt 2 blocks (½ lb.) paraffin in double boiler to prevent spattering and keep it hot over low flame. Boil Madeira and raisins for 1 minute in a small saucepan.

3. Chop pears in the processor to a purée.

4. Combine all ingredients except <u>Certo</u> with Madeira and raisins in a large container.

5. Bring to a rolling boil, stirring constantly. Boil hard 1 minute.

6. Pour in <u>Certo</u> liquid and stir well. Remove from heat.

7. Stir and remove any excess foam by skimming the top with ladle.

8. Ladle jam into <u>hot</u> clean jars.

9. With <u>clean</u>, dampened cloth, wipe the inside of the jar rim from any jelly.

10. Immediately pour ½" of hot wax on top to seal.

11. Let jars sit for about <u>1 hour</u> until wax has a chance to start setting. Place on lid and tighten (do not disturb wax by movement of jar—hold jar firm on table to tighten).

12. Store in a cool, dry, dark place until ready to use. (<u>Never</u> make more than <u>1 recipe</u> at a time.)

Yield: 5 pints
Preparation: 1 hour

The ultimate ecstasy for you jam and jelly lovers.

NECTARINE JELLY

3½ cups ripe nectarines, washed and seeded, leave skins on
¼ cup lemon juice
7½ cups sugar
2 pouches of <u>liquid Certo</u>

1. Sterilize and wash jars in the dishwasher.

2. Melt 2 blocks (½ lb.) paraffin in a double boiler. Keep hot in double boiler over low flame.

3. Chop nectarines in 1″ chunks and <u>squeeze by hand</u> to crush. (<u>Don't</u> use food processor.)

4. Combine all ingredients except Certo in a large container. Stirring constantly, bring to a rapid, hard rolling boil that cannot be stirred down.

5. Pour in <u>Certo</u> pouches, boil hard for 1 minute and remove from heat. Ladle off any excess foam.

6. Ladle into <u>hot</u> jars. With <u>clean dampened</u> dish cloth wipe the inside rim of jar to clean and remove any excess jelly.

7. Pour hot paraffin over jelly ½″ thick to seal. Let sit about <u>3 hours</u>, then place lid on top of jars. Store in a cool, dry, dark place until ready to use.

Yield: 7½ cups
Preparation: 1 hour

A very delicate, rich color and taste that has been a family favorite for years.

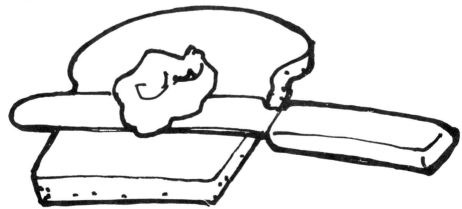

297

MACRINA SUDIMACK
San Rafael, California

APPLE AND BANANA LEATHER

2-3 apples, cored, peeled and sliced
2 bananas
2 Tablespoons honey
2 Tablespoons pineapple juice (no substitute)
1 cup pecans, chopped
1 cup coconut

1. Place Saran Wrap over a cookie sheet (15" x 10" x 1"). Tape edges on bottom to secure Saran Wrap.

2. In a blender, place apples, bananas, honey and pineapple juice. Blend to a purée.

3. Spread purée on Saran wrapped cookie sheet, spreading evenly over whole Saran area.

4. Sprinkle chopped pecans and coconut over purée.

5. Bake in preheated 150° oven with door ajar (use a clothespin) for 8 to 12 hours.

6. The leather is done when it is no longer sticky when touched by finger.

7. Remove from oven and cool completely.

8. When cooled, peel leather off Saran Wrap. Cut and roll into desired lengths and wrap again in Saran Wrap. Store in airtight container.

Yield: 1 large sheet
Preparation: 20 minutes
Baking: 8-12 hours

Addictive.

BOBBIE'S SPICED WINE

BOBBIE LANGER
McDonald, Pennsylvania

2 cups burgundy
1½ quarts dry red wine
2 cups water
1 cup sugar
1½ teaspoons whole cloves
3 cinnamon sticks
1½ lemons, sliced
1½ oranges, sliced

1. Mix all ingredients. Bring to boil, then simmer for 20 minutes. Strain and serve hot.

Serves: 6-10
Preparation: 10 minutes
Baking: 25-30 minutes

A super hot drink after a football game—your guests will love it.

Note: This is an excellent source for beer and winemaking supplies, which are difficult to find. I am in no way compensated or subsidized by Evelyn's Beer and Winemaking Supplies. This information is intended to be a service to the users of my book.

M. Dolly Miller

EVELYN'S BEER &
WINEMAKING SUPPLIES
9220 N. 7th Street
Phoenix, Arizona 85020

BEER RECIPE

1 can malt extract,* unhopped
4 cups corn sugar
1 pack water salts
1 pack hops (10 grams)
1 pack beer yeast

*Munton & Fison, Edme, John Bull, DCL or Blue Ribbon malts may be used.

1. Fill the single-stage fermenter with 3½ gallons of cold water (to a point about 6¾ inches measured up from the outside base). Pour 1 more gallon of water into a large saucepan, bring to a boil and turn off heat. Add the unhopped malt extract and 4 cups of corn sugar and stir until completely dissolved. Stir in one pack each of water salts and the hops. Re-heat mixture to a boil and simmer for 10 minutes. (NOTE: When mix reaches a boil initially it will tend to foam up, so watch for this and reduce heat when it rises. It will fall within a minute and not rise again.)

2. Pour the beer mix into the single-stage fermenter containing the 3½ gallons of water. Sprinkle 1 pack of yeast into the mix and let sit for 10 minutes, then stir the yeast into solution. Secure the air-tight lid. Fill the fermentation lock half full with water and fit it into the hole in the lid. Allow the beer to ferment until the specific gravity is 1.004. (NOTE: Room temperature should be 65° to 80° with 70° being the ideal temperature. The average fermentation time should be four to seven days).

Beer Recipe *(continued)*

3. Siphon beer into a clean priming fermenter, leaving behind the sediment. Pour exactly 1¼ level cups of corn sugar into a small saucepan containing two cups of water. Dissolve and bring to a boil. Stir this sugar solution into the beer to prime it. Bottle and cap and allow beer to age upright at room temperature for at least 15 days. (Peak flavor is reached after two to four months of aging and lasts indefinitely.) Chill beer and pour into glass or mug prior to serving. ENJOY!

Makes: 5 gallons

FRUIT WINE

BOBBIE LANGER
McDonald, Pennsylvania

3 gallons water
3 quarts fresh fruit, cherries, berries or grapes
10 lbs. sugar, less 2¼ cups
3 lemons, sliced
1 small package compressed yeast, crushed
3 lbs. dark raisins
Bottles and caps

1. Combine water, sugar and desired fruit. Bring to a boil and pour into a 5-gallon crock. Cover and cool overnight in a cool, dark place.

2. Next day add sliced lemons and crushed yeast. Cover and let stand for 1 week, stirring once every day.

3. After one week strain through a cheese cloth. Do not squeeze. Strain into an enamel container, not a stainless steel or aluminum container. Rinse out crock.

4. Place juice back into crock and add raisins, stirring well. Let sit another week covered, stirring again every day.

5. Strain again as before, rinse crock, pour mixture back into crock for 2 more weeks until mixture looks clear.

6. Siphon into sterilized bottles, being careful not to disturb sediment, cap and keep in a cool, dark place. (Can buy caps in a hardware store. Use pop bottles, such as gingerale bottles. When capping, just press caps on by hand.) Let sit in a cellar for at least 5 to 6 weeks and then drink. (Again, be careful of sediment on bottom of bottle when pouring.

Makes: 12-14 quarts
Preparation: 3 hours

Cheap and easy to make—delicious to drink—compliments galore.

MACRINA SUDIMACK
San Rafael, California

SUZIE'S HOT APPLE CIDER

1½ qt. sweet apple cider
1 cup sugar
10 whole cloves
6 whole allspice
Nutmeg
Cinnamon sticks

1. Combine all ingredients in saucepan and heat over low heat until sugar is dissolved. Remove from heat.

2. Let stand at room temperature for two hours so that all flavors can marinate together.

3. Strain and reheat when ready to serve.

4. Serve with a cinnamon stick and a dash of nutmeg in a cup.

Serves: 4-6
Preparation: 10-15 minutes
Cooking: 15-20 minutes

Adults and children alike enjoy this on a cold winter night.

303

KAHLUA COFFEE

6 cups strong coffee
1 oz. unsweetened chocolate, melted
½ cup sugar
½ teaspoon cinnamon
1 cup Kahlua*
Dash nutmeg
1 pint whipping cream, whipped

*See page 306.

Makes: 6 cups
Preparation: 15 minutes
Cooking: 10-15 minutes

1. Put all ingredients in saucepan except the last two and heat over moderate heat.

2. Serve in cups with whipped cream topped with a dash of nutmeg.

Serve this marvelous delight instead of dessert.

CHARMAINE WILSON
Scottsdale, Arizona

NORWEGIAN GLOG

2 cups sugar
6 cups water
12 1-inch strips of lemon peel
Juice of 2-3 lemons
12 1-inch cinnamon sticks
40 whole cloves
2 cups brandy
1 gallon burgundy
2 cups claret

Makes: 1½ gallon
Preparation: 15 minutes
Cooking: 2 hours

1. In a large saucepan combine sugar, water, lemon peel, lemon juice, cinnamon sticks and cloves. Simmer for 2 hours.

2. When ready to serve, strain above and add brandy, burgundy and claret. Can serve hot or cold. Can cut in half.

An old Norwegian family recipe enjoyed on Christmas Eve. Thanks, Charmaine.

WASSAIL

GRACE REILLY
Temple City, California

1½ cups sugar
1 48-oz. jar cranberry juice
1 48-oz. can pineapple juice
1½ quarts apple juice, or
1½ quarts cider
1 12-oz. can frozen orange
juice, diluted according to
directions on can
1 12-oz. can frozen lemonade,
also diluted as directed
1½ quarts strong tea
8 cinnamon sticks
18 to 20 cloves

Serves: 30
Preparation: 15 minutes
Cooking: 15-20 minutes

Enjoy.

1. Use a <u>porcelain</u> container. Pour in all liquids and add cinnamon sticks and cloves that have been tied in a small cheesecloth.

2. Bring to a boil and simmer for about 15 minutes. Can be made 2 to 3 days ahead and is really tastier if made ahead. Store in refrigerator.

3. Leave cinnamon sticks and cloves in while storing and reheating. Reheat and serve hot.

FROSTY MARGARITAS

JUDY CASEY
Tempe, Arizona

1½ cups sugar
1 cup water
½ cup Club soda
1 egg white
1 pint bottle regular lime juice
5 oz. tequila
2 oz. orange liqueur (Triple
Sec) or Cointreau*
1 cup crushed ice
1 lime sliced and 1 wedge
of lime
Coarse salt

***See page 309.**

Serves: 4-6
Preparation: 10-15 minutes

A little effort, but well worth the time.

1. Blend all ingredients in blender, except lime slices and wedge and coarse salt.

2. Moisten rim of glass with lime wedge, and swirl rim in mound of salt to coat edge of glass.

3. Pour margarita in glasses, place lime slice over edge of glass and serve.

APRICOT CORDIAL

EVELYN GREER
Melbourne, Florida

1 lb. dried apricots
3 cups sugar
3 cups vodka

1. Place all in a large, wide-mouthed container with lid. Seal securely.

2. Each day for 3 months turn container end over end so that it can mix well and blend.

3. After 3 months, strain into a decanter and serve cordial after dinner.

4. Use leftover apricots in the recipe "Apricot Cordial Bars."*

   *See page 270.

Makes: 1 quart
Preparation: 5 minutes

Very delicate and tasty. Variations: Dried apples for Apple Cordial, dried cherries for Cherry Cordial, dried peaches for Peach Cordial and dried pears for Pear Cordial.

BONNIE'S KAHLUA

BONNIE ZIPPERER
Kissimmee, Florida

4 cups sugar
3¾ cups water
⅓ cup instant coffee
   mixed with ½ cup cold water
½ gallon vodka
½ cup vanilla extract
2 Tablespoons glycerin
   (optional)

1. Bring 4 cups of sugar and 3¾ cups water to a boil. Boil hard for 3 minutes, stirring constantly.

2. Carefully add coffee mixture, stirring constantly and boil hard another 3 minutes. Remove from heat and set aside.

3. Cool at room temperature for about 4 hours. Add vodka and vanilla extract. Bottle and enjoy.

Makes: 2½ quarts
Preparation: 15 minutes
Cooking: 6-10 minutes

Smooth.

POP'S APRICOT BRANDY

1 lb. fresh apricots, washed
3 cups sugar
1 cup water
2 cups brandy
1 bottle white wine
1 quart vodka

1. Poach fruit in water with sugar until soft. Remove from heat and cool at room temperature for about 4 hours.

2. Add brandy, wine and vodka. Pour in gallon container and put in a dark area of cupboard for one month. Stir slightly every 3rd day.

3. At the end of the month strain and restrain over a cheese cloth until brandy is clear. Bottle brandy. Put apricots in refrigerator in another container with some brandy. Use later on ice cream as a dessert.

Makes: 2½ quarts brandy
         1 quart brandied apricots
Preparation: 15 minutes
Cooking: 5 minutes

Another of Pop's recipes — Yummy Good!

RANDY ZIPPERER
Kissimmee, Florida

PEACH GIN

1 small can frozen
   pink lemonade
1 lemonade can full of gin
3 medium fresh peaches
   or nectarines, sliced with skin

1. In a blender, put in frozen lemonade, gin and sliced peaches. Blend at medium speed until peaches are liquid and crushed completely.

2. Serve in champagne glasses on crushed ice.

Makes: 6 drinks
Preparation: 5 minutes

Yummy.

HOMEMADE AMARETTO

2 cups dark brown sugar,
   firmly packed
2 cups white granulated sugar
4 cups water
½ cup almond extract
½ gallon vodka
2 Tablespoons glycerin
   (optional)

1. Combine first 3 ingredients. Bring to a rolling boil and boil six minutes, stirring constantly.

2. Remove from heat and cool about 4 hours at room temperature.

3. Add almond extract, vodka and glycerin. Bottle and enjoy.

4. This recipe can be cut in half.

Makes: ¾ gallon
Preparation: 15 minutes
Cooking: 6 minutes

**If you want to impress someone, serve this.
It is sinfully smooth and delicious; a great gift also.**

GALLIANO LIQUEUR

2 cups sugar
1½ cups water
2 1-oz. bottles of anise extract
   (¼ cup)
8 drops yellow food dye
4 cups vodka
2 Tablespoon glycerin
   (optional)

1. In a large saucepan combine sugar, water, and anise extract. Bring to a boil over medium high heat and boil for 6 minutes stirring constantly.

2. Take off heat and cool to room temperature about 2 hours. Add remaining ingredients, bottle and enjoy. (Can double the recipe.)

Makes: 1¾ quarts
Preparation: 20 minutes
Cooking: 6 minutes

Mama-Mia! Better than the bottle from Italy. (For Brenda.)

COINTREAU

4 cups sugar
4 cups water
½ cup orange extract
   or 4 1-oz. bottles
½ gallon vodka
2 Tablespoons glycerin
   (optional)

Makes: 2½ quarts
Preparation: 15 minutes
Cooking: 6 minutes

Soooo smooth and sooo inexpensive.

1. Bring sugar, water and orange extract to a boil and boil hard for 6 minutes. (Be sure to <u>add the extract in</u>. <u>If added after boiling, it will be cloudy</u>.) Stir constantly.

2. Cool to room temperature, about 2 to 4 hours, add vodka, bottle and enjoy.

INDEX

—A—
APPETIZERS

Artichoke Squares............ 15
Broiled Shrimp in Bacon........ 10
Cheese Pitas................. 23
Crab and Cream Cheese Spread.. 12
Creamy Shrimp Dip............ 11
Deep Fried Zucchini With Creamy
    Garlic Dip................. 14
Guacamole.................. 17
Liverwurst Pâté............. 19
Nachos..................... 16
Pastry Stuffed Brie........... 24
Sauerkraut Balls............. 21
Smoked Oyster Spread........ 13
Special Deviled Eggs......... 25
Spiced Ham Ball............. 18
Sweet 'N Sour Meatballs....... 20
Triple Cheese Ball............ 22

—B—
BEEF

Beef Braicole................. 132
Beef En Brochette............. 115
Beef Rouladen................ 112
Beer Salami.................. 137
Bertie's Beef Stroganoff........ 124
Bologna..................... 138
Cantonese Toss............... 121
Chimichanga................. 118
Chris's Meat Loaf............. 126
Corned Beef Croquettes........ 128
Don's Super Burgers........... 134
Élégante Steak in Marinade...... 119
Fettucini ala Bolognese........ 129
Fillet Mignon in Mustard
    Sauce.................... 109
Fred's Beef Jerky............. 139
Liver, Apples and Onions....... 125
Marion's Beef Burgundy........ 123
Meat Balls Supreme........... 133
Mom's Spaghetti Sauce with
    Meat.................... 130
Onion Beef Roast............. 122
Peppersteak a la Chef Norbert.... 114
Prime Rib Gourmet............ 116
Roth's Nevada Strip Steak...... 117
Roxy's Meat Loaf............. 127
Russian Meat Rolls............ 113
Steak Diane.................. 110

Swiss Austrian Steak.......... 120
Victorian Fillet............... 111
White Hastle Hamburgers....... 135
Yummy Sloppy Joes........... 136

BEVERAGES

Apricot Cordial............... 306
Beer Recipe.................. 300
Bobbie's Spiced Wine.......... 299
Bonnie's Kahlua.............. 306
Cointreau................... 309
Frosty Margaritas............. 305
Fruit Wine................... 302
Galliano Liqueur.............. 308
Homemade Amaretto.......... 308
Kahlua Coffee................ 304
Norwegian Glog.............. 304
Peach Gin................... 307
Pop's Apricot Brandy.......... 307
Suzie's Hot Apple Cider....... 303
Wassail..................... 305

BREADS & DINNER ROLLS

Alligator Bread............... 180
Angel Biscuits............... 193
Bacon Bread................. 185
Cheese Poppy Seed Garlic
    Toast.................... 193
Don's Onion Bread............ 186
French Bread Brioche.......... 184
Homemade Pizza............. 141
Mom's Cheese and Raisin Dinner
    Rolls.................... 189
Mom's Orange Pecan Dinner
    Rolls.................... 191
Onion Buns.................. 192
Pepperoni Bread.............. 182
Potato Refrigerator Rolls........ 190
Spicy Cheese Crisps........... 194
Walnut Cheddar Loaf.......... 188

SWEET BREADS & SWEET ROLLS

Banana Bread Supreme........ 201
Bubba's Kolachy Rolls.......... 204
Caramel Nut Loaf............. 202
Cherry Nibble Bread.......... 199
Danish Rolls................. 205
Finn Nisu Bread.............. 196

310

Grandma Campana's Easter
Bread..................197
Griswold's Bran Muffins........195
Merry Callender Corn Bread.....187
Powdered Orange Puffs........203
Raisin Cinnamon Bread........198
Zucchini Bread..............200

—C—
CAKES & TORTES

Apple Cake..................227
Creamy Banana Torte.........218
Dark Fruit Cake..............231
Dolly's Carrot Cake...........226
Duchess Prune Torte..........216
Easter Egg Fruit Cake.........230
Festive Pumpkin Log..........232
Flourless Chocolate Cake......211
Fruit Gateau.................215
Grandma's Pound Cake........233
Hazelnut Chocolate Torte......217
Hungarian Chocolate Raisin
Cake.....................210
Italian Torte..................224
Orange Pecan Chiffon Cake......228
Orange Pineapple Dream Cake...229
Raspberry, White Chocolate,
Blueberry Mousse Cake......220
Renie's Chocolate Cheesecake...212
Russian Torte................222
Summer Fruit Cake...........225
Wesley's Peanut Butter
Cheesecake...............214

CANDY

Chocolate Creams.............279
Chocolate Grand Marnier
Truffles...................278
Coffee Chocolate Cream Fudge...281
Marshmallow Creams..........280
Ohio "Go Bucks" Buckeyes.....284
Randy's Amaretto Creams.......283
Stuffed Chocolate Covered
Fruit.....................282

CHEESE & EGGS

Artichoke Squares............. 15
Broccoli Fettucine Alfredo......176
Cheese Pitas................ 23
Chilie Rellenos..............169

Fettucini ala Bolognese.........129
Greek a la Cheese Gourmet......166
Macaroni and Cheese Gourmet...167
Mom's Pierogi................164
Quiche Roma.................170
Swedish Onion Quiche.........168

COOKIES

Amaretto Fudge Brownies......275
Apple, Date and Nut Bars.......269
Apricot Cordial Bars...........270
Apricot Pecan Dreams.........259
Aunt Clodie's Sugar Cookies.....268
Cake, Nuts and Booze..........262
Caramel Chocolate Bars........274
Date and Coconut Balls........260
French Bon-Bon Cookies.......265
Hungarian Cookies............266
Italian Nevella Cookies.........263
Italian Wedding Cookies........264
Moist Devilsfood Cookies.......267
Oatmeal Fudge Bars...........273
Polynesian Brunch Bars........271
Pumpkin Squares.............272
Ruth's Coffee Bars.............276
Sesame Cookies..............263
Slate Cookie Bars.............277
Strawberries.................261
Swedish Nut Horns...........258

CRACKERS

Spicy Cheese Crisps...........194

—D—
DESSERTS

Chocolate Coconut Cream
Puffs.....................240
Cointreau Chantilly Triffle.......249
Cold Banana Soup Montego
Bay......................244
Edna's Raisin Pudding.........245
Flan de Queso................242
Indian Pudding with English
Custard...................246
Rice Pudding a la Berry........243
Soufflé Rothschild.............248

—F—
FRUIT LEATHER

Apple and Banana Leather......298

—I—
ICE CREAM & POPSICLES

Chocolate Peanut Pops. 254
Fudgesicles. 255
Homemade Ice Cream—
  8 Flavors. 252
Orange Dreamsicles. 257
Popsicles. 256

—J—
JELLIES

Madeira Pear Butter. 296
Nectarine Jelly. 297

—M—
MISCELLANEOUS

Chow Mein Noodles 288
Court Bouillon/Fish Stock 290
Crêpes. 293
French Fried Vegetable and
  Meat Batter. 286
Lana's Granola. 292
Never Fail Pie Crust. 294
Pâté Brisée. 294
Toasted and Salted Pumpkin
  Seeds. 291
Sea Shell Salad Shells. 289

—N—
NOODLES & PASTA

Broccoli Fettucine Alfredo. 176
Chicken Kiev. 88
Chicken Scampi. 89
Chow Mein Noodles 288
Fettucini ala Bolognese. 129
Fettucine Alfredo. 159
Greek a la Cheese Gourmet. 166
Green Pepper Noodle
  Stuffing. 163
Macaroni and Cheese
  Gourmet. 167
Mom's Spaghetti with Meat
  Sauce. 130
Pasta, Prawns and Scallops. 66
Suzie's Tuna Casserole. 77

—P—
PANCAKES

Blueberry Buttermilk Pancakes
  and Topping. 207
Crêpes. 293
Moms Apple Pancakes. 206
Pumpkin Puff Pancakes 208

PIES & TARTS

Amaretto Mousse Tart. 251
Bavarian Cream Pie—Coconut
  and Banana. 234
Chocolate Buttercrunch Pie. 235
Creamy Peach Pie. 236
Deep Dish Apple Dumplings. 238
Lime Tart, Lime Mousse or Lemon
  Tart and Lemon Mousse with
  Raspberry Sauce. 250
Peanut Crunch Apple Pie. 239
Pecan Rum Pie. 237
Pie Crust and Pâté Brisée. 294

PORK & HAM

Baked Beans and Kielbasa. 143
Baked Pork Chops with
  Barbecued Beans. 144
Crown Roast of Pork with Apricot
  Brandy Sauce. 149
Ham Loaf. 150
Homemade Pizza. 141
Homemade Sausage. 142
Hungarian Pork Chops. 146
Pigs in a Blanket. 145
Pork Chops with White Wine. 148
Sausage, Vegies, and Hard Rolls. . 140
Sweet and Sour Pork. 147

POTATOES

Bacon Almond Potatoes. 154
Baked Creamed Dumplings. 156
Bear Claws Potatoes. 155
Brenda's Irish Potato Casserole. . .152
German Potato Salad. 157
Italian Browns. 154
Sweet Potato Delight. 158
Walker's Au Gratin Potatoes. 153

POULTRY

African Chicken Stew. 96
"Asopaito" Carmen's Style. 98
Big Bucket in the Sky Fried
  Chicken. 91
Chicken Breast with Raspberry
  Sauce. 82

Chicken Divan. 87
Chicken Enchiladas or Crêpes. . . . 102
Chicken Kiev. 88
Chicken Scampi. 89
Cornish Hens Stuffed with Orange
  Pecan Stuffing and Sauce
  Bechamel. 101
Duck of the Bay. 100
Ginger Chicken. 86
Indonesian Chicken Broil. 84
Italian Chicken Stew. 97
Mandarin Cashew Salad (with
  Chicken). 53
Mary Beth's Chicken. 83
Poulet au Citron (Chicken with
  Fresh Lemon). 81
Poulet Geneviese (Chicken
  with Gin). 85
Saffron Cream Chicken. 90
Sautéed Breast of Chicken
  and Shrimp Oscar. 80
Stuffed Chicken Florentine. 92
Sweet and Sour Chicken Wings. . 95
Thin Man's Barbecued Chicken. . . 94

RICE

"Asopaito" Carmen's Style. 98
Lemon Rice. 160
Mimi's Tuna Casserole. 76
Peking Oriental Rice. 161
Rice Pudding a la Berry. 243
Risotto Rice. 162

—S—
SALADS

Brutus Salad. 43
Caesar Salad. 41
Cauliflower Zucchini Salad. 44
Cranberry Salad. 58
Cucumbers in Sour Cream. 54
Flaming Spinach Salad. 52
Grandpa's Antipasto. 42
Hearts of Palm Salad. 40
Joan's "Hell I Don't Know"
  Salad. 49
Mandarin Cashew Salad. 53
Marinated Broccoli and
  Cauliflower. 45
Mediterranean Salad. 56
Overnight Layered Salad. 57
Salade des Asperges aux
  Echalotes. 48

Spinach Salad. 47
Spinach Salad with Hot
  Bacon Dressing. 46
Summer Fresh Fruit Salad. 51
Summer Fruit Salad. 50
Uncle Johnie's Cole Slaw. 55

SANDWICHES

Don's Super Burgers. 134
Sausage, Vegies and
  Hard Rolls. 140
White Hastle Hamburgers. 135
Yummy Sloppy Joes. 136

SAUCES & BLENDS

Apricot Brandy Sauce
  (for Pork). 194
Aunt Mary's Mayonnaise. 287
Barbecue Sauce (for Seafood
  & Meats). 70
Barbecue Sauce (for Chicken
  & Spare Ribs). 94
Béarnaise Sauce
  (for Beef). 105, 293
Bechamel Sauce. 101, 175
Butter Blend. 287
Cherry Sauce (for Chicken). 92
Chocolate Topping. 240
English Custard Sauce. 246
Ginger Sauce (for Chicken). 86
Guacamole. 17
Marinade for Beef. 115, 119
Mom's Spagetti Sauce. 130
Mustard. 292
Mustard Sauce (for Beef). 109
Pizza Sauce. 141
Raspberry Sauce. 295
Sweet and Sour Sauce (for
  Pork, Chicken & Shrimp. 147
Tarragon Sauce (for Beef). 107
Vanilla Sauce. 295

SEAFOOD

Barbecue Sole. 70
Coquille St. Jacques. 65
Crab Crêpe Maxim's. 72
Crepes a la Crab. 73
Flounder a la Maison. 68
Lemon Sole Dumplings. 74
Lobster Thermidor Fondue. 71
Mimi's Tuna Casserole. 76

313

Pasta, Prawns and Scallops...... 66
Sautéed Scampi in Garlic
    Sauce..................... 61
Scallops and Shrimp
    "Marseilles"................ 67
Shrimp in Creamed Mustard
    Sauce................... 60
Shrimp or Scallop Sauté........ 62
Shrimp Pernod............... 64
Stuffed Clams Casino.......... 78
Stuffed Flounder in Wine
    Sauce................... 69
Suzie's Tuna Casserole........ 77
Tish's Salmon Loaf............ 75

SOUPS

Court Bouillon/Fish Stock....... 290
Crème de Laitues (Cream of
    Lettuce Soup).............. 36
Italian Minestrone............ 34
Italian Wedding Soup.......... 35
Leek and Potato Soup and
    Vichyssoise................ 37
Lobster Bisque............... 30
Mom's Barley Soup........... 26
Norton's Favorite Bouillabaisse... 29
Old Fashioned New England
    Clam Chowder............ 31
Russian Cabbage Soup........ 38
Seafood Soup............... 32
Sebastian's Albondigas Soup..... 27

SWEET SOUPS

Austrian Cherry Soup.......... 33
Cold Banana Soup Montego
    Bay..................... 244
Seafood Curry Soup........... 28

STUFFINGS

Chimichanga Stuffing......... 118
Clams Casino Stuffing......... 78
Cornish Hens Stuffing......... 101
Crab Crêpe Stuffing......... 72, 73
Crown Roast of Pork Stuffing..... 149
Flounder or Sole Stuffing....... 69
Green Pepper Noodle Stuffing... 163
Mushroom Sage Stuffing (for
    Turkey and Chicken)......... 163
Stuffing for Mushrooms........ 175
Stuffing for Pierogi........... 164
Spinach Stuffing (for Chicken).... 92
Russian Meat Roll Stuffing...... 113

SWEET BREADS & SWEET ROLLS

Banana Bread Supreme........ 201
Bubba's Kolachy Rolls.......... 204
Caramel Nut Loaf............. 202
Cherry Nibble Bread.......... 199
Danish Rolls................ 205
Finn Nisu Bread.............. 196

Grandma Campana's Easter
Bread...................... 197
Griswold's Bran Muffins........ 195
Merry Callender's Corn
Bread...................... 187
Powdered Orange Puffs........ 203
Raisin Cinnamon Bread........ 198
Zucchini Bread.............. 200

—V—
VEAL

Médallions de Veau au Cognac
    (Medallions of Veal with
    Cognac)................... 108
Veal in Morel Sauce........... 106
Veal Oscar.................. 105
Veal Scaloppine............. 104
Veal in Tarragon Sauce........ 107

VEGETABLES

Barbecue Beans............. 172
Broccoli Charmaine........... 177
Broccoli Fettucine Alfredo...... 176
Carrots Brittany.............. 174
Carrots Del Turco............. 174
Creamy Cheese Onions........ 178
Creamy Sweet Corn.......... 173
Lemon Applesauce........... 173
Stuffed Mushrooms with
    Bechamel Sauce........... 175

RECIPES RATED TEN PLUS
P.O. Box 26610 • Tempe, AZ 85282-0210

Please send me _____ copies of RECIPES RATED TEN PLUS @ $11.95 ea. _____

Plus postage and handling per book . . . . @   2.00 ea. _____

Arizona residents add 6% sales tax . . . . @ $ .72 ea. _____

Very unique gift wrap . . . . @ $ 2.00 ea. _____

Enclosed is my check ☐   or money order ☐ . . . . TOTAL _____

Make checks payable to RECIPES RATED TEN PLUS.
No C.O.D.s, foreign checks or currency accepted.
—PLEASE PRINT OR TYPE—

NAME _____

ADDRESS _____

CITY _____ STATE _____ ZIP _____

- -

RECIPES RATED TEN PLUS
P.O. Box 26610 • Tempe, AZ 85282-0210

Please send me _____ copies of RECIPES RATED TEN PLUS @ $11.95 ea. _____

Plus postage and handling per book . . . . @   2.00 ea. _____

Arizona residents add 6% sales tax . . . . @ $ .72 ea. _____

Very unique gift wrap . . . . @ $ 2.00 ea. _____

Enclosed is my check ☐   or money order ☐ . . . . TOTAL _____

Make checks payable to RECIPES RATED TEN PLUS.
No C.O.D.s, foreign checks or currency accepted.
—PLEASE PRINT OR TYPE—

NAME _____

ADDRESS _____

CITY _____ STATE _____ ZIP _____

- -

RECIPES RATED TEN PLUS
P.O. Box 26610 • Tempe, AZ 85282-0210

Please send me _____ copies of RECIPES RATED TEN PLUS @ $11.95 ea. _____

Plus postage and handling per book . . . . @ $ 2.00 ea. _____

Arizona residents add 6% sales tax . . . . @ $ .72 ea. _____

Very unique gift wrap . . . . @   2.00 ea. _____

Enclosed is my check ☐   or money order ☐ . . . . TOTAL _____

Make checks payable to RECIPES RATED TEN PLUS.
No C.O.D.s, foreign checks or currency accepted.
—PLEASE PRINT OR TYPE—

NAME _____

ADDRESS _____

CITY _____ STATE _____ ZIP _____

Fr. Lemon Taffy
4 c. sugar
2 c. tepid water
1½ tsp. lemon juice
(strain out pulps)
1 tsp. grated lemon peel

Stir sugar, water & lemon juice over med. heat until sugar dissolves. In heat, cook to soft-ball stage. Add lemon peel, cook to hard-crack stage. Pour onto oiled surface; pull quickly toward center w/ narrow spatula. When cool enuf to handle, knead & pull until opaque. Roll into 1 long thin strip. Cut into 1" pieces. Store in airtight container.

Noel Fudge
In lg. pan over low heat, stir until melted and smooth: 2/3 c. whole milk, 1 semi-sw. choc. square. Stir in 2 c. sugar, 1 tsp. light corn syrup, dash salt. Cook gently stirring periodically from bottom to 236° soft ball stage. Remove from heat add 2 T butter. Cool without stirring to lukewarm. Add 1 t. vanilla, beat until thick & no longer glossy. Quickly add 1 c. broken walnuts & pour on buttered plate.

Finlandia Choc. Drops
4 t. grated orange peel
2 eggs, beaten
12 oz. bittersweet choc.
6 T. butter

Melt choc. & butter over low heat. Slowly whisk choc. mixture & orange peel into the beaten egg. Drop by t. on buttered baking sheets, refrig. until firm. 3 doz.

Creole Rosewater Pralines
2 c. sugar
¼ c less 1 t water
4 c. freshly grated coconut
½ t. red food coloring
1 t. rosewater

In heavy saucepan boil sugar & water without stirring. When light syrup starts to form, remove from heat, add coconut. Cook 2-3 min. stirring constantly, until mixture bubbles & forms a thread. Add coloring & water just before taking mixture from heat. Drop spoonfuls on buttered platter, flatten w/ fork into 4" rds.

18-24

RECIPES RATED TEN PLUS
P.O. Box 26610 • Tempe, AZ 85282-0210

Please send me _____ copies of RECIPES RATED TEN PLUS @ $11.95 ea. _____

Plus postage and handling per book . . . . @   2.00 ea. _____

Arizona residents add 6% sales tax . . . . @ $ .72 ea. _____

Very unique gift wrap . . . . @ $ 2.00 ea. _____

Enclosed is my check ☐   or money order ☐ . . . . TOTAL _____

Make checks payable to RECIPES RATED TEN PLUS.
No C.O.D.s, foreign checks or currency accepted.

—PLEASE PRINT OR TYPE—

NAME _____

ADDRESS _____

CITY _____ STATE _____ ZIP _____

- -

RECIPES RATED TEN PLUS
P.O. Box 26610 • Tempe, AZ 85282-0210

Please send me _____ copies of RECIPES RATED TEN PLUS @ $11.95 ea. _____

Plus postage and handling per book . . . . @   2.00 ea. _____

Arizona residents add 6% sales tax . . . . @ $ .72 ea. _____

Very unique gift wrap . . . . @ $ 2.00 ea. _____

Enclosed is my check ☐   or money order ☐ . . . . TOTAL _____

Make checks payable to RECIPES RATED TEN PLUS.
No C.O.D.s, foreign checks or currency accepted.

—PLEASE PRINT OR TYPE—

NAME _____

ADDRESS _____

CITY _____ STATE _____ ZIP _____

- -

RECIPES RATED TEN PLUS
P.O. Box 26610 • Tempe, AZ 85282-0210

Please send me _____ copies of RECIPES RATED TEN PLUS @ $11.95 ea. _____

Plus postage and handling per book . . . . @ $ 2.00 ea. _____

Arizona residents add 6% sales tax . . . . @ $ .72 ea. _____

Very unique gift wrap . . . . @   2.00 ea. _____

Enclosed is my check ☐   or money order ☐ . . . . TOTAL _____

Make checks payable to RECIPES RATED TEN PLUS.
No C.O.D.s, foreign checks or currency accepted.

—PLEASE PRINT OR TYPE—

NAME _____

ADDRESS _____

CITY _____ STATE _____ ZIP _____

Christmas Cherry Divinity

2 c sugar
1/2 c lgt corn syrup
1/8 t. salt
1/2 c. water

2 egg wh beaten till stiff
1 t. vanilla
1 c. candied cherries, chopped
1/2 c. walnuts, chopped

In saucepan over low heat mix sugar, syrup, salt + water. Wipe sugar crystals from sides of pan; cook without stirring to firm ball stage. (248°F) Remove from heat; slowly pour syrup into beaten egg whites, stirring constantly. Add vanilla beat until candy holds its shape when dropped from spoon. Add nuts + cherries, mix well. Drop in lg. spoonfuls onto waxed paper.

RECIPES RATED TEN PLUS
P.O. Box 26610 • Tempe, AZ 85282-0210

Please send me _____ copies of RECIPES RATED TEN PLUS @ $11.95 ea. _____

Plus postage and handling per book. . . . . @ 2.00 ea. _____

Arizona residents add 6% sales tax. . . . . @ $ .72 ea. _____

Very unique gift wrap. . . . . @ $ 2.00 ea. _____

Enclosed is my check ☐ or money order ☐. . . . . TOTAL _____

Make checks payable to RECIPES RATED TEN PLUS.
No C.O.D.s, foreign checks or currency accepted.

—PLEASE PRINT OR TYPE—

NAME _____

ADDRESS _____

CITY _____ STATE _____ ZIP _____

RECIPES RATED TEN PLUS
P.O. Box 26610 • Tempe, AZ 85282-0210

Please send me _____ copies of RECIPES RATED TEN PLUS @ $11.95 ea. _____

Plus postage and handling per book. . . . . @ 2.00 ea. _____

Arizona residents add 6% sales tax. . . . . @ $ .72 ea. _____

Very unique gift wrap. . . . . @ $ 2.00 ea. _____

Enclosed is my check ☐ or money order ☐. . . . . TOTAL _____

Make checks payable to RECIPES RATED TEN PLUS.
No C.O.D.s, foreign checks or currency accepted.

—PLEASE PRINT OR TYPE—

NAME _____

ADDRESS _____

CITY _____ STATE _____ ZIP _____

RECIPES RATED TEN PLUS
P.O. Box 26610 • Tempe, AZ 85282-0210

Please send me _____ copies of RECIPES RATED TEN PLUS @ $11.95 ea. _____

Plus postage and handling per book. . . . . @ $ 2.00 ea. _____

Arizona residents add 6% sales tax. . . . . @ $ .72 ea. _____

Very unique gift wrap. . . . . @ 2.00 ea. _____

Enclosed is my check ☐ or money order ☐. . . . . TOTAL _____

Make checks payable to RECIPES RATED TEN PLUS.
No C.O.D.s, foreign checks or currency accepted.

—PLEASE PRINT OR TYPE—

NAME _____

ADDRESS _____

CITY _____ STATE _____ ZIP _____

If you would like to see **RECIPES RATED TEN PLUS** in your area, please send the names and address of your local kitchen, cooking, housewares or gourmet shops and gift or book stores.

If you would like to see **RECIPES RATED TEN PLUS** in your area, please send the names and address of your local kitchen, cooking, housewares or gourmet shops and gift or book stores.

If you would like to see **RECIPES RATED TEN PLUS** in your area, please send the names and address of your local kitchen, cooking, housewares or gourmet shops and gift or book stores.